ATLANTIC CANADA

ATLANTIC CANADA

A Region
in the Making

Margaret R. Conrad and James K. Hiller

The
Illustrated
History
of
Canada

OXFORD
UNIVERSITY PRESS

OXFORD
UNIVERSITY PRESS

70 Wynford Drive, Don Mills, Ontario M3C 1J9
www.oupcan.com

Oxford University Press is a department of the University of Oxford.
It furthers the University's objective of excellence in research, scholarship,
and education by publishing worldwide in

Oxford New York
Athens Auckland Bangkok Bogotá Buenos Aires Cape Town
Chennai Dar es Salaam Delhi Florence Hong Kong Istanbul
Karachi Kolkata Kuala Lumpur Madrid Melbourne Mexico City Mumbai
Nairobi Paris São Paulo Singapore Taipei Tokyo Toronto Warsaw

with associated companies in Berlin Ibadan

Oxford is a trade mark of Oxford University Press
in the UK and in certain other countries

Published in Canada
by Oxford University Press

Cover & Text Design: Brett Miller
'The Port of Halifax', c. 1835, artist unknown. National Gallery of Canada, Ottawa.
Gift of the Canadian National Railways, Montreal, 1963.

Canadian Cataloguing in Publication Data

Conrad, Margaret
  Atlantic Canada: a region in the making

(The illustrated history of Canada)
Includes bibliographical references and index.
ISBN 0-19-541044-0

1. Atlantic Provinces – History. I. Hiller, J.K. (James K.), 1942–   .
II. Title   III. Series

FC2005.C66 2001   971.5   C00-933065-8
F1035.8.C66 2001

1 2 3 4 - 04 03 02 01
This book is printed on permanent (acid-free) paper ∞.
Printed in Canada

TABLE OF CONTENTS

MAPS

ACKNOWLEDGEMENTS

So many people have helped us with this project along the way that it would be much easier for us to list those who failed to answer our calls for information, photos, and editorial assistance. At the risk of offending someone whose help we have overlooked, we want to thank the following especially: Douglas Baldwin, Josh Beutel, Marion Beyea, Henry Bishop, Phillip Buckner, John Calder, Alex Colville, Michael Deal, Judy Dietz, Fred Farrell, Gerry Friesen, Rob Ferguson, Anne Devlin Fischer, Harry Holman, Gordon Handcock, Peter Haughn, Gerry Gerrits, Olaf Janzen, Chris Haskett, Brian Henderson, Bob Hesketh, David Keenlyside, Deirdre Kessler, Ann Kitz, Peter Laroque, Phyllis LeBlanc, Ronnie-Gilles LeBlanc, Malcolm MacLeod, Regina Mantin, Barry Moody, Ralph Pastore, Peter Pope, Christopher Pratt, Mary Pratt, John Reid, Lynn-Marie Richard, Bert Riggs, Scott Robson, Gary Shutlak, Karen Smith, Jim Snowdon, Caroline Stone, Adrian Tanner, Brook Taylor, James Tuck, Judith Tulloch, Linda White, Duleepa Wijayawardhana. We would also like to thank Phyllis Wilson and Sally Livingston at Oxford.

MRC
JKH

ABBREVIATIONS

CMC	Canadian Museum of Civilization, Ottawa
CNS	Centre for Newfoundland Studies, Memorial University of Newfoundland
MUN	Memorial University of Newfoundland, St John's
NAC	National Archives of Canada, Ottawa
NSARM	Nova Scotia Archives and Records Management, Halifax
PANB	Provincial Archives of New Brunswick, Fredericton
PANL	Provincial Archives of Newfoundland and Labrador, St John's
PEIPARO	Prince Edward Island Public Archives and Records Office, Charlottetown

A Region in the Making

$\mathcal{A}$ joke circulating in Atlantic Canada runs something like this: Following a car accident on the 401 highway, a Toronto businessman dies and goes to heaven. He's relieved, because as he lay on his deathbed he was anything but certain that he would make the final cut. At the heavenly gates he is met by St Peter, who offers to take him on a guided tour of the divine estate. Beatific smiles on the faces of the people they meet indicate widespread contentment, except for one group who are chained to a pole and clearly displeased with their eternal condition. 'Why are these people shackled?' he asks. 'And why are they so unhappy?' 'Oh, they're from Atlantic Canada,' St Peter replies. 'If we didn't restrain them, they would try to go back home.'

This joke, carefully contrived to define Atlantic Canada with reference to Toronto, nicely sums up one contrasting pair of regional identities in contemporary Canada. It also speaks to the deep sense of place that sets Atlantic Canadians apart from many other North Americans. Although there are formal criteria relating to geography, history, and economic condition that may be used to define Atlantic Canada, it is above all the region's

functional relation to the rest of the continent that now fixes its identity. This was not always the case. Nor has the region always been treated as a single geo-political unit. In the nineteenth century, the Maritimes—Nova Scotia, New Brunswick, and Prince Edward Island— were quite distinct from Newfoundland and Labrador. Their distinctiveness manifested itself in differing responses to Confederation. While the Maritime colonies, with varying degrees of reluctance, all became provinces of Canada between 1867 and 1873, Newfoundland and Labrador resisted the modern continental drift until the 1940s. It was only in the second half of the twentieth century that 'Atlantic Canada' became the convenient shorthand term referring to all four of Canada's easternmost provinces.

Despite its common usage, the phrase 'Atlantic Canada' still sits awkwardly with many scholars, who have trouble imagining such a community. Alan Wilson concludes that, apart from fog and underdevelopment, the Maritimes share very little with Newfoundland.[1] In a recent two-volume history of the Atlantic region, Newfoundland and Labrador are an integral part of the pre-1867

Thaddeus Holownia's camera captures two regional realities: the modern port of St John's, Newfoundland, in 1988, and (facing page) the decaying abutments of the Rockland covered bridge in Upper Dorchester, New Brunswick (1981).

volume, but largely absent from the second volume until 1949—as if they had been expelled from the regional fold for their failure, however brief, to conform to their predetermined political destiny.[2] Literary scholars are similarly confounded by the Cabot Strait, with the result that two studies—Patrick O'Flaherty's *The Rock Observed* and Janice Kulyk Keefer's *Under Eastern Eyes*—are required to convey developments in Newfoundland and the Maritimes respectively. Taking a political perspective, J. Murray Beck in the late 1970s could find no regional identity at all—only provincial ones.[3] Others have gone even further, to claim identity primarily in Atlantic Canada's own untidy regionalisms. Mi'kma'ki, Acadie, Africadia, Atlantica, Cape Breton, and Labrador are only the most obvious examples of the regions that exist within, across, and beyond provincial boundaries.

In this volume we work with the current political definition of Atlantic Canada—the sometimes controversial, often artificial bound-

aries marked on a map—but we do not argue for a quintessential Atlantic Canadian regionalism. Instead we chart formal and functional regional identities and take into account the imagined sense of place that has evolved over time among a diverse people. In the documentary evidence left behind by shamans and tourist promoters, poets and photographers, novelists and number-crunchers, it is possible to catch glimpses of 'regions of the mind' in Atlantic Canada that have often had a greater impact on human motivation than more tangible political and economic templates.

Regions of the mind offer a curiously contradictory picture of the Atlantic Canada. As Janice Kulyk Keefer reminds us, one lens frames 'white clapboard church in scarlet autumn dale, dories in the very shape of indolence nesting in placid harbours, the subtle rot of grey-shingled shacks in dense spruce groves'; another captures 'senile, ruined faces, large families in two-roomed shacks.'[4] Bards, both ancient and modern, have often empha-

The remains of the Rockland bridge are a poignant reminder of an earlier era when covered bridges were a common feature of the New Brunswick landscape. Photo by Thaddeus Holownia.

sized the Arcadian quality of the Atlantic landscape, while flint-eyed critics such as Patrick O'Flaherty have reflected on a brutal geographical legacy that in Newfoundland makes it impossible for 'one generation to tame the environment for the benefit of the next'.[5] O'Flaherty's comment may be less applicable to the Maritimes, where the landscape has been more receptive to human industry, but it touches on a problem that pollsters suggest is endemic in the region: a low sense of efficacy. Atlantic Canadians, past and present alike, have combined regional pride and relentless optimism with a Sisyphean resignation to the idea that it may well be their lot to struggle rather than to arrive.

'To be a scholar of Atlantic Canada,' Ian McKay has observed, 'is to wrestle, often at the very outset of one's inquiries, with a subtle, pervasive and durable language of disparagement and marginality.'[6] Even the region's history, as it has been interpreted in the twentieth century, may have helped to sell the re-

gion at a discount. In his provocative book *The Quest of the Folk,* McKay traces the processes by which in the difficult inter-war years (1919–39) Nova Scotians succumbed to the myth of a golden age when innocent fisherfolk lived in harmony with an idyllic rural landscape. Romanticized notions of pre-industrial utopias have been common enough in Western societies, McKay argues, but they have proved particularly pernicious in Nova Scotia, and by implication in all of Atlantic Canada, reducing real people to static essences represented by stereotypical figures: Glooscap, Loyalist Pioneers, Rugged Fishermen, Scottish Bagpipers. In Newfoundland, celebrations of outport life have been dangerously combined with a long-standing sense of victimization, with a parade of historical scapegoats—from the fishing admirals to Water Street merchants— used to explain relative backwardness and failure. At the beginning of the twenty-first century, fictional characters—Evangeline, Anne of Green Gables, La Sagouine—seem to

Bruce MacKinnon, 'Oh Please, Oh Please', 1992. As this award-winning cartoon, published in the *Halifax Herald*, suggests, regional fortunes were increasingly tied to those of the United States following the Free Trade agreements of 1989 and 1992.

loom larger on the region's historical landscape than more complex realities do.

When they venture outside their natural habitat, Atlantic Canadians often find that their 'folk' images work against them, the first impression being that they are quaint rustics in a modern world of sophisticated go-getters. David Weale notes that some people from Prince Edward Island still take a perverse pleasure in boasting that they have never been to 'the other side', by which they mean 'the mainland'.[7] At the same time, it seems, nothing so becomes the Atlantic region as the leaving of it. Writing in 1912 from Leaskdale, Ontario, the popular writer L.M. Montgomery conceded

that her new home was 'a very pretty country place—would be almost as pretty as Cavendish if it had the sea. . . . At times—generally in the winter twilight—I am very homesick and feel as if I would exchange all the kingdoms of the world and the glory thereof for a sunset ramble in Lover's Lane.'[8]

Gary Burrill argues that the idea of leaving home is inseparable from the Atlantic regional identity. As the 'light infantry of capital', Atlantic Canadians have sailed the oceans of the world and crisscrossed the continent in search of work and greener pastures. Both Prince Edward Island ('Prince Edward Island Adieu') and Nova Scotia ('Farewell to Nova

Mi'kmaq at Rocky Point, Prince Edward Island. By the turn of the twentieth century, the Mi'kmaq and Maliseet were frequently sought out by photographers eager to capture their 'vanishing' culture on camera. PEIPARO, 2320/9-11, Charlottetown Camera Club Collection.

Scotia') have inspired 'leaving' songs that are now canonized in folklore. The 'Ode to Newfoundland' is sung with as much enthusiasm in the taverns of Toronto and Edmonton as in the province that so many of its sons and daughters have been forced to leave. Such evidence of social cohesion notwithstanding, Atlantic Canadians have generally been quick to assimilate to other North American cultures and have left little permanent record of a distinctive legacy from a beloved homeland. This should come as no surprise. Despite their nostalgia for the 'home place', Atlantic Canadians have a great deal in common with their North American neighbours.

Identities are not inbred; they are learned. Moreover, they vary over time and are usually shaped by cultural factors. In a study of identity formation in Cape Breton in the 1970s, Stephen Ullman discovered that pride in Cape Breton (as opposed to pride in Nova Scotia or Canada) increased with age, was stronger among Mi'kmaq than Euro-Canadians, and was also more pronounced among the working than the middle class.[9] Had he included gender among his variables, it is likely that, given their socialization to separate spheres, women and men too would have revealed differing levels of regional awareness. Marilyn Porter's work on outport Newfoundland suggests that family and community concerns among women may well have a bearing on the findings of many quantitative studies purporting to measure regional or provincial traits.[10]

The foregoing suggests that 'region' and 'regionalism' are slippery concepts, ones that should be understood as reflecting shifting cultural and historical contexts rather than fixed and static 'truths'. The two terms also need to be distinguished. While the Atlantic 'region' can be easily found on a map, 'regionalism' implies a political stance, a consciousness of a shared outlook that can be summoned up when other structures—familial, communal, provincial, national, global—fail. Regional identity may manifest itself as friendliness in distant ports, but so far it has not been the stuff of political cohesion at home. Over the years, calls for union of the Maritime or Atlantic provinces have been voiced by policymakers desperate to find a quick fix for real or imagined ills. That no such union has ever materialized suggests not only that there are other powerful identities in Atlantic Canada competing for dominance, but also that regionalism has limited value as a vehicle for common action.

Although Atlantic Canadians have so far rejected political union, they have increasingly come to share an angle of vision on the world they inhabit. This common perspective derives in large measure from the fact that, compared to the rest of Canada, the Atlantic region is both economically poor and politically weak. Indeed, sociologist Wallace Clement has gone so far as to argue that in Canada all regionalisms are largely geographical expressions of more deeply rooted inequalities in the nation as a whole.[11] Relative poverty and political impo-

tence are not unique to Atlantic Canada; until recently, much of Canada was a hinterland of the golden triangle framing Toronto, Montreal, and Ottawa. Only in the second half of the twentieth century has a common experience with Canadian federalism served as a force for unity in the Atlantic region.

It might well be asked why 2.3 million people inhabiting a resource-rich area that is larger than most of the world's nation-states are not wallowing in wealth. Small countries off the edges of continents—among them Great Britain, Japan, even Iceland—have proven that economic success is possible without vast hinterlands or favoured climates. In the past, much of the responsibility for the region's economic plight has been laid at the feet of Atlantic Canadians themselves. Perhaps the first to so assign blame was the Nova Scotia judge Thomas Chandler Haliburton, who, through his fictional character Sam Slick, commented in the 1830s that 'these Bluenoses have no motion in 'em, no enterprise, no spirit, and if any critter shows any symptoms of activity, they say he is a man of no judgment, he's speculative, he's a schemer, in short, he's mad.'[12] Haliburton's view has often been echoed, most recently by neo-liberal theorists eager to abandon regional development programs.

Given the industry displayed by Atlantic Canadians at home and abroad, it is difficult to put much stock in the notion that laziness is the cause of the region's economic difficulties. One might just as convincingly blame capitalist exploitation, federal policies, resource endowment, or acts of God. More useful is a conclusion reached by economist Donald Savoie: that community life in Atlantic Canada is richer than modern statistical analyses, based on narrow notions of economic well-being, suggest.[13] It is, after all, a moot point whether wage-earners forced to spend most of their annual income on survival in more favoured regions of the continent are any better off than their counterparts in the Atlantic region, where the scale of living is smaller but may be equally rich in material and psychological well-being. Before his death in 1980, David Alexander, who perhaps contributed more to the understanding of his adopted region than any scholar of his generation, suggested that 'a new notion of happiness' based on the idea of regional self-reliance was emerging.[14] This suggestion has yet to be fully realized, but the rising tide of globalism may well advance the process of regionalization more rapidly than even he could have imagined.

What exactly is Atlantic Canada? A shared location is obviously the cornerstone of any region, but even geography is an uncertain ally in the quest for definition. Consisting of islands, peninsulas, and fringes of the North American continent, the Atlantic region is not defined solely by its exposure to the North Atlantic; if it were, the Magdalen Islands, St Pierre and Miquelon, and the Gaspé would all be integral parts of it. Geographic diversity rather than homogeneity is the region's most obvious feature. Extending over 17 degrees of both longitude and latitude, Atlantic Canada contains 539,101 square kilometres of land and fresh water, and 16,000 kilometres of saltwater shoreline. Mount Caubvick in Labrador's Torngat Mountains is the region's highest point, at 1,652 metres, while no part of Prince Edward Island rises above 142 metres. In western Newfoundland, New Brunswick, and Nova Scotia, the Appalachian range dominates

In Cape Breton, ancient mountains of the Appalachian range offer some of the Atlantic region's most dramatic scenery. Barrett and MacKay Photography, Inc.

the landscape. These mountains are so old that they have been eroded into stumps, the highest of which is Mount Carleton in New Brunswick (820 metres). In Cape Breton and Newfoundland the Appalachians rise steeply from the sea, helping to make the Cabot Trail and Gros Morne National Park two of the most spectacular tourist attractions in the world.

Fishing stages clinging to the cliffs at Pouch Cove, Newfoundland (north of St John's), in the 1950s. Although industrialization was already under way, the traditional inshore fishery persisted. PANL.

Several millennia ago, the Atlantic region was much larger than it is today, and its ancient contours can be seen in the rough outlines of the continental shelf. The relative shallowness of the shelf has, until recently, provided a rich habitat for fish, and still yields undersea deposits of oil and natural gas.

Climate also ranges widely in the region, from the subarctic conditions of northern Labrador to the temperate ranges of southwestern Nova Scotia. Although weather is influenced primarily by continental systems moving eastwards, these are modified by the ocean, which gives Atlantic Canada warmer winters and cooler summers than areas of North America in the same latitudes farther west. Most of the region lacks the warming influence of the Gulf Stream that keeps Great Britain pleasantly mild compared to Newfoundland and Labrador, though they are in roughly the same latitude. When the Gulf Stream meets the cold Labrador Current carrying ice from the north, it produces the fog for which the Grand Banks are infamous. The humourist Ray Guy imagined that a Newfoundland angel would miss 'a bit of fog' while strolling along the Celestial Landwash.[15]

Labrador makes up 54 per cent of the total land mass of the Atlantic region, but its rugged landscape, which is part of the Canadian Shield,

Atlantic Canada seen from a satellite. Canada Centre for Remote Sensing, Ottawa/National Atlas of Canada.

The Moravian mission station at Hebron, Labrador, 1962. The settlement was closed down in 1959 and its inhabitants relocated. James Hiller.

Chepstow, Prince Edward Island. Red soil, potato fields, and blue sea compose a familiar summer scene on the island. Barrett and MacKay Photography, Inc.

Tantramar Marsh, Sackville, New Brunswick. The natural marshlands created by the region's high tides were greatly prized in the era of early settlement. They produced rich crops of hay once dykes were built to keep out the sea. Barrett and MacKay Photography, Inc.

The Tablelands, Gros Morne National Park, Newfoundland. Photo Wayne Barrett, Parks Canada, 1996.

The Confederation Bridge finally linked the mainland to Prince Edward Island in 1997. Barrett and MacKay Photography, Inc.

has never supported a large population. By contrast, the rich soils of Prince Edward Island, and the valleys of the St John and Annapolis-Cornwallis rivers yield agricultural crops in modest abundance. Most of the region sustains a forest cover, much of it a mix of deciduous and coniferous trees. Over the past 500 years, the forests have been so thoroughly exploited that few old-growth stands are left. By contrast, the mineral wealth of the region, with the exception of the coal deposits of Nova Scotia and New Brunswick and the iron deposits of Labrador, has yet to be fully exploited.

Fish, timber, minerals, and agricultural land provided immigrants with the material conditions for a degree of economic well-being and cultural commonality. Yet instead they nurtured dependency and diversity. With no internal metropolitan centre to impose a homogenizing influence, Atlantic Canada has historically been loose-jointed and vulnerable to outside forces. In the eighteenth century the region became the site of a struggle between France and Britain (and their satellites on the St Lawrence and in New England) for imperial domination. The losers in this contest were the Aboriginal peoples and the Acadians—the region's first European settlers—who saw most of their lands taken over by immigrants from Europe and the Thirteen Colonies/United States, who settled in the Maritimes between 1713 and 1867.

By the time of Confederation, more than 90 per cent of Atlantic Canadians could trace their origins to France or Great Britain (a proportion that still holds), and more than 80 per cent were native-born (the figure is much higher today). Except in Labrador, boundaries were also firmly in place by 1867, having been drawn well before the provinces in the rest of Canada took their final form. Rooted in the land and shaped by the sea before the Industrial Revolution had its way with them, Atlantic Canadians developed a sense of place more reminiscent of time-bound European nations than the frontier-driven empires of North America.

Provincialism and social rootedness had become defining features of Atlantic Canada by the middle of the nineteenth century. By that time too, according to some pundits, the region had begun to exhibit signs of a debilitating conservatism that made it resistant to progressive change. Historian E.R. Forbes and others have challenged the use of 'conservatism' to describe developments in the region, not so much because it is inaccurate as because it is inadequately explored. If Atlantic Canadians are

---

Facing above. Reconstructed Norse dwellings at L'Anse-aux-Meadows, Newfoundland. The only authentic Norse site in North America was discovered in 1960 by Helge and Anne Stine Ingstad. Subsequent excavations revealed eight structures from the eleventh century—houses, workshops, and a forge—of the same kind as those built in Iceland and Greenland. The buildings were made of sods laid over a frame, with long, narrow fireplaces in the middle of the floor. These replicas were built a short distance from the actual ruins. Photo J. Steeves, Parks Canada, Department of Canadian Heritage.

Facing below. Lunenburg, Nova Scotia. Declared a UNESCO Heritage Site in 1995, Lunenburg retains significant elements of its original town plan and the culture of its founding people, including Lutheran churches, exquisite detailing on its wooden buildings, and traces of German syntax in the speech of many citizens. Photo Gerry Hallowell.

In the 1950s, when this picture was taken, the family-based mixed farming-fishing economy that had long sustained many rural areas of the Atlantic region was rapidly disappearing. Such scenes nevertheless attracted visitors and tourist promoters eager to find evidence of what they considered a simpler and happier age. NSARM Norwood #175.

more conservative than other North Americans, how does their conservatism manifest itself? Scholars who would confirm the conservative stereotype point to the comparative reluctance of Atlantic Canadians to support radical political movements, the tendency of the region's artists and creative writers to cling to realism, and a commitment to the notion of 'social good' in law and social policy. Scholars who dispute this view draw attention to the region's

leadership in the movement for responsible government, its early commitment to higher education for women, pitched battles between capital and labour in mining and steel-making communities, and the outrageously radical efforts of the region's governments, in the second half of the twentieth century, to impose modernization through wholesale resettlement programs, sweeping municipal reform, and state-run enterprise. For our part, we contend that emphasizing radical departures serves the region no better than belabouring the conservative ones. The wiser course is to concede that Atlantic Canada is a complex region with a history long and deep enough to accommodate most academic prejudices. What we can say with certainty is that in recent years formal, functional, and imagined Atlantic regions have coincided more completely than ever before in recorded history. That coincidence is the basis on which this volume is predicated. Indeed, in lumping the four Atlantic provinces together in one volume—the four westernmost provinces are treated in two while Ontario and Quebec each have their own—Oxford University Press is helping to promote the idea of a cohesive region where, arguably, one does not exist.

History is a subjective enterprise, and what follows is only one way of 'seeing' Atlantic Canada. Our task has been made easier because one of the manifestations of a new sense of regional awareness in recent years has been an outpouring of historical literature. A

focus and stimulus for a growing interest in regional history has been provided by the academic journal *Acadiensis,* founded in 1971, and the related conferences that began on a regular basis in 1974. Since then, articles and books have appeared at such a rate that it is difficult to keep up with the field. *The Nova Scotia Historical Review, The Newfoundland Quarterly, Newfoundland Studies, Them Days, The Island Magazine, Les Cahiers de la Société historique acadienne,* and *The Cape Breton Magazine* have joined *Acadiensis* in exploring aspects of the region's past. So too have the historians based outside the university who have added immeasurably to our knowledge, and the archivists who have collected the documents and images that make our work possible. Thus, while we have selected what we consider relevant to our narrative, this book is indebted to the work of colleagues who, like ourselves, have been caught up in developing a better historical understanding of a region in the making.

CHAPTER ONE

Beginnings

In 1855 J. William Dawson, a native of Pictou, Nova Scotia, published a book entitled *Acadian Geology*. In it he reflected on a time millions of years earlier when 'multitudes of large animals now extinct' inhabited the Maritimes, and 'submerged tropical forests' laid the foundation for the region's rich coal deposits. Dawson was a pioneer in the emerging fields of geology and palaeontology, two of

'Reptiles of the Coal Period', an illustration from the 1891 edition of J.W. Dawson's *Acadian Geology*.

the sciences that, in the nineteenth century, were transforming everything people had hitherto believed about the earth and its inhabitants. A strict Presbyterian, he refused to accept the theory of evolution as expounded by his famous contemporary Charles Darwin. Dawson nevertheless helped to advance new scientific ideas about the origins of the earth and the emergence of an 'Atlantic region'.

In Dawson's time most people living in the British North American colonies subscribed to a biblical interpretation of the origins of the universe. God, they believed, had created heaven and earth in six days—some thought 4,004 years before the birth of Christ—and placed Adam and Eve in the Garden of Eden, from which they were eventually expelled to people an imperfect world. Since God was all-powerful, there was little need to account for the evolution of the earth or its peoples in his cosmic blueprint.

Aboriginal creation stories also attributed the earth's origins to powerful gods. According to one account passed down by the Mi'kmaq, Kji-kinap made the world and breathed life into a large, flat stone that he named Kluskap

(Glooscap). With the help of a young man and a young woman, Kluskap cleaned out the silt-choked river beds, made the trees grow, summoned birds and animals from the Sky World, and shaped various geological features. The Bird Islands in Cape Breton, for instance, were said to be the remnants of a canoe that he threw into St Anne's Bay in one of his epic battles with an evil wizard. Like the Christian God, Kluskap established a gendered social order. 'I am going to marry you together,' he told the two young people who helped him to form the earth. 'You will live together and have children, and they will have children. Go and make yourselves a wigwam. The man can go out into the forest and hunt animals. The woman can cook them.'[1]

The implications of the scientific view of creation that now dominates most textbooks also take a leap of faith to grasp. In the 1830s, Abraham Gesner, another Nova Scotia-born scientist, had discovered fossils in the Bay of Fundy region. These drew the attention of Charles Lyell, the founder of modern geology, and in 1852 Lyell and Dawson explored the cliffs around Joggins on Chignecto Bay, where they found the earliest reptilian remains discovered in North America to that time. These findings helped to confirm the view that the earth and its inhabitants were far older than the Book of Genesis suggested.

Scientists now think that the earth is at least 4.5 billion years old, and explain the creation of continents and oceans through the theory of plate tectonics. According to this theory, continents are in constant movement, colliding and breaking apart as they float on the planet's soft, molten interior. The Canadian Shield, of which Labrador is a part, contains some of the

Sir J. William Dawson (1820–99) was one of the most respected scientists of his generation. In 1855 he was appointed Principal of McGill University, a position he held until 1895. Natural Resources Canada.

earth's oldest land forms; at Saglek Bay in Labrador, rocks have been found that date back some 3.6 billion years. The rest of the Atlantic region is younger and forms a separate geological province, known as the Appalachian Orogen. Some 400 to 200 million years ago, the Atlantic region took shape at the centre of a large continent named Pangaea, which itself was formed when two ancient continental plates—Laurentia on the west and Gondwana to the east—collided. Evidence of the collision can be seen in many parts of the Atlantic

Fossil trees, still standing in the positions in which they once grew, are exposed in the coastal cliffs around Joggins, Nova Scotia. No fewer than 65 coal-forming periods and 40 drowned forests have been identified in the Joggins area. Photo John Calder, Nova Scotia Department of Natural Resources.

region, most notably in Gros Morne National Park, which UNESCO declared a World Heritage Site in 1987 because of the richness of its geological resources.[2] Two hundred million years ago Pangaea broke apart to form the present Atlantic Ocean, but the break was not clean. Fragments of Gondwana remained attached to

Laurentia, including the Eastern Zone of Newfoundland, much of Nova Scotia (the Megumba Zone), and parts of New Brunswick and the northeastern United States. The terrain stretching from northern Africa to Scandinavia bears a striking resemblance to the Atlantic shores of the Maritimes and Newfoundland because they were once part of the same land mass.

In the 200 million years since Pangaea divided and the North American continent began drifting northward, adjustments of the earth's crust and the forces of erosion have eaten away the once rugged mountains of the Appalachian chain and built up the continental shelf, with its rich reserves of oil and natural gas. Water flowing from mountains along the coastal margins and the interior of the continent created the Gulf of St Lawrence, carved out the Cabot Strait and Strait of Belle Isle, and laid down the iron-rich sandstone deposits that are responsible for the red soils of Prince Edward Island. Where water drained into basins creating lakes, life forms emerged. One such lake occupied what is now Albert County in New Brunswick. Lake Albert once teamed with fish and algae, and it is their remains, locked up in the lake sediments, that are the source of the hydrocarbons extracted from an oil and gas field near Moncton.

The exposed rocks along the Bay of Fundy reveal dramatic evidence of the last 360 million years of the earth's history. During what is known as the Carboniferous period (286 to 360 million years ago), the region was subjected to repeated buckling and faulting. When the buckling and sediment accumulation were slow, the vegetation that grew on the river flood plains was preserved as coal beds; when these processes occurred more rapidly,

Rock formations at Hopewell, Albert County, New Brunswick. These 'flower pots', carved by the high tides of the Bay of Fundy, are left exposed at low tide. They became popular tourist attractions in the nineteenth century. PANB, P93A1-14.

forests were drowned, trapping reptiles in hollow tree stumps. The reptiles that Dawson and Lyell discovered in drowned forests were the ancestors of the dinosaurs that would dominate the region for nearly 200 million years until they suddenly became extinct—perhaps as a result of an asteroid hitting the earth—some 66 million years ago.[3]

The final shaping and scraping of the Atlantic landscape occurred during the last Ice Age, which gripped the continent from 2 million to 10,000 years ago. During the Wisconsinian glaciation (75,000 to 10,000 years ago), the Laurentide Ice Sheet gradually expanded to cover most of what is now Canada, including Labrador and the tip of Newfoundland's Northern Peninsula. The rest of Newfoundland and the Maritimes were covered by an independent ice cap, which formed part of the Appalachian Glacier Complex. Ice flowed over earlier river valleys, cut deep valleys and fiords, and dumped boulders, gravel, and fine sand throughout the region. Erratics—glacial debris dropped by the moving ice cap—still litter the landscape in some areas, including along the road to Peggy's Cove, Nova Scotia.

About 20,000 years ago the glaciers of the last ice age began to melt, but they took several millennia to disappear entirely. The sea level rose, fell, and rose again as the ice retreated and the land rebounded from the weight of the glaciers. Prince Edward Island began as three islands; later it was connected to the mainland by a land bridge. In periods when the sea level was low, sections of the continental shelf and what is now the floor of the Bay of Fundy lay exposed. The Atlantic region took the geological form we recognize today as recently as 3,000 years ago.

The early history of human habitation in the Atlantic region is difficult to determine because many areas of coastal settlement have sunk below sea level, and the region's acidic soils tend to destroy any organic materials that have not been submerged. As a result there are few sites that offer evidence of continuous occupation over long stretches of time. Archaeological discoveries in recent years have enabled us to imagine the broad outline of the region's early human history, but we may never know the full story.[4]

The earliest North American peoples are called Palaeo-Indians. Hunting species such as mammoths, mastodons, and long-horn bison, they moved across the continent from the south and west as the retreating glaciers permitted, adapting their culture to the changing climate, animal species, and vegetation. The oldest discovered remains of human settlement in the region were found near Debert, Nova Scotia, in the 1960s. Dated to about 10,600 years ago, the site is believed to be a seasonal encampment near a caribou trail passing through the Cobiquid Bay region. Although these Palaeo-Indians may have relied primarily on caribou for survival, their descendants pursued diverse hunting, fishing, and gathering subsistence patterns, gradually making their way to the rich maritime life of the Strait of Belle Isle, where archaeological evidence dating back nearly 9,000 years has been found at Pinware Hill in southern Labrador.

Palaeo-Indian culture, based on chipped-stone technology, gave way to a sequence of what are termed Archaic cultures, distinguished from their predecessors by the fact that their stone tools were ground and polished. While it is believed that Archaic peoples inhabited the region from 10,000 to 2,500 years ago, until recently very little was known about the first 5,000 years of their occupation. Because of evidence found near lakes and rivers and from drowned coastal sites in the Bay of Fundy and off Prince Edward Island, archaeologists now agree that the Early and Middle Archaic cultures they have identified in New England also existed in the Maritimes. By the late Archaic period, beginning about 5,000 years ago, there were two distinct groups inhabiting the Atlantic region: the Interior Late Archaic and the Coastal Late Archaic.

The Interior Late Archaic peoples represented an eastern version of the Laurentian tradition that extended from the Great Lakes to the shores of what are now Maine and New Brunswick. The Coastal Late Archaic marks a distinct phase in what archaeologist James Tuck calls a Maritime Archaic tradition. With local variants, it extended from Maine to Northern Labrador, and from Newfoundland to the Gulf of St Lawrence, and reflects a continuous occupation of coastal areas from the Palaeo-Indian period to European settlement. There has been considerable debate on this

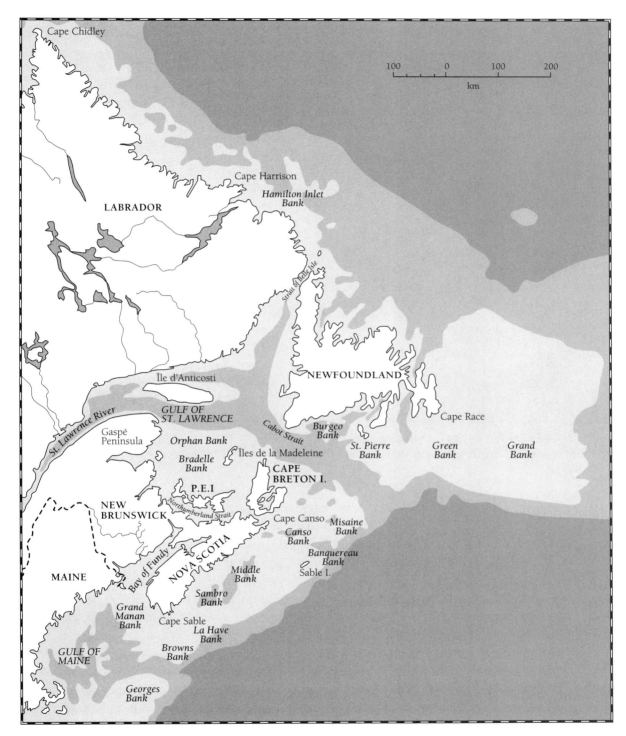

Cape Chidley

LABRADOR

Cape Harrison

Hamilton Inlet Bank

Strait of Belle Isle

NEWFOUNDLAND

Île d'Anticosti

GULF OF ST. LAWRENCE

St. Lawrence River

Gaspé Peninsula

Orphan Bank

Cabot Strait

Burgeo Bank

Cape Race

St. Pierre Bank

Green Bank

Grand Bank

Bradelle Bank

Îles de la Madeleine

P.E.I

CAPE BRETON I.

NEW BRUNSWICK

Northumberland Strait

Cape Canso

Misaine Bank

Canso Bank

Banquereau Bank

Sable I.

MAINE

Bay of Fundy

NOVA SCOTIA

Middle Bank

Sambro Bank

Grand Manan Bank

Cape Sable

La Have Bank

GULF OF MAINE

Browns Bank

Georges Bank

100   0   100   200
km

The continental shelf and fishing banks. Adapted from Innis, *The Cod Fishery*, 7.

Discovered by Roland Jones in the 1960s, near the entrance to St Peter's Bay, Prince Edward Island, this site contains late Palaeo-Indian materials that are 9,500 to 10,000 years old. Photo by David Keenlyside, Canadian Museum of Civilization.

issue, in part because times and tides have eroded areas where these people once lived. B.J. Bourque, for instance, maintains that the Late Archaic in the southwestern Maritimes and Maine represents a separate cultural tradition that he calls the 'Moorehead phase'.

The evidence is more firm in Labrador and Newfoundland, where archaeologists have been able to document an unbroken Maritime Archaic tradition running from 7,500 to 3,500 years ago. Surviving artifacts from such sites as L'Anse Amour and Port au Choix indicate that a Northern Branch of that tradition spread from the Strait of Belle Isle along the coast of

Labrador, eventually reaching Saglek and Ramah bays. The Southern Branch people occupied southern Labrador and were the first humans to colonize the island of Newfoundland, where they established themselves some 5,000 years ago (or perhaps even earlier), spreading around the entire coastline with the possible exception of the Avalon Peninsula.

There is also evidence that people belonging to the Broad Point (or Susquehanna) culture, first defined in the Middle Atlantic states of North America, moved into the southwestern extremes of the Maritimes in the late Archaic period. What makes them distinct, apart from the broad points of their artifacts, is the fact that they cremated their dead and buried their ashes and bone fragments in pits. The Broad Point peoples seem not to have penetrated much beyond southwestern New Brunswick and the Yarmouth-Tusket region of Nova Scotia.

Whatever their specific tradition, all Archaic cultures depended—as their Palaeo-Indian predecessors had—on some combination of hunting, fishing, and gathering. Their highly mobile communities consisted of bands made up of a few related families, 50 people on the average. Although they carved out territorial jurisdictions, there was probably significant cultural exchange between the sea-based and interior peoples who shared the region's bounty. Surviving tools suggest that they adapted their resources of stone and bone to the job at hand. In the sea-based societies, people fashioned toggling harpoons to spear seals and swordfish, which were then killed with lances tipped with bone and ground slate points. Animals were butchered with stone knives and the skins dressed with bone scrapers. From the bones of small birds and animals people crafted fine needles and awls with which to make shelters, clothing, footwear, and carrying bags. Ground and polished axes, adzes, and gouges were used to fashion wooden spear shafts, traps, and other hunting devices, as well as wooden bowls, dugout canoes, house frames, and small decorative objects.

Archaic peoples had highly developed spiritual beliefs, burying their dead, accompanied by red ochre, tools, weapons, and decorative objects, in cemeteries. If the surviving carved charms, tokens, and amulets are any

In 1973 a road maintenance crew found this mound of rocks near L'Anse Amour in southern Labrador. The following year archaeologists discovered that it was a burial mound—the oldest known in North America—marking the grave of a Maritime Archaic child who died some 7,500 years ago. The body was placed face down, with a stone, sprinkled with red ochre, on the back. Among the artifacts buried with the child were a flute made from a wing bone of a large bird, a quartz knife or spear point, a pestle made of antler (probably used to grind the ochre), and a toggling harpoon. James Hiller, MUN.

indication, the Archaic peoples living in the Atlantic region had great respect for the fish, sea birds, whales, and seals upon which they depended for survival. At Port au Choix, for example, some of the graves included the remains of a particular bird species, which may have served to identify family lines.

Population movements and cultural evolution in the Maritimes appear to be linked to climatic change. About 3,500 years ago, rising sea levels and cooling temperatures encouraged an increased reliance on shellfish and fur-bearing animals, and the adoption of new practices and technologies from other cultures. The Maritime Archaic culture as such disappeared and, absorbing influences and perhaps

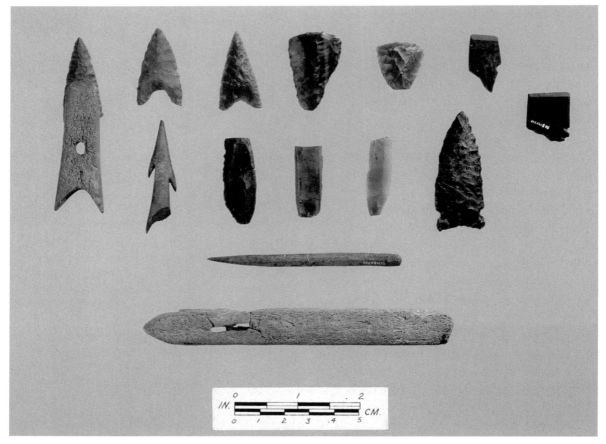

Dorset Palaeo-Eskimo artifacts, 1,300 to 2,000 years old, from Port au Choix in northwestern Newfoundland. Clockwise from top left: a bone harpoon head tipped with a stone end-blade, two typical Dorset triangular end-blades, two end-scrapers, two ground nephrite engraving tools, a chipped-stone knife, three microblades, and a bone point. At the bottom is a segment of a whalebone sled-runner, and above that a stone awl. M.A.P. Renouf, MUN.

immigrants from the south and west, the Maritime peoples moved into the Woodland (or Ceramic) period, characterized in part by the use of clay pottery. Modern Maliseet and Mi'kmaq almost certainly derive from the Woodlands peoples who predominated in the Maritimes from 500 to 2,500 years ago.

The appearance of ceramics may be an indication that Archaic peoples borrowed technology from adjacent cultures in the New England and St Lawrence regions to meet changing circumstances. Such a theory is supported by burial mound sites found on the Red Bank Reserve on the Miramichi and at Skora, near Halifax. Similar to sites associated with the Adena in Ohio, they suggest either that people from the interior of the continent swept through the region 3,000 years ago or that Maritime Archaic people had learned new ways to inter their dead relatives.

The Augustine Mound excavation site, near the Red Bank reserve in New Brunswick. In 1972 Joseph Augustine, following up information given to him by his father about a 'special place' thought to have been used for ceremonial dancing, discovered a burial mound near the Miramichi River system. Subsequent archaeological excavations, in which Augustine and other members of his family participated, revealed human remains and artifacts, including stone pipes, clay vessels, copper and shell beads, and remnants of woven fabric, dating back some 2,400 years. The Augustine Mound reflects burial practices similar to those of the Adena peoples of the Ohio River Valley and raises questions about the transfer of cultural practices among First Nations in North America. Photo David Keenlyside, Canadian Museum of Civilization.

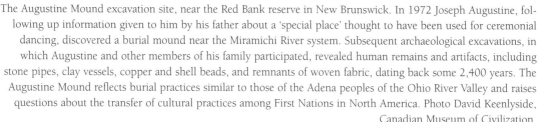

Most Woodland sites are located along the coast or on rivers where fish were abundant. From the available evidence, there seems to have been considerable continuity in the seasonal rhythms. For example, some bands in eastern New Brunswick regularly made late winter expeditions to Prince Edward Island to catch sea mammals. While most bands were highly mobile, the discovery of more than a hundred semi-subterranean pit-houses in the Passamaquoddy Bay area suggests that people living there were based in the same village for most of the year. These pit-houses were conical structures framed with poles or saplings covered with skins or sheets of bark, and sometimes banked with a mixture of shells and soil, presumably to keep out the cold.

The peoples of southeastern New Brunswick developed somewhat different cultural patterns, but they shared with their

Thule culture artifacts excavated at Saglek Bay, northern Labrador. Bones of sea mammals were fashioned into hunting weapons and other implements. James Tuck, MUN.

neighbours a dependence on shellfish and the use of clay pots. Shell middens—accumulations of discarded shells of clams, quahogs, mussels, and occasionally scallops or oysters— are found throughout the region and offer valuable evidence about the evolution of Woodland material culture. At a midden site at Sellar's Cove, on the shores of St Margaret's Bay, Nova Scotia, remains from nearly the

entire span of the Woodland period indicate that pottery techniques declined, perhaps because people were becoming more mobile. By the time of European contact, both the semi-permanent dwellings along the coast and pottery had disappeared, for reasons that have yet to be fully explained.

Mobility was greatly advanced by the use of birchbark for making dishes, baskets, and especially canoes. Ribs for canoes were made from cedar and thwarts from maple or other hardwoods. Woodland peoples apparently used their canoes primarily for river and coastal travel, but they were clearly able to navigate the Northumberland Strait, the Strait of Canso, and perhaps the Cabot Strait as well. Before the arrival of Europeans, the region's Aboriginal peoples had also adopted the bow and arrow.

Newfoundland and Labrador experienced the same climatic shift that affected the Maritimes, but received successive immigrants from the north rather than the south and west. The first of these were the Palaeo-Eskimos, who arrived in coastal Labrador nearly 4,000 years ago and later spread to the island of Newfoundland, replacing the Maritime Archaic peoples. In turn, their culture was replaced about 2,000 years ago by the Late Palaeo-Eskimo, usually called Dorset, who probably originated in the Hudson Bay–Foxe Basin area. They disappeared from the island of Newfoundland by the ninth century and from Labrador by 1300. Skilled in crafting stone, bone, and ivory tools, the Dorset peoples produced distinctive soapstone lamps and cooking vessels as well as whalebone 'shoes' to protect the runners on their sleds, which they probably hauled themselves.

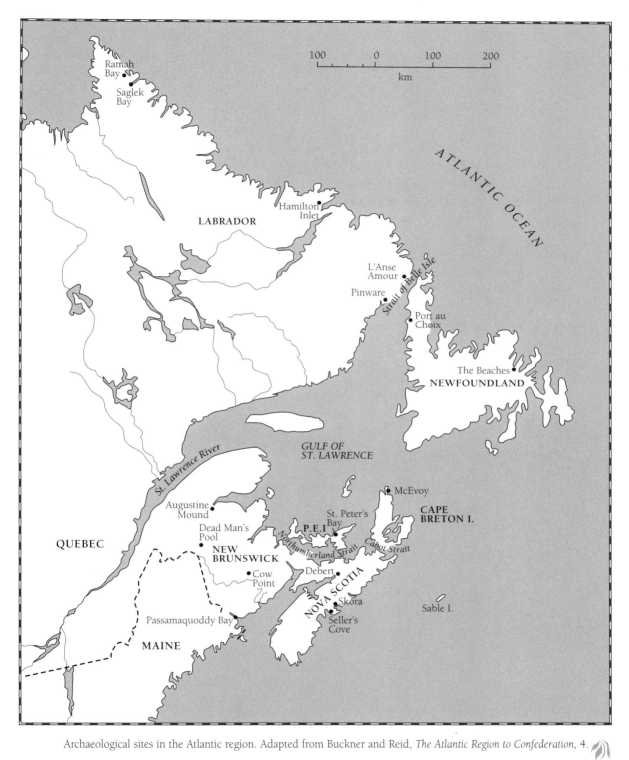

Archaeological sites in the Atlantic region. Adapted from Buckner and Reid, *The Atlantic Region to Confederation*, 4.

The direct ancestors of the modern Labrador Inuit were the Thule, the last major group to migrate there from the western Arctic. Adept at catching whales with their large toggling harpoons, kayaks, and umiaks, they moved quickly across the High Arctic. Their success was facilitated by a warming trend about 1,000 years ago, which reduced the sea ice and drew both bowhead and right whales into the northern waters. Arriving in the extreme north of Labrador between 1250 and 1450, the Thule reached Saglek by 1500, and soon after that encountered Europeans in the Strait of Belle Isle.

Since the material culture of the Thule peoples has been well preserved, we know more about their lifestyles than those of most early peoples in the region. The typical house was an oval-shaped, semi-subterranean structure with three levels, entered through a tunnel leading to a slightly elevated flagstone floor. At the rear was a raised sleeping platform. A low earthen exterior wall supported a whalebone interior frame, which was covered with baleen and sod to create a domed roof. It seems likely that the Thule people also built snow houses. The Thule had teams of dogs trained to pull their sleds. In 1500 right whales were the mainstay of their diet, supplemented by the sea mammals, birds, fish, land animals, and wild berries that flourished in the region.

The origins of the modern Labrador Innu are imperfectly understood, but have been traced back about 1,000 years to a tradition known to archaeologists as Recent Indian, whose remains have been found at Point Revenge. On the island of Newfoundland, the Little Passage people, named for the site near Gaultois on Newfoundland's south coast, were also Recent Indians and the direct ancestors of the Beothuk.

The history of the peoples of Atlantic Canada before European contact shifts constantly as new archaeological evidence and, with it, new theories appear. Many questions remain to be answered, but the main outlines of a story of continuous human occupation since the arrival of Palaeo-Indians over 10,000 years ago, are beginning to take shape. What we can say for certain is that archaeologists have opened a fascinating window on past cultures in the Atlantic region, which has a long history of peoples encountering environmental change, new technologies, and new populations.

CHAPTER TWO

Aboriginal Peoples

To preserve the fire, especially in winter, we would entrust it to the care of our war-chief's women, who took turns to preserve the spark, using half-rotten pine wood covered with ash. Sometimes this fire lasted up to three moons. When it lasted the span of three moons, the fire became sacred and magical to us, and we showered with a thousand praises the chief's woman who had been the fire's guardian during the last days of the third moon. We would all gather together and, so that no member of the families which had camped there since the autumn should be absent, we sent out young men to fetch those who were missing. Then, when our numbers were complete, we would gather round and, without regard to age or rank, light our pipes at the fire. We would suck in the smoke and keep it in our mouths, and one by one we would puff it into the face of the woman who had last preserved the spark, telling her that she was worthy above all to share in the benign influence of the Father of Light, the Sun, because she had so skilfully preserved his emanations.[1]

With the arrival of Europeans, the daily life of the Atlantic region's Aboriginal peoples

suddenly comes into sharper focus, but the evidence is often incomplete and contradictory. We have no way of knowing, for example, how the cultural practice described here developed, or when, or how widespread it may have been Moreover, by the 1740s, when Chief Arguimaut (Ľkimu) recounted this ceremony in an interview in what is now Prince Edward Island, Europeans had already been in the region for over 200 years. While it is now widely recognized that oral traditions are more reliable than text-bound historians had earlier believed, it is impossible to tell how accurate this account may be. For all their seeming authenticity, Chief Arguimaut's words were preserved for posterity by a missionary, the Abbé Pierre Maillard. The evidence of ethnographers is rarely accepted without scrutiny today, and we must not lose our critical perspective when we discover a rare archival document, even— or perhaps especially—one written by a priest. The Europeans who first came into contact with Aboriginal peoples had a Christian worldview, a sense of cultural superiority, and a gendered perspective that often led them to misinterpret—perhaps deliberately, perhaps unconsciously—what they heard and saw. Although the above description of the problems posed by a Maritime winter for the pre-contact Mi'kmaq offers insights impossible to deduce from an inert artifact, it must be treated like any other historical source: as evidence from a particular time and place, not necessarily a key to universal truths.

Nevertheless, we can paint a much clearer picture of Aboriginal societies in the period after the arrival of Europeans than in earlier times. Europeans were intrigued by the 'New World', and often wrote detailed descriptions of the peoples they encountered. When these accounts are combined with the surviving material culture and oral traditions of indigenous peoples, a picture emerges of vibrant pre-contact societies that, like their European counterparts, were neither static nor without their faults.

A word about nomenclature is in order here. Europeans encountered at least five cultural groups in the Atlantic region, which they called Eskimo and Montagnais-Naskapi in Labrador, Beothuk in Newfoundland, Micmac and Malecite in the Maritimes. These were not necessarily the names that Aboriginal peoples gave themselves. In recent years, for example, northern peoples have objected to 'Eskimo', which means 'eater of raw meat'; they prefer to be called 'Inuit', meaning simply 'the people'— a term many Aboriginal groups used at the time of contact to distinguish themselves from the other creatures with whom they shared the land. Similarly, the 'Montagnais-Naskapi' are now called 'Innu'. Aboriginal peoples have also begun adopting names and spellings that reflect their own language structures rather than imposed Europeanized versions. Thus 'Micmac' and 'Malecite' become 'Mi'kmaq' and 'Maliseet'.

In 1500 the Americas were populated by peoples as varied and as numerous as could be found in Europe. Natives of the Atlantic region lived on the eastern edge of a world that included complex empires, city-states, confederacies, chiefdoms, and band communities like their own. The Labrador Inuit were a branch of a culture that stretched from Alaska to Greenland, while the Mi'kmaq, Maliseet, Beothuk, and Innu belonged to the Algonkian language group, which occupied an extensive territory from the Atlantic to the Rockies.[2] Essentially communal societies, they were largely self-sufficient, though in contact with each other.

All pre-contact peoples in the Americas shared a world-view according to which humans were part of a cosmological order that included the land and its animals, the stars, and the sea. The universe functioned harmoniously only when natural forces were in balance—a condition that could be maintained by elaborate rituals. Because of their strong spiritual beliefs, most of the surviving evidence of pre-contact Aboriginal societies takes the form of burial sites, not monuments to the living. What today would be called the natural and social sciences were highly developed. Before the arrival of Europeans, North Americans had calculated the movement of the sun and stars and understood the medicinal properties of plants.

As hunter-gatherers, the peoples of the Atlantic region followed a seasonal round that allowed them to make the most effective use possible of the resources around them. The Maliseet, who lived in what is now southwestern New Brunswick and northeastern Maine, grew corn in the early contact period, and may have done so for some time before then. They shared characteristics with other northeastern

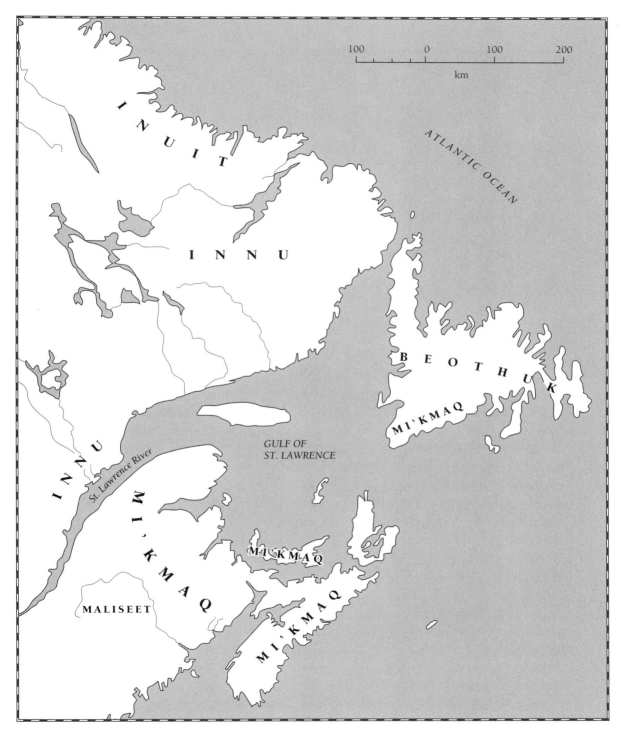

100   0   100   200

km

I N U I T

ATLANTIC OCEAN

I N N U

B E O T H U K

INNU

MI'KMAQ

St. Lawrence River

GULF OF
ST. LAWRENCE

MI'KMAQ

MALISEET

MI'KMAQ

MI'KMAQ

Aboriginal peoples in the sixteenth century.

Maliseet spearing salmon, by Sir George R.A. Levigne (1811–89). This method of catching fish was prohibited by fish and game laws in the late nineteenth century. NAC, C-30873.

Woodland cultures that dominated present-day New England and Quebec, but like other peoples in the region, the Maliseet also depended heavily on ocean resources.

The Mi'kmaq, first known to Europeans as the 'Souriquois', were the most numerous of the Aboriginal groups living in the Atlantic region in 1500. While estimates of their numbers at the time of contact range from 3,500 to 50,000, the scholarly consensus now suggests a figure of about 12,000. The extended family, sometimes supplemented by a few unrelated individuals, was the basic unit of their society. Headed by a chief, or sagamore, this unit formed the summer village that ranged from

30 to 200 people, but broke up into smaller groups during the winter. Summer was also a time for sagamores to come together to consult among themselves on matters of common interest. By the eighteenth century the Mi'kmaq were divided into seven districts, each governed by a chief who presided over a council of chiefs from each district's communities. This form of political organization probably developed in response to European trade, but the significance of chiefs seems to have been deeply rooted among the Mi'kmaq. Nicolas Denys, a French fur trader who spent several decades in the Maritimes in the seventeenth century, noted that the Mi'kmaq greatly

Petroglyphs in Kejimkujik National Park. The rock art in this central Nova Scotia park was carved by the Mi'kmaq in the post-contact period. Photo Brian Molyneaux, 1981, for Parks Canada, cat. #9B-1122-M.

valued the genealogical traditions that linked them to 'ancient chiefs' going back for more than twenty generations.[3]

At the time of European contact, the Mi'kmaq relied heavily on the moose for survival. Every part of the animal was used. Its meat was eaten fresh and dried. Women rendered a highly nutritious moose butter, called *cacamos*, from the bones, and fashioned the skin into clothing, moccasins, carrying bags, and snowshoe webbing. Antlers and bones became tools, weapons,

and needles. Moose brains were used in tanning skins, dew-claws became rattles, shin bones were carved into dice, tendons served as thread, hair was used in embroidery, and hoofs yielded an ingredient used in a treatment for epilepsy. Although moose were killed throughout the year, they were most easily caught in winter, when snowdrifts impeded their escape from hunters speeding along on snowshoes.

The Mi'kmaq were highly skilled hunters. Men and boys used dogs to help them track

Mi'kmaq playing a gambling game called waltus, early in the twentieth century. The discs in the shallow bowl were tossed like dice and the sticks were used to keep score. Similar discs made of antler, stone, bone, or pottery are often found in pre-contact burial sites. University of Pennsylvania Museum, Philadelphia, neg. #S4-13840.

down their prey, which were then dispatched with spears and arrows. Fish were so plentiful that they were easy to catch with three-pronged spears, loosely-woven nets, and weirs. The Mi'kmaq had an ingenious method for trapping birds. Under the cover of darkness, men floated their canoes among a flock of ducks or geese; they would then light torches, which confused the birds and caused them to circle the light, enabling the hunters to knock them down with long poles.

By the time of European contact the Mi'kmaq no longer used clay pots to cook their food, but fashioned watertight containers from birchbark stitched with spruce roots and sealed with spruce gum; heated stones from the fire would be placed in the pot until its contents boiled.[4]

Europeans were fascinated by Aboriginal gender roles, courtship practices, and family relationships. According to Chrestien Le Clercq, a Jesuit who ministered in the Gaspé region in the late seventeenth century, the Mi'kmaq were patriarchal, subordinating women and 'mooseless' younger males to the authority of adult men:

> The women have no command among the Indians. They must needs obey the orders of their husbands. They have no rights in councils, nor in the public feasts. It is the same, as to this, with the young men who have not yet killed any moose, the death of which opens the portal to the honours of the Gaspesian nation, and gives to the young men the right to assist at public and private assemblies. One is always a young man, that is to say, one has no more rights than the children, the women, and the girls, as long as he has not killed a moose.[5]

Polygamy was practised and marriages were easily dissolved, especially when no children were involved.

Women reputedly took motherhood literally in their stride. According to Le Clercq, whose expertise in these matters is perhaps questionable, a woman would simply 'retire a little apart in order to bring the child into the world', and then proceed with her regular duties. He continued:

> They never give birth to a child in the wigwam, for the men never give it up to them. The men remain therein whilst the wife is delivered in the woods at the foot of a tree. If she suffers pains, her arms are attached above to some pole, her nose, ears and mouth being stopped up. After this she is pressed strongly on the sides, in order to force the child to issue

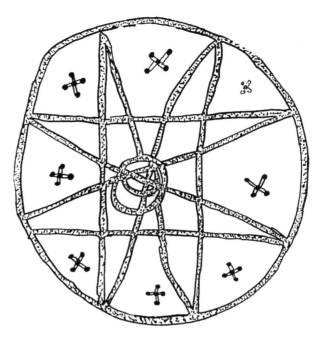

Sun design from a petroglyph near Bedford, Nova Scotia. For the Mi'kmaq the sun was an especially powerful force, the 'father' of light and life. This motif, carved in a rocky spine of the Bedford Barrens near Halifax, may be more than 500 years old, making it one of the few examples of rock art that survive from the pre-contact period. Drawing by R.H. Whitehead, History Collection, Nova Scotia Museum, Halifax.

> from the belly of its mother. If she feels it a little too severely, she calls upon the [shamans], who come with joy, in order to extort some smoking tobacco, or other things of which they have need.[6]

The method of carrying infants drew particular attention. 'In place of a cradle,' Le Clercq explained, 'they make the children rest upon a little board, which they cover with the skins of beaver or with some other furs.' Both the cradleboard and the infant's clothing were adorned with beadwork, porcupine quills, and

This engraving of an 'homme Acadien' shows a Mi'kmaq marked with various symbols, including both a sun and crosses. NAC, C-21112.

painted designs, which Le Clercq believed were used 'to beautify it, and to render it just so much the finer in proportion as they love their children'.

Le Clercq, like his fellow countrymen, had few good words for shamans. Although Native spirituality was rooted in a highly developed cosmology, Europeans spent more time trying to eradicate what they considered paganism than trying to understand it. Most Mi'kmaq eventually embraced Roman Catholicism, but traditional beliefs persisted. As late as the eigh-

teenth century, their prayers still acknowledged the role of the sun and moon in the creation of the world.[7]

The Mi'kmaq considered the sun and moon to be the ancestors of 'People', who lived on the Earth, which was part of a spiritual universe made up of Six Worlds. In addition to the Earth World, there was the World beneath the Water, the World beneath the Earth, the World above the Sky, and the World above the Earth. After death, the People went to the Ghost World, which a very few managed to visit while still living. The universe formed itself out of Power, which was manifested in people, animals, plants, and phenomena such as winds, weather, seasons, and directions. Not only could one form of power change into another—a person into a wolf, or a stone into a person, for example—but the character or state of mind of the power force could also change—from good to evil, or from strong to weak. This notion of power made for a very unpredictable universe, but it encouraged the Mi'kmaq to acquire and use power responsibly through proper behaviour. Legends conveyed their sense of the world and appropriate ways of living in it. Signs representing natural phenomena, such as the sun, communicated important spiritual concepts and were often incorporated as intricate designs on clothing, adornments, and other material possessions.

Until recently not a great deal was known about the Beothuk, an Algonkian people who chose to remain apart from Europeans and became extinct in the 1820s. Probably numbering no more than 1,000 at the time of contact, they were among the first Aboriginal peoples that Europeans encountered, and because they painted themselves with red ochre, they may have inspired the term 'Red Indian'. For food and clothing the Beothuk depended heavily on caribou, which they hunted during the herds' fall migrations.[8] Marine resources—seals, seabirds, fish, and shellfish—were also important. Moving frequently to accommodate the seasonal round, the Beothuk could travel long distances in distinctive, light-weight birchbark canoes and lived in easily assembled conical, oval, and multi-sided wigwams, covered with hides or birchbark.

The Beothuk were probably in contact with the Innu, who by 1500 were living on the south coast and interior of Labrador. Both the Beothuk and the Innu avoided the Inuit, who, for the most part, occupied the coastal area north of Hamilton Inlet, ranging further south on a seasonal basis, especially after Europeans arrived in the Strait of Belle Isle. The Innu relied heavily on what the interior could provide, principally caribou and a variety of freshwater fish, which they caught in the winter and spring. During the summer months they gathered on the coast in large groups to hunt whales, seals, and saltwater fish before breaking into small bands to winter in the interior.

Like other Aboriginal groups in the region, the Innu shared the rewards of a successful hunt and encouraged egalitarian values. Open displays of anger were repressed, decisions were made through discussion and consensus, and conformity was encouraged through joking and ridicule. Patience and good humour were considered important virtues. In contrast to the harsh discipline typical of European society, much of it aimed at breaking children's will, the Innu spared their children physical punishment. Although gender roles were clearly defined, Europeans

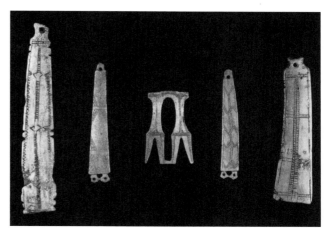

These pendants, made of caribou bone coloured with red ochre, are among the few surviving Beothuk artifacts. Since most of them have holes at the top, it seems likely that they were attached to clothing or hung around the neck. Whether they had any spiritual significance is not known. Collection of the Newfoundland Museum.

remarked on the independence and relative power of Innu women, who dominated the life-sustaining lodge hearth, controlled the distribution of food, and readily left husbands who were not good providers.

Even so, Innu men still took precedence over women. Revered for their hunting skills, men not only received the best pieces of meat, but excluded women from their feasts, and were allowed to take more than one wife. From the Aboriginal perspective, polygamy had advantages for women. Paul Le Jeune, a Jesuit priest who lived among the southwestern Innu in the 1630s and 1640s, remarked: 'Since I have been preaching among them that a man should not have more than one wife, I have not been well received among the women; for since they are more numerous than the men, if a man can only marry one of them, the others will have to suffer. Therefore

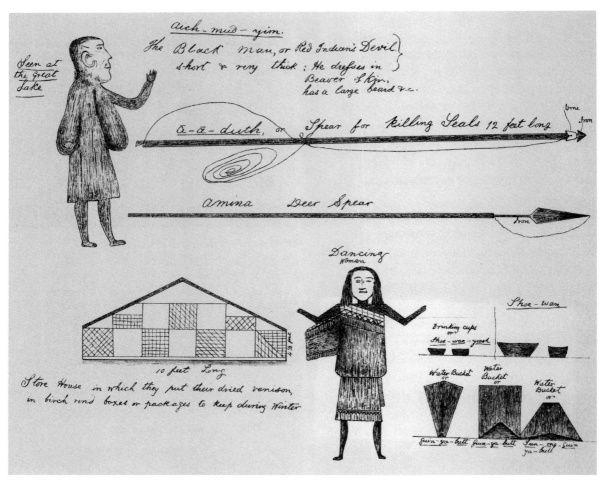

auch–mud–yim.

The Black man, or Red Indian's Devil,
short & very thick; He dresses in
Beaver Skin,
has a large beard &c.

Seen at
the Great
Lake

ā–ā–duth, or Spear for killing Seals 12 feet long

a̅mina   Deer Spear

Dancing
Woman

Shoe–wan

Drinking cups
or
Shoe–wan–yeash

Water Bucket
or

Water
Bucket
or

Water
Bucket
or

Guin–ya–butt   Gun–ya–butt   Gun–ong–Guin
ya–butt

Store House in which they put their dried venison,
in birch rind boxes or packages to keep during Winter

10 feet Long

Before her death in 1829, Shanawdithit, the last surviving Beothuk on the island of Newfoundland, drew these images depicting aspects of her culture. NAC, C-28544.

this doctrine is not according to their liking.'[9]

The Labrador Inuit were primarily a coastal people, though caribou were also important to them for both food and clothing. During the fall and winter they lived in semi-subterranean sod houses at the mouths of fiords, the men hunting whales and seals from their kayaks and umiaks until the sea froze, when they would hunt seals through the ice. In the spring some Inuit fished through lake ice, while others moved to the outer islands building snow houses and living on seals, fish, and mussels. In early summer everyone moved to the islands, where skin tents replaced sod huts and snow houses. In July the Inuit congregated at places where salmon was plentiful before migrating inland to hunt caribou. The success of the hunt was assisted by shamans, or *angakut*, who mediated between the human and spirit worlds. In 1772, the Moravian missionaries at Nain reported that a female shaman 'fell into a trance, when her soul took a tour through the inland parts, where she saw a vast quantity of Rain Deer. Upon this the Esquimaux went to the inlet as directed by her, where they saw and got many deer.'[10] Shamans also treated sickness, which was thought to be caused by evil spirits, and in general helped Inuit to make sense of their lives and deaths.

One of the earliest European images of North America is a woodcut of an Inuit mother and daughter, probably from Labrador, who were captured by French fishermen and taken to Europe in 1566. The kidnappers had killed the woman's husband before taking their captives, foreshadowing the hostile relations that quickly developed between Inuit and newcomers. Writing in the early seventeenth century, Samuel de Champlain noted that the Inuit were 'very malicious . . . [attacking] fishermen, who in self defence arm small vessels to protect the boats which put to sea to fish cod.'[11] In later years the French would be slow to establish fishing and sealing stations on the Labrador coast, in part because of their justified fear of the Inuit.

Every Aboriginal group in the Atlantic region would have tales to tell once Europeans began to frequent their coasts in the early sixteenth century. In each case the encounter brought disease, death, and social and economic dislocation, even to those who, like the Mi'kmaq and Maliseet, initially welcomed the Europeans and what they had to offer. The least affected were the most remote—the Inuit

Printed in Augsburg in 1567, this woodcut is the first known European depiction of Inuit drawn from life. The woman and child had been put on exhibition in Europe after being captured on the Labrador coast the previous year. From W.C. Sturtevant, 'The First Inuit Depiction by Europeans', *Etudes Inuit Studies* 4, 1–2 (1980), 47-9.

and northern Innu bands. Those who lived around the Gulf of St Lawrence bore the brunt of the first European efforts to explore, fish, trade, and spread the Christian faith.

CHAPTER THREE

European Encounters: 1000–1598

Then there were no people in this country but Indians, and before any others became known, a young woman had a singular dream. . . . A small island came floating in towards the land, with tall trees on it, and living beings. [The shaman] pondered the girl's dream but could make nothing of it. The next day an event occurred that explained all. What should they see but a singular little island, as they supposed, which had drifted near to the land and become stationary there. There were trees on it and branches to the trees, on which a number of bears . . . were crawling about. . . . What was their surprise to find that these supposed bears were men.[1]

This account, by Josiah Jeremy, of one Mi'kmaq community's first sighting of hirsute Europeans and their tall-masted sailing ships was recorded by Silas Rand, a nineteenth-century Baptist missionary who collected the Mi'kmaq's oral history. What encounter this story describes is impossible to determine, but as far as we know, the first Europeans to reach Atlantic Canada were the Norse. Their arrival in the region around 1,000 years ago marked

the final stage in a process that had begun in Scandinavia several centuries earlier. Waves of migrants, often preceded by the raiders we know as Vikings, spread across northern Europe, and then westward over the North Atlantic. Unlike their successors five hundred years later, they were looking not for Asia but for land that they could settle.

Late in the tenth century, Eirik the Red colonized southeastern Greenland. Then in 986 a merchant-shipowner named Bjarni Herjolfsson was blown off-course while travelling to the new settlement. Finding himself sailing along an unknown coastline, he headed north and then east to Greenland without taking time to explore, but his voyage was remembered. A few years later Leif Eiriksson retraced Bjarni's route in reverse. According to the saga, Leif found three lands. The first he called Helluland; consisting primarily of rock and ice, it was probably Baffin Island. The second, Markland, flat and wooded, was almost certainly part of southern Labrador. Leif then reached a country he called Vinland, with grassy meadows and well-stocked rivers. The expedition over-wintered there in sod and timber houses, before returning to Greenland.

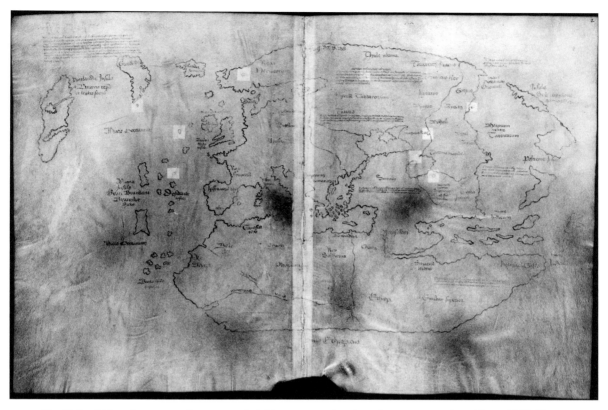

The Vinland Map. Controversy has surrounded this map ever since its existence was made public in 1965. If it was actually drawn around 1440—which many scholars doubt—it is the oldest European map to show a part of North America. Beinecke Rare Book and Manuscript Library, Yale University.

Where was Vinland? The sailing route and some of the physical features described in the sagas suggest a Newfoundland location, a theory bolstered by the discovery in 1961 of a Norse habitation at L'Anse-aux-Meadows on the island's Northern Peninsula. Yet the sagas also mention lush vegetation, grain, self-sown wheat, and grapes—none of which can be found in Newfoundland today—and archaeologists at the habitation have discovered the remains of butternuts, which do not grow any farther north than what is now New Brunswick. The current scholarly consensus reconciles this evidence by arguing that L'Anse-aux-Meadows was a base camp at the entrance to Vinland, a region that encompassed the Gulf of St Lawrence.[2]

The sagas indicate that Leif Eiriksson made several later expeditions, and others followed his lead. The most ambitious of the known Norse ventures was that of Thorfinn Karlsefni, who attempted to establish a settlement in Vinland and remained there for several years. Like at least one of its predecessors, Thorfinn's expedition found it impossible to co-exist with the people living in the region,

According to medieval legend, in the sixth century St Brendan, with a party of Irish monks, made a long and marvellous voyage across the Atlantic in a curragh. These woodcuts, first published in Germany in 1499, show the monks meeting a siren and a holy man, and being attacked by a sea monster. From André Vachon, *Dreams of Empire: Canada Before 1700* (Ottawa: NAC, 1982), 18.

whom the Norse called Skraelings, a highly derogatory term meaning 'wretches' or 'savages'. Largely as a result of conflicts with the Skraelings, Thorfinn retreated to Greenland.

Reasons for the Norse failure to create a permanent settlement in Vinland are not difficult to imagine: the location was remote, the journey was difficult, and the Native inhabitants were hostile. Moreover, as the Greenland settlements became increasingly fragile the Norse lost interest in colonization to the west. In any case, their encounter with America seems to have had little, if any, impact in Europe. It neither changed the European view of the world nor stimulated further voyages westward. Although there are stories of Atlantic crossings before the time of Christopher Columbus, no firm evidence exists to support any of these often far-fetched claims.

Systematic exploration of the Atlantic began in the fifteenth century with the Portuguese. First probing south along the African coast, they then reached out farther to the west. Their goal was to develop new sea routes to India and other parts of Asia, in an effort to share in the lucrative spice trade hitherto monopolized by the Italians. By the end of the century the Portuguese had rounded the Cape of Good Hope and reached India, sparking increasing interest all along the Atlantic seaboard in the possibility of reaching Asia by sailing west. Europeans had known for centuries that the earth was round, but for good reasons were reluctant to venture too far out to sea. With the development of more seaworthy vessels and improvements in navigational instruments in the fifteenth century, captains were better able to establish their positions, set their courses with reasonable accuracy, and sail for days without sighting land. These advances in marine technology enabled Christopher Columbus, sailing in the name of the Spanish Crown in 1492, to reach what he (and everyone else in Europe) thought was Asia, but was in fact the Caribbean. Five years later another Italian mariner, Zuan Caboto (known to the English as John Cabot) also reached what was assumed to be Asia, where he raised a cross along with the banners of England and Venice.

Cabot had sailed from Bristol, England, on 2 May 1497, in a small vessel called the *Matthew*. Commissioned by King Henry VII to 'sail to all parts, regions, and coasts of the eastern, western, and northern sea' and authorized 'to conquer, occupy, and possess whatever towns, castles, cities, and islands, he discovered', Cabot returned to England in August bringing tales of 'new founde landes' whose adjacent waters swarmed 'with fish which can be taken not only with the net, but in baskets let down with a stone. . . .'

Because the evidence relating to Cabot's voyage is scanty, the location of his landfall has been the subject of considerable debate. There are, roughly speaking, three groups of interpretations: those that favour a landfall in the Strait of Belle Isle region; those that argue for the east coast of Newfoundland; and those that champion Cape Breton or points further south. Most Canadian historians used to support the claims of Cape Breton, arguing that Cabot would have been carried south by storms and ocean currents, and that cartographic evidence supports their case. Newfoundlanders have consistently dismissed these arguments, holding it as an article of faith that Cabot's first landfall was Cape Bonavista. How, they ask, could he have missed Newfoundland? And does not John Mason's 1617 map bear the legend 'Bona Vista Caboto primum reperta'? Today, most scholars lean towards a northern

John Cabot's *Matthew* was described as a *navicula* (a small vessel) of fifty *toneles*, meaning that it could carry fifty tuns of wine or other cargo. Like a Portuguese caravel, the *Matthew* had flush decks, a sterncastle, and three masts, the rear one rigged with a lateen sail to help the ship sail into the wind.
The model shown here was commissioned by the Newfoundland Historical Society in 1947 to mark the 450th anniversary of Cabot's first voyage. Photo Ned Pratt, Newfoundland Historical Society.

landfall, somewhere on either side of the Strait of Belle Isle. It is agreed that Cabot would have sailed north along the Irish coast before turning west, and, as a skilled navigator, could have held his latitude.[3]

Pleased by Cabot's apparent success, Henry VII authorized a larger expedition in 1498, financed by Bristol merchants. Virtually nothing is known about this voyage, in the course of which Cabot himself disappeared. It seems likely that his ships would have returned to the lands found in 1497 and then sailed south, looking for 'Cipango' (China).

Instead they found 'primeval tracts and Indian tribes, no great state or government, no cities, seaports, ships or trade, no spices and silks for barter—in a word, no Asia.'[4] Information on early sixteenth-century maps suggest that some of Cabot's ships returned to describe their findings. Although there were a few more voyages from Bristol to North America, the city's merchants were, for the most part, more interested in trade than fishing. England effectively dropped out of the exploration sweepstakes, and it was not until the second half of the sixteenth century that its interest in what North America had to offer revived.

Meanwhile, Spain and Portugal had established that the Atlantic was the highway to the immense resource-base of the Americas.[5] In 1494, by the Treaty of Tordesillas, they divided the non-Christian world between them (with the blessing of the Pope). A north-south line was drawn west of the Cape Verde Islands; territory west of the line was awarded to Spain, east of it to Portugal. Cabot, it seems, had been trespassing.

Assuming that the 'new' lands in the North Atlantic lay within his sphere, King Manoel of Portugal authorized a number of voyages by inhabitants of the Azores. In 1499 João Fernandes, a small landowner or 'labrador', reached Greenland, which as a result was called 'Labrador' on some early maps. In the sixteenth century, the name was transferred to the coast of North America, where it has since remained. In 1500 Gaspar Corte-Real reached 'Terra Verde'—probably Newfoundland—and returned with three ships in 1501, but his vessel disappeared on this voyage. A similar fate befell his brother Miguel, who sailed to find him in 1502. A

third brother made a futile attempt to find them both in 1503.

Although these voyages provided cartographers with important new information, it was not yet understood that the 'new founde landes' were part of a new continent. Contemporary maps show the 'discoveries' of Columbus, Cabot, and the Portuguese either as islands in the ocean, or as connected with Greenland and Asia. By the 1520s, though, the shape of the Americas was emerging. An important contribution to this process was made by Giovanni da Verrazzano, who in 1524, on behalf of the French king, explored the coast between the Carolinas and Cape Breton, and possibly part of Newfoundland as well. His purpose had been to find a passage to Asia, but instead he ascertained the existence of a continuous coastline and established the first formal link between France and North America. Similar voyages were made in 1524–5 on behalf of Spain by Estevão Gomes (who kidnapped a large number of Native people, probably on the Nova Scotian coast), and for England's Henry VIII by John Rut, who in 1527 sailed from Labrador to the Caribbean.

In 1534 the king of France, François I, commissioned Jacques Cartier to sail beyond Newfoundland to 'discover certain islands and countries where it is said a great quantity of gold and other precious things are to be found'. From a landfall near Bonavista, Cartier sailed through the Strait of Belle Isle and circumnavigated the Gulf of St Lawrence, which he took to be an inland sea. On his second voyage, in 1535, he found its true nature, and entered the St Lawrence River. In 1535 he and his men wintered near present-day Quebec City, and in 1541–2 he participated in an

Palaeo-Indian artifacts
from the Debert site, Nova
Scotia, radiocarbon-dated
to about 10,600 years ago.
They include spear points,
engraving tools, knives,
and scrapers, all made
from Minas Basin chal-
cedony. Archaeological
Survey, Canadian Museum
of Civilization, from James
Tuck, *Maritime Provinces
Prehistory*, colour plate I,
© Canadian Museum of
Civilization.

Archaic artifacts from Cow
Point, New Brunswick,
dated to between 3,600
and 3,800 years ago.
Shown here are a plum-
met, slate spears or bayo-
nets, and two woodwork-
ing tools. Archaeological
Survey, Canadian Museum
of Civilization, from James
Tuck, *Maritime Provinces
Prehistory,* colour plate II,
© Canadian Museum of
Civilization.

Anonymous, 'Micmac Indians', c. 1850. This idealized rendering of the Mi'kmaq depicts the crafts with which they were most often identified: quillwork baskets, snowshoes, toboggans, canoes, and wigwams. National Gallery of Canada, Ottawa, purchased 1957, #6663.

John T. Stanton, 'Indians in New Brunswick Making Baskets', watercolour over red chalk on paper, c. 1840. The New Brunswick Museum, Saint John, NB.

Mushuaunnu Innu painted caribou-skin coat from Labrador, *c.* 1800. Made for a boy or small man, this coat is unusual in that the skin was smoked, making it darker than usual, and the pattern was based on a European model. Collection of the Newfoundland Museum.

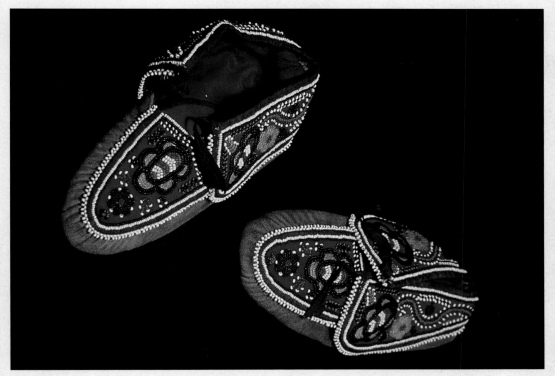

Moccasins made of leather, wool, glass beads, cotton, and silk, 1885, attributed to Mary Acquin. From the earliest contact period, the Mi'kmaq and Maliseet incorporated European materials into their beautifully ornamented clothing. Gift of the Estate of Sir Douglas Hazen. The New Brunswick Museum, Saint John, NB, 59.88.7.

A portrait of 'Mary March' by Lady Henrietta Hamilton, watercolour, 1819. Demasduit, captured at Red Indian Lake, was later taken to St John's, where she was painted by the wife of the governor. This is the only known authentic portrait of a Beothuk. Demasduit died of tuberculosis in 1820. NAC, C-87698

John Russell, 'Esquimaux Lady', oil on canvas, 1769. Mikak and her son were captured on the south Labrador coast by British troops in 1767 and later taken to England. She is clothed in a dress given to her by the Dowager Princess of Wales. Mikak was returned to Labrador in 1769, and later helped the Moravian mission become established there. Völkerkundliche Sammlung der Universität Götttingen, Germany.

TRAMONTANA // TERRA DE LABORADOR

PARTE INCOGNITA

ISOLA DE DEMONI.

ONENTE

TERRA NVOVA.

LA NVOVA FRANCIA·

LEVANTE

TERRA DENVR VMBEGA

Baccalaos.

Bonne uiste.

C. de.despera

Isola de Brettoni.

Isola della rena.

OSTRO

This imaginative woodcut map of the Atlantic region was made by Jacoma di Gastaldi and published in Venice in 1556. Like other maps of this period, it shows Newfoundland as a group of islands, and narrow off-shore banks; Gastaldi obviously had no knowledge of Cartier's explorations in the Atlantic region. CNS, MUN.

unsuccessful attempt to establish a permanent European settlement there.

With Cartier's voyages the first phase in the European discovery of North America came to an end. The coastline from Mexico to Greenland had been explored, described, and mapped. For most of the explorers, who had no intention of staying, their voyages ended in disappointment. They found neither gold nor spices, and the Native people were often hostile.[6] Even the northwest passage to Asia eluded them, although for many years English

explorers, beginning with John Cabot's son Sebastian (1508–9), tried to find it.

Nevertheless, the first generation of explorers had located a region that some Europeans believed to be potentially profitable. Cabot might not have found spices or precious metals, but he had located a rich new source of fish. This was a valuable resource in its own right—so much so that more Europeans of the period worked in the fisheries than in any other occupation except agriculture. Fish was an important source of protein, easy to preserve and transport, and often replaced meat on Roman Catholic fast days. Moreover, fishing trained mariners for service on sea in time of war. As a result, James Axtell argues, the Atlantic region rapidly became 'a pole of European activity in every way comparable to that of the Caribbean and the Gulf of Mexico'.[7]

Although the English had sponsored Cabot, they were not the first to make significant use of the new fishing grounds. English markets were adequately supplied by local and Icelandic fisheries, and the major fishing ports were on the northeast coast—not the best starting point for transatlantic voyages. The ports of northern and eastern France were better positioned, and French markets for North Sea cod were already in place before the Cabot voyage. Vessels from Channel ports in Brittany and Normandy were therefore the first to fish regularly in Newfoundland waters. In their wake came fishermen from Atlantic ports such as Bordeaux and La Rochelle, joined after 1520 by Basques from southern France and northern Spain. By the 1520s, between 60 and 90 French vessels were crossing the Atlantic each year.

The role of Portugal in the north Atlantic fishery of the sixteenth century is a subject of some controversy.[8] Certainly there was a Portuguese presence in the region, but whether it included a fishery of any significance is debatable. In the current state of knowledge, the most that can be said is that the Portuguese sent over relatively few vessels and seem, on the whole, to have been more interested in the region's landward potential than in codfish. Nevertheless, they were among the first to visit Newfoundland's Avalon Peninsula, and Portuguese-derived place names line the shore south of St John's, among

them Cape Spear (Cauo da espera), Ferryland (Farilham), and Cape Race (Capo raso).

Although the French too fished off the Avalon Peninsula, they ranged widely throughout the region. Bretons and Normans fished at Cape Breton and Gaspé, and later in the sixteenth century they moved along the coast of the Nova Scotia peninsula and into the Bay of Fundy. Bretons in particular were interested in the potential of Newfoundland's northeast and southern coasts. French and Spanish Basques often fished together, congregating in southeast Newfoundland between Trepassey and Placentia Bay, on the Gaspé Peninsula, in the Gulf of St Lawrence, and in the Strait of Belle Isle (la Grande Baye).

These were initially shore-based fisheries, but later in the century France also began to exploit the offshore banks—first the Grand Bank, then those off southern Newfoundland and in the Gulf—sending about 100 vessels annually by the 1590s. Another form of mid-century diversification was the Basques' development of a whaling industry in the Strait of Belle Isle. They established stations on the Labrador coast between Cape Charles and the St Paul River, the most important at Red Bay (Butus, or Hable des Buttes), where archaeologists have recently excavated both the buildings and the wreck of the *San Juan,* a galleon that sank there in 1565. At the height of the industry, some 30 Basque ships hunted right and bowhead whales annually, employing about 2,500 men. Although whalers sometimes remained in Labrador for the winter, such sojourns were usually involuntary, the result of delaying departure so long that the ships became icebound. Perhaps it was during one such enforced stay that on Christmas Eve

The Descelliers Map, 1546 (detail). This detail depicts whaling in the general area of the Strait of Belle Isle, and a ship similar to the one used by Jacques Cartier. Newfoundland is represented as an archipelago, as was often the case in sixteenth-century maps. NAC, NMC-40461; original in the University of Manchester.

1584, at Carrol's Cove (then known as Puerto Breton), Joanes de Echaniz dictated his will—one of the earliest in Canada.

In the late sixteenth century the Iberian fishery declined. Not only had the Spanish government begun imposing new taxes and restrictions on trade and shipping, but inflation was increasing costs. Moreover, the war with England, which culminated in the disaster of the Spanish Armada in 1588, caused serious disruptions and financial losses. Annexed by Spain in 1580, Portugal saw its fortunes decline as well. Having depleted the

whale stocks off Labrador, Basque whalers moved elsewhere. Spanish Basques continued to fish in the Gulf and off southeastern Newfoundland throughout the seventeenth century, but in decreasing numbers. An important result of these developments was that Iberia now needed to import significant quantities of fish.

In response, the French fleet expanded to approximately 500 vessels, a level at which it would remain until the mid-seventeenth century. At the same time French fishermen began using the Gulf much more extensively than

A reconstructed Basque *chalupa* at Red Bay, Labrador. Crewed by six men, and powered by either sails or oars, shallops such as this one were used for whaling in the Strait of Belle Isle. Photo Kevin Redmond, Parks Canada, 1998.

they had before, steadily moving farther west into the St Lawrence River itself. The same market opportunity caught the attention of ports in southwestern England (the West Country) such as Poole, Plymouth, and Dartmouth. Anthony Parkhurst, a merchant who first came to the island in 1574, estimated in 1578 that no more than 50 English vessels made the trip to Newfoundland; by the early seventeenth century that number had increased to at least 200.[9]

At first there appears to have been relatively little conflict between the English and French fisheries, which differed significantly.

The French, sailing from ports along the coast from Normandy to the Pyrenees, produced both a 'wet' (or 'green') cure, in which the fish was heavily salted in a ship's hold or packed in brine, and a 'dry' cure, in which the fish was split, lightly salted, and then dried on shore. The French market, particularly in the north and east, generally preferred green fish, but in response to demand from Spain, Portugal, and the Mediterranean, French Basques in particular began to produce dry-cured fish, which kept better in hot climates.

By contrast, the English, sailing almost exclusively from West Country ports, produced only a dry cure (known as saltfish) and ignored the domestic market in favour of Iberia and southern Europe. For the English, saltfish was above all an article of trade, a commodity to be exchanged for bullion, fruits, wines, and exotic Mediterranean goods. If production of a dry cure was dictated largely by market considerations, it also used less salt—which was in short supply in England—than a wet cure did.

The production of saltfish demanded the building of seasonal fishing stations where the catch could be cleaned, salted, and dried. Increasingly, the English began to establish themselves on the eastern shores of the Avalon Peninsula, gradually extending as far north as Bonavista. This 'English Shore' was the first English foothold in what is now Atlantic Canada.

In the sixteenth century there were no permanent, year-round European settlements anywhere in the Atlantic region. The fisheries were seasonal extensions of a European industry, reliant on a European workforce and European markets. Moreover, Europeans were not persuaded that overseas colonies were desirable. One factor that helped to change this attitude was the development of the fur trade. Native people were usually eager to barter with the newcomers. Basque whaling stations, for instance, attracted Inuit, Innu, and St Lawrence Iroquoians, all of whom placed a high value on metal objects, especially knives and axes. Although Natives sometimes pilfered metal items when Europeans were absent, by mid-century the practice of trading furs had become well-established, and it was further stimulated after 1580 by the European demand for felt made of beaver fur, which was fashioned into hats. The Basques

seem to have established a good relationship with the Innu in the region. In the last decade of the sixteenth century, the West Country sea captain Richard Whitbourne reported that the Innu were 'an ingenious and tractable people (being well used)',[10] who worked in the whale fishery, helping to hunt and process the catch. Relations between Europeans and the Inuit were not usually so cordial.

The decline of the Basque whale fishery and the subsequent westward shift of the St Lawrence fur trade produced a relatively distant relationship between Europeans and the Labrador Innu and Inuit. On the island of Newfoundland, the Beothuk increasingly withdrew from areas used by Europeans. They had not always been so reclusive. In the sixteenth century, they occasionally traded with French and Basque fishermen, and John Guy recorded meeting Beothuks in Trinity Bay in 1612, who greeted him with 'signes of ioy, & gladnes' and signalled their willingness to trade by setting up poles on which skins had been fastened. As the numbers of Europeans increased, however, the Beothuk avoided direct contact, instead scavenging for metal goods in the debris left behind by migratory fishing crews. The fur trade in Newfoundland, therefore, was conducted not by the Beothuk, but by Europeans over-wintering there.

By contrast, the Mi'kmaq and Maliseet seem to have been eager to trade, and gradually established close relations with the Europeans. The early contact period is not well documented, but it is clear that by the time of Cartier's first voyage the Mi'kmaq in the Gaspé region were familiar with the rituals of the fur trade. In July 1534 Cartier met a group of Mi'kmaq near the Bay of Chaleur:

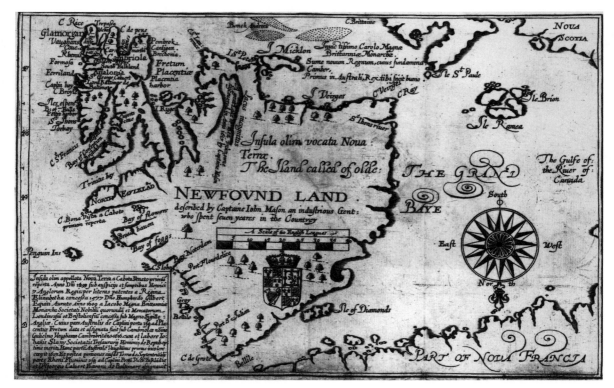

The John Mason Map, 1617. When Mason was appointed governor of the English colony at Cupids, Conception Bay, in 1616, he was already familiar with Newfoundland. His map—the first English depiction of the island—constitutes an important piece of evidence for those who believe that John Cabot made his landfall at Cape Bonavista. On the left, just below the peninsula named 'North Falkland' (now the Bonavista Peninsula), is the legend *C. Bona Vista a Caboto primum Reperta*. NAC, NMC-21046.

The next day some of these Indians came in nine canoes to the point at the mouth of the cove where we lay at anchor with our ships. . . . As soon as they saw us they began to run away, making signs that they had come to barter with us; and held up some furs of small value, with which they clothe themselves. We likewise made signs to them that we wished them no harm, and sent two men on shore, to offer them some knives and other iron goods, and a red cap to give to their chief. Seeing this, they sent on shore part of their people with some of their furs; and the two parties traded together.[11]

According to James Axtell, some Mi'kmaq became middlemen, 'sailing in Basque shallops, wearing various items of European clothing . . . speaking a half-Basque, half-Indian trade jargon', and bartering furs from as far south as the coast of Maine with French or Basque traders in the Gulf of St Lawrence and at Tadoussac.[12]

In a pattern that would be repeated in the

region and across the continent, the Mi'kmaq and Maliseet saw their way of life transformed by interaction with European traders. They replaced their stone and bone implements with metal ones, began to use guns and copper pots, and adopted European foodstuffs and cloth garments. These changes may have made everyday life easier, but they also encouraged over-hunting, changed seasonal rhythms, and disrupted social organizations. Increasing respect, for example, was accorded those who had close relationships with Europeans. While it has been pointed out that trade partnerships between Aboriginal peoples and Europeans were not at first grossly imbalanced,[13] that would change when the French and English decided to stake territorial claims in their 'new world'.

CHAPTER FOUR

Colonial Experiments: 1598–1632

On 26 August 1621 Edward Wynne wrote to his employer, Sir George Calvert, outlining his plans for planting a colony at Ferryland, on the east coast of the Avalon Peninsula:

> The place whereon I have made choice to plant and build upon is . . . the fittest, the warmest, the most commodious of all about the harbour. As soon as the [Mansion] house and fortification is fitted and finished, I shall (God willing) prepare and fence in a proportion of seed ground and a garden, close by the house. It may please your Honour not to send out any cattle next year, because I cannot fodder for them so soon, before there be some quantity of corn [grain] growing, but it may please your honour to send some goats, a few tame conies [rabbits] for breed, as also pigs, geese, ducks and hens. I have some hens already. Some spades from London were necessary, if of the best making, also some good pick-axes, iron crows [crowbars], and a smith, and also such as can brew and bake.[1]

Like other would-be European colonizers, Wynne hoped to recreate the old world in the new, but this project would prove more challenging than any of them could have imagined.

The eventual success of Europeans in colonizing the Americas and Australasia is one of the most significant developments in modern history. Until recently, historians assumed that the outcome was predetermined by European superiority—moral, technological, and institutional. It is true that Europeans had the advantage of what Stephen Greenblatt has described as 'a complex, well-developed, and, above all, mobile technology of power' characterized by 'writing, navigational instruments, ships . . . and highly lethal weapons'.[2] They could not colonize a strange new environment, however, until they had learned how to survive in it. This knowledge they obtained in part from experience, but above all from the Native peoples. Two sixteenth-century colonization efforts in the Atlantic region failed, and the small settlements established in the seventeenth century were vulnerable in that they depended on the tolerance of both the Aboriginal populations and other Europeans. This situation was not to change until the eighteenth century, by which time Europeans—

along with their animals, plants, and diseases—had become familiar features of the North American landscape.[3]

The failure of early colonial initiatives also reflected the weakness of the European powers—primarily France, England, and Scotland—competing for ascendancy in the region. As Elizabeth Mancke and John Reid have pointed out, in the sixteenth and early seventeenth centuries the rulers of these emerging nation-states had neither the financial nor the institutional resources required to undertake empire-building directly. Instead they delegated colonization and governance to private individuals or companies. This approach, coupled with persistent international conflict, made the Atlantic region vulnerable to economic, political, and religious rivalries defined in Europe. As much linked to Europe by the Atlantic as distanced by it, the eastern margins of North America served as a stage on which imperial characters acted out their competing roles.[4]

Given the environmental and political challenges, it is not surprising that colonization efforts in the Atlantic region between 1578 and 1632 yielded bold characters, high drama, and meagre results. In 1578, Elizabeth I of England gave Sir Humphrey Gilbert, an early enthusiast for overseas ventures, a patent to explore and occupy those parts of eastern North America not already taken by the Spanish. Gilbert's dream was to plant a colony in some part of what is now Massachusetts. In 1583 he set out on a reconnaissance expedition, sailing from Southampton with four ships. Arriving off Newfoundland, they made for St John's harbour to obtain food and other necessities. After convincing the captains of

Sir Humphrey Gilbert, by an unknown engraver, 1620. Courtesy National Portrait Gallery, London, neg. 3253.

the forty or so fishing vessels there that he was not a pirate, Gilbert was allowed to pass through the Narrows, where one of his ships anticlimactically ran aground. Whether he had originally planned the ceremony is unclear, but on 5 August he went ashore and formally claimed the land for the English Crown. He erected a pillar with the arms of England fixed to it, issued licences to non-English ships, and appropriated and leased back shore premises. Before he reached the mainland, the expedition began to fall apart. Eventually admitting

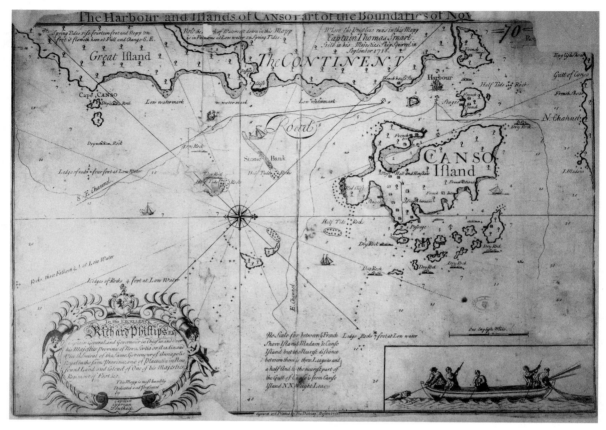

Cyprian Southack, 'The Harbour and Islands of Canso . . .', 1720. From the early sixteenth century, Canso Harbour was a major site for the French fisheries. Cyprian Southack was a member of a British expedition sent to take possession of Canso in 1718. PRO, CO 700, Nova Scotia No. 6.

failure, Gilbert decided to return home without reaching his destination. In the course of the voyage he drowned, having last been seen sitting on board his vessel with a book in his hand, shouting, 'We are as neare to Heaven by sea as by land.'[5] Nineteenth-century historians tended to see Gilbert's performance in St John's harbour as a significant event in the evolution of the first British empire, but since neither his successors nor the English Crown followed up his assertion of sovereignty, it meant little in practical terms.

It was not the English but the French who began the European settlement of the Atlantic region. In 1598 Henri IV ascended to the throne following a bloody civil war that had raged between Protestants (Huguenots) and Roman Catholics in France since 1562. Emulating the model established by other monarchs, he tried to restore his own treasury and the glory of France through overseas ventures financed by private interests. Entrepreneurs were offered a monopoly of the fur trade in territories claimed by France if they would agree to transport settlers and support Christian missions among the local inhabitants. The first settlement attempt was on Sable Island, where in 1598 the Marquis de la Roche left 40 settlers from Rouen and ten soldiers. Only eleven were left by the spring of 1603, when the colony was abandoned.

The next, ultimately more successful, initiative was led by a Huguenot. In 1603 Pierre Du Gua, Sieur de Monts, was appointed by Henri IV as his viceroy in 'la Cadie', Canada, and 'autres terres de la Nouvelle France'. In return for a ten-year fur-trade monopoly, de Monts undertook to take out at least 60 settlers annually and to support efforts to convert the Natives to Christianity. The next year, de Monts set out to establish a colony in 'la Cadie'.[6] His entourage included two Roman Catholic priests, a Protestant minister, several noblemen, masons, carpenters, a miner, a surgeon, and an apothecary, as well as sheep and hens. It also included seasoned explorers, among them Samuel de Champlain, a veteran of the religious wars and an enthusiastic proponent of European colonization, and probably Mathieu d'Acosta, an African who was subsequently described as an interpreter of 'Acadian tongues' (Aboriginal languages). After exploring the south coast of Nova Scotia and the Bay of Fundy (named la Baie Française by de Monts), they finally chose Dochet Island in the mouth of the St Croix River as the site for a settlement. The choice seems to have been dictated by a concern for military protection, but it proved disastrous. The harsh climate, lack of firewood, and inadequate provisions brought singular hardship. By the spring, 35 of the 79 men who had wintered on the island had died of scurvy.

All but three of those who survived the ordeal returned to France. One of the few determined to remain was Champlain, who spent the summer of 1605 helping de Monts to find a more suitable location for a settlement. After exploring the coast as far as Cape Cod, they finally fixed upon a sheltered basin on the south shore of the Baie Française. The previous year, Champlain had described Port-Royal (today the Annapolis Basin) as 'the most suitable and pleasant for a settlement that we had seen'.[7] While the natural military protection, agricultural potential of the soil, and temperate climate were all good reasons for choosing Port-Royal, the location offered another advantage as well: the Mi'kmaq in the area, under their chief Membertou, were prepared to tolerate the intruders. Having experienced a hostile reception from the Aboriginal people in the Cape Cod region, the French recognized that friendship with the local inhabitants was a decided asset in any effort to establish a colony.

The would-be colonizers built their second 'habitation' on the north shore of the basin and, with the assistance of the Mi'kmaq, quickly adapted to life in North America. In the spring of 1606 the governor, Jean de Poutrincourt et de Saint-Just, brought skilled workmen to Port-Royal as well as several aristocratic relatives and friends who would play important roles in the development of New France. These included his son, Charles de Biencourt; a cousin from Paris, Louis Hébert, who was an apothecary and horticulturalist; a cousin from Champagne, Claude de Saint-Etienne de La Tour, and his fourteen year-old-son, Charles; and Marc Lescarbot, a lawyer from Paris who recorded the activities of this charmed circle in his *Histoire de la Nouvelle*

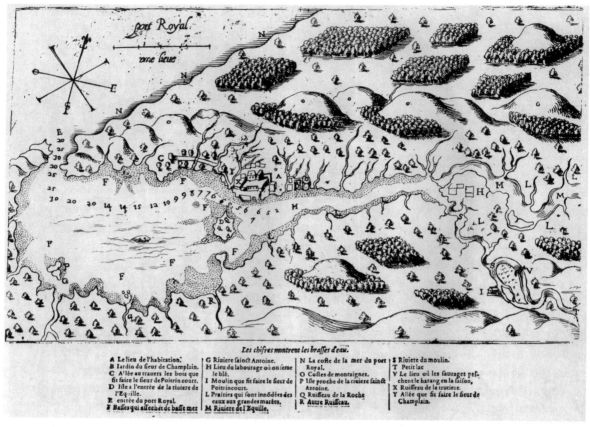

Les chifres montrent les brasses d'eau.

A Le lieu de l'habitation.
B Iardin du sieur de Champlain.
C A'lée au trauers les bois que fit faire le sieur de Poitrin court.
D Isle a l'entrée de la riuiere de l'Equille.
E entrée du port Royal.
F Basses qui assechét de basse mer

G Riuiere sainct Antoine.
H Lieu du labourage où on seme le blé.
I Moulin que fit faire le sieur de Poitrincourt.
L Prairies qui sont inñodées des eaux aux grandes marées.
M Riuiere de l'Equille.

N La coste de la mer du port Royal.
O Costes de montaignes.
P Isle proche de la riuiere sainct Antoine.
Q Ruisseau de la Roche.
R Autre Ruisseau.

S Riuiere du moulin.
T Petit lac
V Le lieu où les sauuages peschent le harang en la saison,
X Ruisseau de la trutiere.
Y Allée que fit faire le sieur de Champlain.

Champlain's map of the first Port-Royal. The habitation is flanked by a trout brook (X) and Champlain's garden (B). The wheat fields (H) would become the site of Fort Anne, and the mill is located on the Allain River (I). National Library of Canada, NL 15325.

France, published in 1618.[8] The French planted wheat, built a grist mill, and did their best to recreate a European agricultural settlement. Delighting in the relatively warm winters at Port-Royal, the French developed innovative responses to the challenges of survival. Champlain founded the Ordre du Bon Temps, which obliged each gentleman to take his turn providing game and fish for the table. In the fall of 1606 Lescarbot wrote and produced a masque, the *Théâtre de Neptune*,

which the colonists performed to welcome Poutrincourt back to Port-Royal.

Notwithstanding his success in planting the colony, de Monts was in trouble. His fur-trade monopoly was impossible to enforce, and under attack from rivals. In 1607 it was revoked. Faced by financial losses, de Monts ordered the abandonment of Port-Royal. The French focus now shifted to the St Lawrence, where both de Monts and Champlain concentrated their efforts. However, Poutrincourt—to whom de Monts had given the Port-Royal area—remained interested in Acadia. In 1610 he returned there with his son Charles de Biencourt and some twenty colonists, including a priest named Jessé Fléché. The Mi'kmaq had looked after the habitation while the French were sorting out their difficulties. In short order Poutrincourt collected a shipload of furs, Fléché baptized Membertou and other members of his band, and Biencourt set off for France to obtain support for his enterprise by demonstrating that it could be both financially and spiritually profitable. He managed to find a patron in the person of Antoinette de Pons, the Marquise de Guercheville, but her support was tied to the condition that the Jesuits, who had become influential at the French court, would control missionary work in Acadia and become partners in the trade. In May 1611 Biencourt returned to Port-Royal with 36 colonists and two Jesuit priests, Pierre Biard and Énemond Massé.

The colony was soon thrown into turmoil. While Poutrincourt was absent in Paris, serious quarrels broke out between young Biencourt and the Jesuits. The Marquise de Guercheville, who was determined to see the Jesuits prevail, obtained control over territories outside of Poutrincourt's jurisdiction and financed an expedition to move the Jesuits from Port-Royal to Saint-Sauveur, a new colony established on a site opposite what is now known as Mount Desert Island on the Penobscot River in Maine. Alarmed by developments to the north, the governor of the English colony of Virginia, established in 1607, instructed Samuel Argall to attack the French settlements. In the fall of 1613 he took the Jesuits prisoner, destroyed Saint-Sauveur,

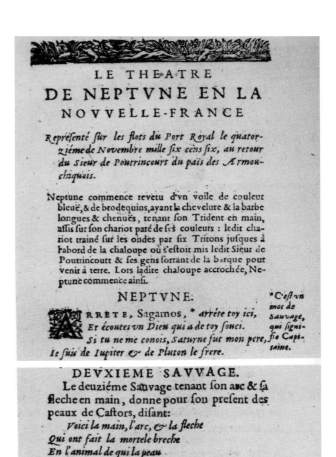

'Le Théâtre de Neptune en la Nouvelle France'. Marc Lescarbot's masque, performed on 14 November 1606 and published in Paris in 1609, was the first European theatrical performance in North America. Bibliothèque de la ville de Montréal.

and put Port-Royal to the torch. Returning the following year to find complete devastation, Poutrincourt took most of the colonists back to France. Only Biencourt, his cousin Charles de Saint-Étienne de La Tour, and a few others stayed on.

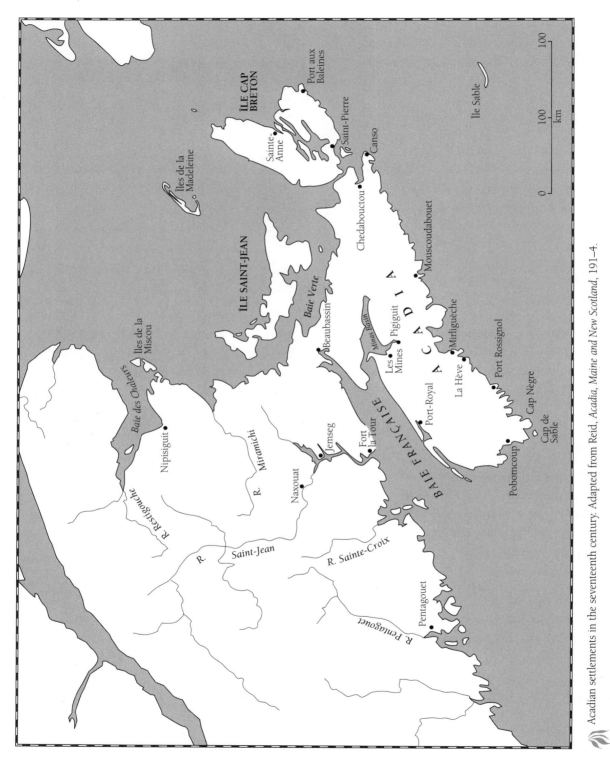

Acadian settlements in the seventeenth century. Adapted from Reid, *Acadia, Maine and New Scotland*, 191–4.

Backed by merchants in La Rochelle, Biencourt and his partners built a successful business in fur and fish. They developed good relations with the Mi'kmaq and extended their activities into the harbours of Cap Nègre, Cap de Sable, Port Lomeron, and La Hève on the south shore of Acadia. Following the death of Biencourt in 1623, the direction of the colony was entrusted to Charles de La Tour who, with his father Claude, continued to make Acadia his home. Charles married a local woman who was likely a chief's daughter and their union, later blessed by a Récollet priest, produced three daughters, all of whom were baptized; one eventually entered a convent in Paris.[9]

French claims to Acadia were directly challenged by Sir William Alexander, a Scot who in 1621 received from King James a grant of 'New Scotland', defined as extending from the St Croix to the St Lawrence. After his first attempt to found a colony failed, Alexander persuaded the king in 1624 to create 150 knights-baronet who, in return for payment, would each receive a title and a land grant of 30,000 acres. There were few takers, and many vicissitudes, but eventually a fleet set sail for New Scotland in the spring of 1628. Although small colonies were established the following year at Port-aux-Baleines on Cape Breton Island under the command of Lord Ochiltree and at Port-Royal under Sir William Alexander's son, also named William, they both failed. War broke out between England and France in 1627, and in September 1629, Ochiltree's settlement was destroyed by a French expedition under Captain Charles Daniel. Alexander's colony survived by making accommodations with both the Mi'kmaq and Claude de la Tour, who toyed

One of several women in France whose wealth helped to finance the French empire in North America, Madame de Guercheville was the pious wife of the governor of Paris and chief lady-in-waiting to the queen. Bibliothèque nationale de France, Paris.

with the idea of becoming one of Alexander's knights-baronet. Had the war not come to an end in 1632, the Scottish settlement at Port-Royal might well have become permanent. Instead it was abandoned when Acadia was recognized formally for the first time as French territory by the Treaty of Saint-Germain-en-Laye, which ended the war. Alexander's legacies are a name, a flag, and a coat of arms still used by the province of Nova Scotia.

The Newfoundland and Nova Scotia Coats of Arms. The oldest provincial coats of arms in Canada, they are the only ones to include Aboriginal people, though the images are rather fanciful. The Nova Scotia arms (bottom) were originally granted to Sir William Alexander in 1626, and the Newfoundland arms to Sir David Kirke and others in 1638. College of Arms, London, MS 1.79, p. 259; and MS Misc. Grants 4, f.7.

The other, equally precarious, node of European settlement in the region was Newfoundland's Avalon Peninsula. Here the London and Bristol Company decided in 1610 to sponsor England's second overseas plantation—the first was in Virginia—at Cupid's Cove, Conception Bay. The investors hoped to establish a fur trade with the Beothuk and create a series of permanent settlements that would enable the company to control a substantial proportion of the Newfoundland fishery and trade. On behalf of the company, a merchant from Bristol named John Guy brought out 39 men in 1610, followed by 16 women in 1612. The son born to the wife of Nicholas Guy in March 1613 was probably the first English child born in what is now Canada.

Although the colony's early years were quite promising, problems soon developed. The settlement was harassed by the pirate Peter Easton. The soil and climate were not as good as expected, with the result that agriculture proved difficult. The settlers had virtually no contact with the Beothuk, for trade or any other purpose. In addition there was friction with the migratory fishermen. These factors, together with internal dissension, led to the plantation's break-up in the early 1620s. A few colonists remained in Cupids, some moved to Bristol's Hope (now Harbour Grace), while others left Newfoundland behind them.

Cupids may have been a business failure, but it marked the beginning of permanent English settlement on the Avalon Peninsula. To recoup some of its investment, the company began to sell tracts of land to other potential colonizers. The first of these was Sir William Vaughan, a Welsh lawyer and scholar who saw in overseas colonization a solution to social and economic problems at home. In 1616 he purchased the Avalon Peninsula south of a line from Caplin Bay (now Calvert) across to Placentia Bay and called his land New Cambriol. A flimsy settlement was established at Aquaforte, which Richard Whitbourne later moved to Renews. By 1621 the colony was finished. Vaughan sold off sections of his property to Sir George Calvert and Lord Falkland, and retired to his library to write *The Golden Fleece* (1626), a fanciful book promoting the colonization of Newfoundland.

Falkland did nothing with his holdings, but the wealthy and influential Calvert established a settlement at Ferryland in 1621. Known as the Colony of Avalon, it became one of the earliest permanent European settlements in northeastern America, and among the best capitalized. Lord Baltimore (as he was known from 1625) viewed the colony as a business enterprise, but he also wanted Ferryland to be a haven of religious toleration. Himself a convert to Roman Catholicism, Baltimore allowed both Protestant and Catholic clergy to serve the colonists. He spent part of 1627 and winter of 1628–9 in Ferryland before deciding 'to shift to some other warmer climate of this new worlde'. As he complained to King Charles I:

> *from the middest of October, to the middest of May there is a sadd face of wynter upon all this land, both sea and land so frozen for the greatest part of the tyme as they are not penetrable, no plant or vegetable thing appearing out of the earth untill it be about the beginning of May nor fish in the sea besides the ayre is so intolerable cold as it is hardly to be endured.[10]*

The Ferryland Cross. This ornate iron cross was excavated at Lord Baltimore's Ferryland settlement. It was once gilded and embedded with gems. James Tuck, MUN.

A North Devon bowl decorated with intricate *scgraffito* designs. Also excavated at Ferryland, it probably dates from about 1673. James Tuck, MUN.

After an interval in England, Baltimore departed for Maryland in 1632, leaving the Ferryland property, in which he had invested over £20,000 (about $4 million today), in the hands of agents, and a village of some 30 people.

Despite valiant efforts, the European presence in the Atlantic region in the early seventeenth century remained largely seasonal and migratory. Settlement was not necessary for catching fish and trading furs; indeed, much of the good agricultural land was far removed from the best harbours for trading and fishing. If formal colonization schemes in Newfoundland and Acadia were to be successful, they had to generate profits that would satisfy investors and at the same time provide enough resources to support year-round habitation. There also had to be compelling reasons, ideological or self-interested, for Europeans to leave their homelands to settle in the unknown and potentially dangerous 'new world'. Religious persecution unleashed in the wake of the Protestant Reformation and population pressures in Europe served as important stimuli to overseas colonization, but other regions of North America were more easily adapted to European settlement.

After more than a century of contact, it was clear that unfavourable agricultural conditions made Newfoundland unsuitable for extensive colonization, even in the absence of a large Aboriginal population. The eventual emergence of a permanent population on the island was the result of informal settlement. Residents depended on imported foodstuffs, though locally-grown potatoes became an important dietary staple by the middle of the eighteenth century. In Labrador there were no European settlers at all. Barren and forbidding, with a subarctic climate and a seemingly hostile Native population, it held little attraction for Europeans.

The story in Acadia, the present-day Maritimes, was quite different. On the periphery of the rapidly developing North Atlantic trading system, Acadia was bypassed by Puritans from England, who fetched up further south in the Massachusetts Bay area, and even by the French, many of them Huguenots, who emigrated to the West Indies. But it had potential. Although its climate was more extreme than Europe's, with hotter summers and colder winters, Europeans could survive there, particularly with the help of the Mi'kmaq. The sheer abundance of resources—fish, fowl, and fur in profusion, trees growing down to the shoreline, and pockets of potentially productive agricultural land—and relative proximity to Europe commended the region to prospective immigrants.[11]

The French were the first to explore Acadia's agricultural potential. As Ramsay Cook has pointed out, French colonizers in Acadia were determined to cultivate the North American wilderness.[12] Lescarbot, for example, was clearly pleased with his efforts at Port-Royal: 'I can say with truth that I have never done so much bodily work through the pleasure which I took in digging and tilling my gardens, fencing them in against the gluttony of the swine, making terraces, preparing straight alleys, building storehouses, sowing wheat, rye, barley, oats, beans, peas, garden plants, and watering them. . . .' In creating his European oasis, Lescarbot was participating in a crucial part of the colonization process: the introduction of European animals, plants, and—through their very presence—diseases.

By Lescarbot's time, European ecological imperialism was already well under way. Weeds, such as the dandelion, were among the early

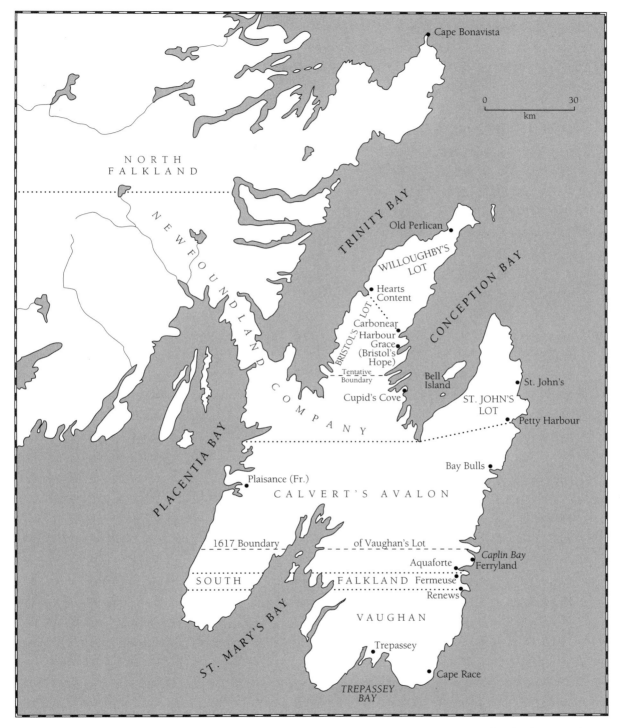

The English Shore of Newfoundland, seventeenth century. Adapted from Gillian Cell, ed., *Newfoundland Discovered: English Attempts at Colonisation, 1610–1630* (London: Hakluyt Society, 1982), 21.

Champlain's map of New France, published in *Les Voyages de la Nouvelle France*, 1632, gives a relatively accurate rendering of the contours of the Atlantic region. NAC, NMC-15661.

passengers on fishing vessels; and European diseases were taking their toll among the Aboriginal population. Père Biard noted in 1612 that the Native people 'are astonished and often complain that since the French mingle with and carry on trade with them, they are dying fast and the population is thinning out. . . . One by one the different coasts according as they have begun to traffic with us, have been more reduced by disease. . . .'[13] Within another century, European rats, cats, rabbits, cattle, sheep, pigs, and deer would be competing with bears, caribou, moose, and mice for the region's resources.[14]

Europeans were notoriously careless of the abundance they found around them. When Sir Humphrey Gilbert and his group arrived in Newfoundland in 1583, Stephen Parmenius, a young Hungarian poet who accompanied the expedition, noted that they considered burning down the forests 'so as to clear an open space for surveying the area'. Fortunately, this ill-conceived plan was abandoned after 'some reliable person asserted that, when this had occurred by accident at some other settlement post, no fish had been seen for seven whole years, because the sea-water had been turned bitter by the turpentine that flowed down from the trees burning along the rivers.'[15] Whether by accident or by design, Europeans were gradually making their mark on the North Atlantic landscape.

CHAPTER FIVE

Imperial Designs:
1632–1713

$\mathcal{F}$ollowing the Treaty of Saint-Germain-en-Laye in 1632, the French government established firm control over its North American colonies. Most of its attention was focused on the St Lawrence, but efforts in Acadia also quickly bore fruit, and the French base at Plaisance in Newfoundland reached new levels of settlement and institutional development under imperial auspices. By contrast, the English government showed little interest in sponsoring colonial endeavours of any kind in the Atlantic region and even began to wonder whether the English Shore in Newfoundland should support any permanent settlers at all. Nevertheless, the Atlantic colonies figured prominently in England's negotiating strategies during its periodic wars with France—a testimony not only to the significance of the fisheries but also to the Atlantic region's strategic location at the junction of competing territorial claims for imperial control of North America.

France's new attitude towards Acadia became apparent when Louis XIII's chief minister, Cardinal Richelieu, appointed Isaac de Razilly to take the surrender of Port-Royal in 1632—with a force of three ships and 300

men—and further commissioned him as the royal lieutenant-general in New France. Over the next three years Razilly, with the assistance of his lieutenants Charles de Menou d'Aulnay and Nicolas Denys, laid the groundwork for a lasting Acadian colony to serve as 'a defensive bulwark against New England'.[1] Razilly established his main base at La Hève on the south shore, which was better suited to his military and commercial interests than Port-Royal. Denys engaged in fishing, lumbering, and fur-trading, eventually concentrating his efforts at Canso, Saint-Pierre (St Peters), and Nepisiquit on the Bay of Chaleur.[2]

Razilly managed to maintain harmonious relations with Charles de La Tour, who also claimed title to Acadia and conducted major trading operations from his bases at Cape Sable and the mouth of the St John River. Essentially dividing Acadia between them, Razilly and La Tour dealt separately with the Compagnie des Cent Associés, the Paris-based seigneurs of New France. Razilly brought with him some 300 people, mainly indentured single men, but also priests, and a few women. Many of these pioneers, believed to have come from Touraine and Brittany, returned to France following the sudden death of Razilly in December 1635.

Razilly's successor, Charles de Menou d'Aulnay, was equally committed to the development of Acadia, arranging the migration of settlers from his seigneury near Loudon in Poitou. Because he believed that agriculture should be the colony's mainstay, he moved most of the remaining settlers at La Hève to the potentially more productive Port-Royal area. Families formed by marriages between the French and Mi'kmaq apparently remained at La Hève. By 1650, when d'Aulnay died, there were roughly 400 Europeans living in Acadia. Some of them returned to France, but most of them stayed to become the founding families of the French Acadie.

The death of d'Aulnay brought to a close what has been described by the geographer Andrew Hill Clark as 'a minuscule civil war between rival fur-trading seigneurs'.[3] Unlike Razilly, d'Aulnay was not prepared to accommodate La Tour's territorial claims in the Atlantic region, and a vicious power struggle ensued. It culminated in d'Aulnay's attack in 1645 on La Tour's St John River fort, which was defended in La Tour's absence by his spirited and resourceful second wife, Françoise-Marie Jaquelin. She eventually surrendered and, so the story goes, was forced to watch the hanging of those of her men who had survived the battle. She died soon after, and La Tour went into exile in Quebec.[4]

The dispute with La Tour had driven d'Aulnay deep into debt, and on his death his chief creditor, Emmanuel Le Borgne, seized Port-Royal and attacked other settlements in the region. Meanwhile, the equally debt-ridden La Tour was attempting to consolidate his interests and get his property back. To this end, he married d'Aulnay's widow, Jeanne Motin, and resumed his position as governor—this time of all Acadia. The La Tours were joined in opposition to Le Borgne by Nicolas Denys, who by this time had substantial interests in the fishery and the fur trade between Canso and the Gaspé. Incipient civil war was averted in 1654 when an English force led by Robert Sedgwick plundered Port-Royal and other settlements and took La Tour prisoner. The English government agreed that La Tour could reoccupy his posts in Acadia on the condition that he swear allegiance to England and pay off his huge debts to Boston and other English creditors. Finally beaten, La Tour agreed. To raise the money, in 1656 he sold most of his rights in Acadia to Thomas Temple (who became governor in 1662) and William Crowne, and retired to Cape Sable. The English regime proved to be short-lived. In 1667 the Treaty of Breda returned Acadia to France, and three years later a reluctant Temple was finally persuaded to permit the French to assume control.

King Louis XIV of France began to take a direct interest in overseas colonization following his decision in 1661 to take the reins of government into his own hands. As a result, most French colonies were subjected to a bureaucratic regime that was headed by a governor supported by a standing army; a legal system based on the Custom of Paris; a seigneurial system of land distribution that concentrated wealth in the hands of an aristocratic élite; a Roman Catholic church closely allied to the state; and a closed mercantile trading system designed to advance France's economic inter-

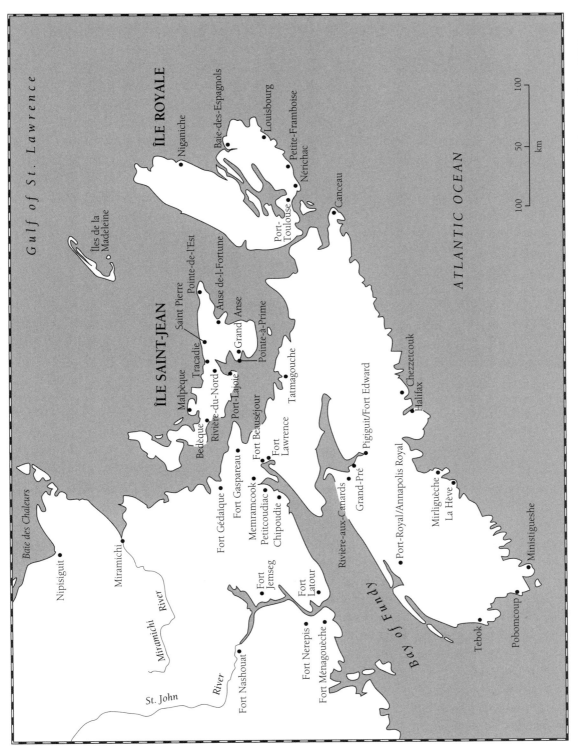

Gulf of St. Lawrence

ÎLE ROYALE

Niganiche

Baie-des-Espagnols

Louisbourg

Petite-Framboise

Nérichac

Port-Toulouse

Canceau

ATLANTIC OCEAN

Îles de la Madeleine

Pointe-de-l'Est

Saint Pierre

Anse-de-l'Fortune

Grand Anse

Pointe-a-Prime

ÎLE SAINT-JEAN

Malpeque

Tracadie

Bedèque

Rivière-du-Nord

Port-Lajoie

Tatmagouche

Fort Beauséjour

Chezzetcouk

Fort Lawrence

Pigiguit/Fort Edward

Halifax

Fort Gaspareau

Grand-Pré

Rivière-aux-Canards

Mirliguèche

La Hève

Baie des Chaleurs

Fort Gédaïque

Memramcook

Petitcoudiac

Chipoudie

Port-Royal/Annapolis Royal

Nipisiguit

Miramichi

Fort Jemseg

Fort Latour

Ministigueshe

Miramichi River

Fort Nerepis

Fort Ménagouèche

Tebok

Pobomcoup

St. John River

Fort Nashouat

Bay of Fundy

100   50   100
km

Acadian settlements, 1755. Adapted from Daigle, ed., *Acadia of the Maritimes*, 33; *Historical Atlas of Canada*, I (Toronto: University of Toronto Press, 1987), plate 30.

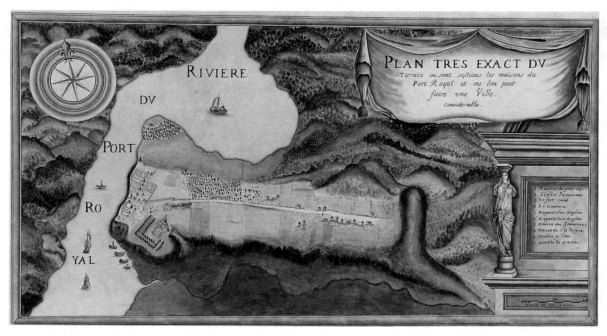

Jean-Baptiste-Louis Franquelin, plan of Port-Royal, 1686. By that time the main settlement at Port-Royal consisted of one-storey wooden houses with enclosed yards and symmetrical gardens, a windmill, church, presbytery, and graveyard, as well as English warehouses left over from the period of English rule in the 1660s and a large house for the governor. NAC, C-35567.

ests. In 1670 Acadia was declared a royal colony like the others, with an administration subordinate to officials based in Quebec, but it had missed the crucial decade of the 'Sun King's' interest in overseas colonization. His attention increasingly taken up with European affairs, Louis XIV had few resources, either financial or military, to spare for Acadia. Governor Hector d'Andigné de Grandfontaine established royal authority in the colony with only a handful of soldiers, while the 60 settlers he brought with him nearly equalled the 66 (of whom only five were women) who would migrate to the neglected colony over the next forty years. Without support from France, the 55 seigneuries granted in the region failed to sus-

tain social organization, and trade regulations were openly flouted. The few priests in the area sometimes took on legal duties in the absence of judicial officers. Meanwhile the settlers, especially those who moved beyond the confines of Port-Royal, learned to fend for themselves.[5]

Despite the lack of imperial interest, a small colonial society managed to take root in Acadia. Port-Royal was the heart of French settlement in 1670, but other communities were developing at Pubnico (Pobomcoup), Cape Negro (Cap Nègre), Pentagouet, Musquodoboit Harbour (Mouscoudabouet), and St Peters (Saint-Pierre). In the 1670s and 1680s, young families moved to Beaubassin on the Isthmus of Chignecto, and around the Minas

The size of this work crew, photographed at the turn of the twentieth century at Boyd Creek, New Brunswick, suggests how much work was required to maintain the dykes originally built by Acadians in the seventeenth and eighteenth centuries. PANB, P61-439.

Basin. Geographical expansion reflected the spectacular population growth that characterized early French settlements.[6] Well-adapted to their environment, 'Acadians' were a well-nourished people, and mercifully free of the plagues that periodically ravaged European communities. People married young, few remained single, and the death rate was low by European standards.

One of the most enduring features of early Acadia was its dykeland agriculture. Instead of clearing the forests for planting, the settlers reclaimed the rich alluvial soils flooded by the high tides of the Bay of Fundy. This practice was introduced to the Port-Royal area in the mid-seventeenth century, by immigrants from Poitou who knew how to drain and cultivate marshlands. As settlement spread, so too did the construction of dykes, creating the distinctive landscape that still characterizes the Bay of Fundy region. The marshland farms were highly productive, allowing the settlers to grow wheat and barley, as well as fodder for livestock, and the salt produced in the drainage process was used to cure fish. Although agriculture was central to the Acadians' survival, fishing and fur trading supplemented their well-rounded economy.

Pen drawings of Jesuit missions in the Miramichi, published in Chrestien Le Clercq's *Nouvelle Relation de la Gaspésie*, 1691.

Roman Catholic clergy were present from the earliest days of French settlement and remained a significant force even after the British conquest of 1713. In the first half of the seventeenth century, Acadia was an open field for competing clerical orders. Récollet, Jesuit, and Capuchin priests all conducted missions among the Native people, ministered to French settlers and sojourners, and clashed both with one another and with the secular authorities. The Capuchins were particularly active, sending at least 40 priests and 20 lay brothers to Acadia between 1632 and 1656.[7] Most priests spent only a few years in Acadia, but they achieved their goals. French settlers

remained committed to Roman Catholicism, and many Mi'kmaq and Maliseet gradually adapted their belief system to accommodate the teachings of the persistent Christians in their midst.

In 1676 Father Louis Petit was appointed vicar-general of Acadia, under the jurisdiction of the Bishop of Quebec. Bishop Saint-Vallier visited his Acadian province in the spring of 1684, and resident priests were subsequently appointed to communities outside Port-Royal. From 1701 to 1710, a sister of the Congregation of the Holy Cross conducted a school for young girls at Port-Royal. Legal and clerical records suggest that most people followed clerical injunctions relating to marriage and sexual conduct. In a highly controversial case at Beaubassin in 1688, the local priest responded to a paternity suit by insisting that not only the reputed father but 19 members of his family be expelled from the community and their confiscated goods given to the girl's father.[8]

Because, for the most part, Acadians did not settle on Native hunting and fishing grounds, and provided valued opportunities to trade, their relations with the Mi'kmaq and Maliseet were amicable. In some cases, intermarriage between Native women and French immigrants played a significant role in cementing military alliances. In 1670, for example, a young soldier named Bernard-Anselme d'Abbadie de Saint-Castin accompanied Grandfontaine to Pentagouet (in present-day Maine) and married the daughter of a Pentagouet chief. He then devoted himself to extending French influence among the Abenaki who lived in what is now the state of Maine. Fighting a rearguard action against New England, the Abenaki welcomed the French support provided by Saint-Castin against New England expansionism, and valued his advice.

Cultural exchange between Natives and French immigrants was extensive and long-lasting. Acadians adopted those elements of local cultures that they found most useful, including canoes, moccasins, and knowledge of local herbs and vegetables, while European metal products, foods, clothing, religious rituals, and military support became standard elements of Aboriginal society. According to historian Naomi Griffiths, 'The Indians, in Acadian eyes, were permanent neighbours, neither the middlemen in commercial enter-

Archaeological excavations at Bellisle and Melanson, two Acadian sites on the north shore of the Annapolis River, have added greatly to our understanding of Acadian life in the pre-Deportation period. Most of the houses had exterior bake ovens, and the ceramics in their kitchens came not only from France but from Germany, England, and New England. This round-bottomed French earthenware cooking pot was found at the Melanson site. Parks Canada/Landmark Designs Inc.

prise nor a hostile force.'[9] It was a symbiotic relationship, highly unusual in the story of European settlement in North America.

A more ambiguous relationship developed with the Acadians' other neighbours, the English settlers in Massachusetts. Regarding Acadia as falling within their sphere of influence, the New Englanders were hostile to the French presence and periodically attacked Acadian settlements. At the same time they fished along the Acadian coastline and traded with Acadian settlers, who exchanged furs and surplus agricultural produce for a variety of manufactured goods and foodstuffs. Both La Tour and d'Aulnay traded with merchants in

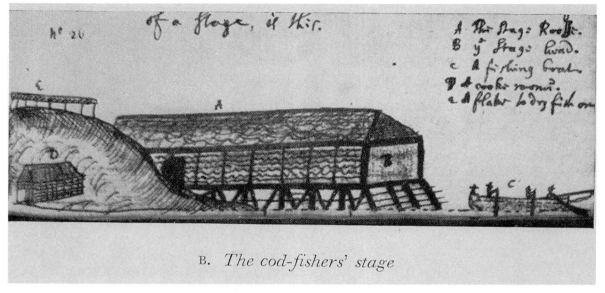

B. *The cod-fishers' stage*

A Newfoundland fishing room, *c.* 1663, sketched by the surgeon James Yonge at either Renews or Fermeuse. The key reads: 'A The Stage Roofe. B ye Stage head. C A fishing boat. D A cooke room. E A flake to dry fish over'. From F.N.L. Poynter, ed., *The Journal of James Yonge, 1647–1721, Plymouth Surgeon* (London: Green and Co., 1963).

Boston, and these dealings continued after 1670 despite royal injunctions against foreign trade. Since few French merchants were interested in Acadia—there had been some heavy losses in the past—and because administrators lacked the resources to control the trade, the colony emerged as an economic satellite of New England. In the Acadian phrase, the English became 'our friends the enemy'.[10]

By the turn of the eighteenth century, the settled population of Acadia was approaching 1500 and, with a balanced population of men and women, was doubling every generation. Most of the inhabitants were connected to each other, at least through marriage, giving a society of varied origins the closely knit character of an extended family. A common language and religion further cemented the Acadians' interdependence, which was also encouraged by the political vacuum. With a government that was always distant and often ineffectual, sometimes English, sometimes French, the Acadians became singularly self-reliant and pragmatic. Periodic attacks on Acadian communities—mostly conducted by the English, but also by the Dutch in 1674—drove home the reality that their political situation was precarious. Learning to live with their neighbours, and with whatever regime was in power, they kept their own counsel. Frustrated French administrators thought them 'republican', lacking in deference and respect.

Acadia was a permanent French colony, and it was viewed as such in Paris. The British attitude towards Newfoundland was not so clear-cut. While officials in London were not opposed to formal settlement, it was an option that had few, if any, influential backers, especially after the failure of the proprietary colonies. Instead, the government listened to a lobby mounted by some of the West Country merchants engaged in the Newfoundland trade. They argued that settlement on the island would threaten the viability of the migratory fishery, since settlers, called 'planters', would take over the best fishing places. Because the fishery was considered to be of great economic and naval importance, their opinions were treated with respect. The issue remained unresolved during the politically troubled years of the mid-seventeenth century, when England was preoccupied with civil war between royalist and parliamentarian forces, and its aftermath.

In 1637 Lord Baltimore's Ferryland plantation was appropriated (with Charles I's tacit approval) by Sir David Kirke, who, with a number of associates, formed the Company of Adventurers to Newfoundland, the object being to trade in fish. As Governor of Newfoundland from 1638 to 1651, Kirke levied taxes and held courts at Ferryland. A royalist, Kirke represented a suspect figure to the republican regimes that ruled England after 1649. He lost the governorship, was recalled to London, and died there in 1654, while still embroiled in litigation with the Calverts. Oliver Cromwell's republican government replaced him, but otherwise left Newfoundland alone.

Following David Kirke's death, the Ferryland plantation was managed by his widow, Lady Sara Kirke, while her sons developed their own plantations at Ferryland and Renews. In effect, the Kirkes functioned as a local gentry. The number of people who by this time had some sort of permanent attachment to New-

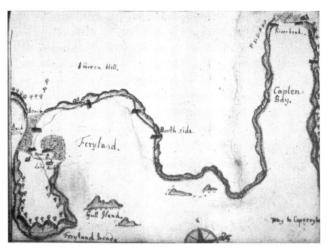

James Yonge's map of Ferryland, about 1663, showing the location of Lady Sarah Kirke's house. From F.N.L. Poynter, ed., *The Journal of James Yonge, 1647–1721, Plymouth Surgeon* (London: Green and Co., 1963).

foundland was small: between one and two thousand living in some thirty settlements along the English Shore. Around this core group of planters moved a shifting, seasonal, overwhelmingly male population, who during the summer helped to produce saltfish and cod oil for export. Whether permanent or migratory, everyone in Newfoundland relied heavily on England, New England, and Ireland for provisions, livestock, fishing equipment, and other goods.[11]

Since the basis of their own society was land rather than sea, the English had difficulty conceiving how a colonial society could exist without an agricultural foundation. If Newfoundland was 'productive of no commodities as other Plantations, [n]or affords anything of food to keep men alive', as West Country merchants maintained in 1668, then it was probably not fit for European habitation. Such arguments supported the view that settlement should be prevented, and the issue was debated

The remains of Fort Royal. Built at Plaisance during the 1690s, the fort overlooked the settlement—now the town of Placentia—and the beach then used for drying fish. Photo Dale Wilson, Parks Canada, 1996.

at length after the restoration of the English monarchy in 1660.

Finally, under pressure from West Country interests, the English government ordered all British settlers to leave Newfoundland in 1675. The naval commodore sent to implement the order reported that the policy was both impractical and mistaken: 'if the habitants are taken off and the French left solely in possession . . . they will in a short time invest themselves of the whole at least of Ferryland and St John's, where harbours are almost naturally fortified, to the disadvantage of the trade, if not the loss of all.'[12] Nor were the French the only threat to the English Shore. In 1665 and

1672, Ferryland and St John's were attacked by Dutch naval squadrons attempting to advance their nation's imperial interests. Sensibly reconsidering its position, the government adopted a compromise. Settlement in Newfoundland would be accepted and tolerated, but not encouraged. Eventually enshrined in the 1699 statute known as King William's Act, this policy was to remain on the books until 1824. There is an old and hardy myth that the British government opposed settlement in Newfoundland and made it illegal. The truth is more complex. Until the 1660s the government supported settlement. Thereafter, British policy reflected the assumption that Newfoundland was an industry, not a colony, and settlement was largely ignored.

By contrast, France placed a far higher value on the Newfoundland fisheries than it did on Acadia or even Canada. Determined to protect its interests in Newfoundland, France established a colony and fort at Plaisance, on the island's southeast coast, in 1662. Theoretically subordinate (like Acadia) to Quebec, Plaisance was designed to act as a base for the French fishing fleet, to monitor English activity on the Avalon Peninsula, and to protect the approaches to the Gulf. Plaisance became home to a governor and other administrators, a military force, Roman Catholic priests, and, on its beach properties, bona fide settlers. By the end of the seventeenth century, Plaisance boasted 52 resident fishing families and served a fleet of more than 400 vessels, employing over 1,000 men. As in Acadia, clandestine trade with New England flourished.

When war was declared between England and France in 1689, Acadia and Newfoundland were seriously affected. The origins of the conflict, known as King William's War or the War of the League of Augsburg, were European, but North Americans—both Native people and newcomers—could not avoid involvement. The Comte de Frontenac, Governor of New France, organized midwinter raids along the New England frontier, while French privateers attacked English shipping. In response, New Englanders raided their nearest French neighbour. In 1690 a force commanded by Sir William Phips attacked French posts along the coast, and then plundered Port-Royal. Another devastating attack on the colony by the New Englanders followed later in the year. Unable

to occupy the territory, Phips induced a number of Acadians to swear allegiance to the English Crown, and appointed a council of residents to act as a local government. The French and their Native allies continued to conduct damaging raids on New England from bases on the St John River. In retaliation, Benjamin Church and a force of New Englanders burned and pillaged the Beaubassin settlements in 1696, and the Massachusetts General Court forbade trade with Acadia. The latter measure proved a futile gesture, and trade between New England and Acadia continued throughout the war.

In Newfoundland there were French raids on Ferryland and St John's, and repeated English raids on Plaisance. The main French campaign, designed to drive the English out of Newfoundland, began in November 1696, when Pierre Le Moyne d'Iberville and a force of Canadians, Acadians, Mi'kmaq, and Abenaki marched overland from Plaisance to meet a force of French regular troops at Renews. The French rapidly moved north, and by the end of the month had occupied St John's, which they destroyed along with 80 fishing vessels. In January 1697 d'Iberville and Testard de Montigny moved against the English settlements in Conception and Trinity bays. The French terrorized the scattered settlements, driving all before them except a group of defenders on Carbonear Island. Only Bonavista remained beyond their reach. In all, the French destroyed 36 settlements, killed 200 people, took 700 prisoners, and captured 300 fishing vessels. The campaign, which has been described as 'the cruellest and most destructive of d'Iberville's career',[13] marked a new level of European conflict in North America.

If the French had capitalized on their success, Newfoundland would have become a wholly French island, with important strategic consequences. But France lacked the resources necessary to follow up its victory. D'Iberville retreated to Plaisance, and was then despatched to campaign against the English in Hudson Bay. While Newfoundland's English population had suffered a severe blow, the survivors were able to reoccupy their territory without difficulty and a garrison was established at St John's.

The Treaty of Ryswick, which ended the war in 1697, was in effect a truce. In North America, each side was simply awarded what it had held in 1689 and prepared for the inevitable next round. The War of the Spanish Succession began in 1702. As before, Canada and Acadia became bases for attacks on New England, again prompting a trade embargo and retaliatory raids. In the summer of 1704, Benjamin Church led an attack against Acadia in response to the 'Deerfield Massacre' of the previous year, in which 50 New Englanders had been killed and 112—many of them women and children—taken prisoner to Montreal. Church and his men devastated the major Acadian settlements with the exception of Port-Royal, which was defended by its fort and garrison. Leaving a trail of broken dykes, burned homes, slaughtered cattle, and ruined crops at Chignecto, Cobequid, Pisiquid, and Minas, the New Englanders also took some 50 Acadian captives to Boston; they were returned in 1706. New Englanders mobilized a force of 1,600 men to attack Port-Royal again in 1707, but the new governor, Daniel d'Auger de Subercase, managed to repulse the attackers with the help of a hastily assembled Acadian militia.

Although his position, both militarily and economically, was precarious, Subercase continued to hold out. Port-Royal became the base for privateers from the French West Indies who attacked trading vessels from Massachusetts, securing much-needed foodstuffs and manufactured goods. In 1709 the privateers seized 35 vessels and took about 300 prisoners, fuelling New Englanders' resolve to rid themselves of their French tormentors. Supported by a detachment of British marines, General Francis Nicholson stormed Port-Royal with 2,000 men, and on 13 October 1710 forced Subercase and his demoralized garrison of fewer than 300 soldiers to surrender.

In Newfoundland, settlers along the English Shore again suffered raids from Plaisance, which also served as a base for privateers. A repeat of d'Iberville's 1697 raid in 1705, led by Subercase and Montigny, caused widespread destruction as far north as Bonavista—they took 1,200 prisoners—and in 1709 French forces captured the fort at St John's, burning most of the town and forcing the inhabitants to pay a huge ransom. Yet once again the French found it impossible to secure their advantage. They withdrew to Plaisance, where they were blockaded by British naval vessels and suffered severe privation.

In the negotiations leading up to the Treaty of Utrecht, which would end the War of the Spanish Succession in 1713, the British demanded that France abandon its claims to both Acadia and Newfoundland. After long and intense bargaining, France recognized British sovereignty over Newfoundland, agreed to abandon Plaisance, and ceded mainland Acadia, but retained Cape Breton (renamed Île Royale) and Île Saint-Jean (Prince Edward Island).

These islands, it was reasoned, would protect the route to Canada and provide the site for a new French base in the Atlantic region. As for the Newfoundland fisheries, France extracted a valuable and clever concession: the right to fish in season on the Petit Nord, defined as extending from Cape Bonavista to Pointe Riche on the northwest coast.

The treaty contained some troubling loose ends. The precise nature of French fishing rights in Newfoundland was unclear, and the definition of boundary lines between French and English possessions—Acadia was ceded according to its ill-defined 'ancient boundaries'—was left for future discussion. Although France now accepted British sovereignty over Hudson Bay, that territory was also left undefined, the parties agreeing only that sometime in the future a boundary should be drawn in the Labrador peninsula.

The Treaty of Utrecht was severely criticized in both England and France—'an indication', writes John Reid, 'of the virtually irreconcilable interests at stake'.[14] The rivalry between Britain and France remained unresolved, and the two powers were left uneasily and resentfully to share northeastern America. For people living in the Atlantic region, the future was uncertain. French settlers in Acadia were faced with the choice of swearing allegiance to a Protestant monarch who was hostile to France or moving to French-controlled territory, while some Native people found their land 'given away' to their enemies. For English settlers in Newfoundland and New England, the prospect of the French re-establishing themselves on Île Royale and Île St Jean was troubling, since any future war between Great Britain and France would almost certainly make them vulnerable to attack. The Treaty of Utrecht, in short, settled little, and left a great deal open to dispute.

CHAPTER SIX

Renegotiating the Atlantic Region: 1713–1763

$\mathcal{F}$ifty years separated the treaties of Utrecht (1713) and Paris (1763). The first officially endorsed Britain's initial acquisition of territory in the Atlantic region; the second confirmed Britain's ascendancy. In the interim, the British and French jostled for position in Nova Scotia/Acadia, often spurred on by the ambitions of colonial officials based in Quebec and Boston. Their battles involved both Acadians and Aboriginal peoples, who were the real losers in the imperial contest.

Britain's acquisition of Nova Scotia/Acadia in 1713 presented an unprecedented imperial dilemma. How were British authorities to deal with a possession whose borders were disputed, where the European colonists were French and Roman Catholic, and where the Native people, also Roman Catholic, were allied with the enemy? These difficulties were compounded by French efforts to re-establish dominance in the region. No sooner was the ink dry on the Treaty of Utrecht than France began constructing a base on Île Royale intended to trump British power in North America and to support the migratory fishery that was considered so essential to national interests.

Following the conquest of Acadia, British officials based in Annapolis Royal (formerly Port-Royal) attempted to reach accommodations with the Acadians and the Native people. Both groups refused to swear allegiance to the British Crown, and neither wanted to sever their ties with the French, who remained a potent force in the region. To further complicate matters, France disputed the 'ancient boundaries' of Acadia, claiming that the area north of the Bay of Fundy (present-day New Brunswick) and even Canso, on the eastern end of the Nova Scotia peninsula, were still French territory. When they began to claim that their fishing rights on the Newfoundland French (or Treaty) Shore were exclusive, the British countered that their vessels had every right to fish there concurrently, so long as they did not interfere with French operations. Both disputes rumbled on for years.

Despite a scattered resident population of nearly 3,000, the British had no intention of establishing a regular colonial administration in Newfoundland. Local problems were sufficiently serious, however, to warrant something more than the often-ignored provisions of King

View of Louisbourg, 1731, by Verrier fils. Dominating the skyline are the King's Hospital (left) and the King's Bastion Barracks (right). Bibliothèque nationale, Paris, Cartes et plans, Ge C 5019.

William's Act. Under that law, the fishing admirals—masters of migratory vessels who acquired authority by being the first to arrive in a given harbour—were empowered to decide local disputes, with commanders of the naval warships sent out each summer acting as appeal judges. This administrative structure, such as it was, disappeared in winter. In 1718, a known murderer in Torbay could not be arrested because no one had the legal authority to do so. At Placentia (as the British called Plaisance), which was placed under the government of Nova Scotia in 1713, the eccentric Colonel Samuel Gledhill seemed immune from outside control. In the winter of 1728–9, convicts left behind by a passing ship harassed the inhabitants of St John's, who had long complained about the lack of winter authority. It was decided, finally, that the commodore of the annual naval squadron would double as governor and commander-in-chief. The first such migratory naval governor was Captain Henry Osborne, who in 1729 appointed magistrates and constables along the shore from Bonavista

to Placentia, which in the same year was put under his jurisdiction. In summer these new authorities were supplemented by naval officers acting as surrogate magistrates, and the fishing admirals in time disappeared as an independent force. Thus was born what has been called a 'naval state'; 'the island was not the desolate frontier described by most historians,' writes Jerry Bannister, '[though] it does not fit the orthodox account of imperial development.'[1]

For their headquarters in the Atlantic region, the French chose the ice-free port of Havre L'Anglois, renamed Louisbourg, on the south shore of Île Royale. The fortress of Louisbourg cost a fortune to build, fell both times it was attacked, and proved ineffective in protecting the St Lawrence, but in other respects it succeeded admirably. Perched on the edge of the North Atlantic, it quickly became a major fishing port and a thriving commercial entrepôt. Indeed, the colony's combined import and export trade soon grew to equal Canada's in value. Louisbourg also served as an effective base for maintaining

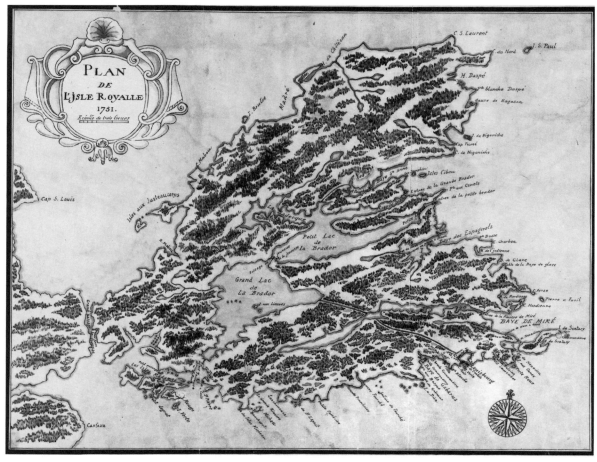

Map of Île Royale by Louis Franquet, 1751. This carefully labelled plan shows French settlement on the island before its final capture by the British in 1758. NAC, NMC-148.

channels of communication with the Acadians and Mi'kmaq, thereby undermining the British position in Nova Scotia.

By 1744, with a population approaching 3,000, Louisbourg was the largest and most cosmopolitan community in the Atlantic region. Its citizens included evacuees from Plaisance, French and Basque fishermen, German and Swiss soldiers, a few Irish, Scots, and Spanish sojourners, and Native and Black servants and slaves. The latter catered to the town's administrative and commercial élite, most of them from France, who lived in comfort if not opulence. Eager to maintain their standard of living when they returned home, many of them enhanced their personal fortunes by bilking the colonial treasury and engaging in clandestine trade with the English colonies. The troops, required to work long hours maintaining the fortifications, were only too aware that they were being cheated. In the winter of 1744–5 they took over the town, demanding better food, more firewood, and adequate uniforms. Order was eventually restored, but for days civilians lived in terror.

The Treaty of Utrecht had given Acadians a choice. They could stay where they were and accept British rule, or move to Île Royale and Île Saint-Jean. French authorities hoped that they would chose the second option and produce the foodstuffs that Louisbourg needed, but most Acadians preferred to remain in British territory. This is hardly surprising. Acadians had established some of North America's most productive agricultural communities, and by 1713 they were beginning to reap the benefits. Pragmatic as ever, they saw little point in moving onto the thin soils of Île Royale, or clearing forests on Île Saint-Jean. Only 67 Acadian families (about 500 people) eventually moved to Île-Royale. A few lived in Louisbourg, but the majority settled in outlying communities, such as Saint-Pierre (St Peters), Rivière de Miré (Mira), and Baie-des-Espagnols (Sydney), where they farmed, fished, built boats, and mined coal. Unlike Nova Scotia, Île Royale did not develop a significant agricultural base and depended on imported foodstuffs, a fact that threatened the colony's security. Cod fishing, both sedentary and migratory, remained the chief economic activity, producing most of the colony's exports to France and, importantly, to the West Indies, where slave plantations were becoming lucrative markets for saltfish.

Acadians initially showed little interest in Île Saint-Jean, where the French government had left development to private interests. In 1719 the Comte de Saint Pierre was granted the right to pursue the cod fishery on Saint-Jean, Miscou, and the Îles de la Madeleine in return

This pyx, used for carrying the host to the sick, was made in Acadia by a silversmith named Jean Frémont, who worked from 1751 to 1775. It attests to the artisanship achieved in the Acadian community in the eighteenth century. Musée acadien de l'Université de Moncton.

for sponsoring settlement. The following year his Compagnie de l'Île Saint-Jean sent out more than 250 colonists, who established themselves at Port LaJoie (near present-day Charlottetown), Havre Saint-Pierre (St Peter's), and other coastal locations. Like most private ventures sponsored by France, this one failed within a few years, and the settlers drifted away.

To confirm its sovereignty, in 1726 France installed a detachment of 30 naval fusiliers in the dilapidated buildings formerly occupied by Saint-Pierre's company. During the 1730s Jean-Pierre Roma, an energetic Parisian merchant, established fishing operations on the island. Building roads to connect his base at Trois Rivières with Havre Saint Pierre and Port LaJoie, he hoped to develop his colony into a great trading centre and might well have succeeded if the War of the Austrian Succession had not intervened.

Between 1713 and 1744, the Acadians lived a relatively peaceful existence, described

St Anne's Day celebrations, 26 July 1930, Chapel Island, Cape Breton. The site of an early French mission to the Mi'kmaq, Chapel Island has remained the location of an annual gathering on St Anne's Day. Photo Clara Dennis, History Collection, Nova Scotia Museum, Halifax, NSM 73.180.654/N-14-775.

in retrospect as a 'golden age'.[2] Family life flourished, economic opportunities beckoned, Roman Catholic priests were still permitted to minister to their flocks, and the empires that dominated the region resisted the temptation to declare war. By 1750 there were over 9,000 Acadians in Nova Scotia and 3,000 more on Île Saint-Jean and Île Royale. A few ambitious Acadian families married their daughters to British officers, signalling their willingness to take advantage of the new political order, but most Acadians were wary of aligning themselves too closely with the British. While culture and tradition predisposed them to support French objectives, their political history was such that neutrality seemed the best option. By 1730 a majority of Acadians had signed an oath of allegiance, but only on the condition—either noted in the margin or expressed verbally—that they would not be required to take up arms against France.

Following the Treaty of Utrecht, France vigorously nurtured alliances with Native peoples throughout North America, using subsidized trade, annual gift-giving, and missionary influence to achieve their goals. In the Atlantic region, two priests in particular were effective both as missionaries and *agents-provocateurs*: Pierre-Antoine-Simon Maillard and Jean-Louis Le Loutre. By the 1750s Abbé Maillard's base at Chapel Island on Île Royale had become the site for an annual Mi'kmaq celebration combining worship, gift-giving, and trade. Le Loutre ministered to mainland Mi'kmaq from his base at Shubenacadie, some 50 kilometres north of Halifax, until 1750, when his political manoeuvrings forced him to move to the Isthmus of Chignecto.

Native people did not need priests to encourage them to defy the British. After more than a century of French settlement, trade, and missionary activity, the Mi'kmaq and Maliseet (now closely aligned with the Passamaquoddy who lived in the area of present-day St Andrews, New Brunswick) had little interest in an alliance with the British, whose language and religion were foreign. With New England settlement moving up the coast, France offering better terms of trade, and British authorities demanding that they take an oath of allegiance, the Mi'kmaq and Maliseet-Passamaquoddy soon made their position clear. During the summer of 1715, the Mi'kmaq seized Massachusetts fishing vessels off Cape Sable, declaring that 'the Lands are theirs and they can make War and peace when they please.'[3] Governor Richard Philipps, who arrived in 1720, managed to extract a promise of friendship from the Maliseet, but the Mi'kmaq remained hostile. They drove New England fishermen out of Canso in 1720 and in the summer of 1722 captured 36 trading vessels off Nova Scotia.

The New Englanders were quick to retaliate, setting off an 'Indian War' along the New England-Nova Scotia frontier. In the summer of 1724, the Mi'kmaq attacked Annapolis Royal, burning part of the town and killing several British soldiers. Hostilities were finally brought to an end by a treaty concluded in Boston late in December 1725 and ratified at Annapolis Royal in June 1726. The Mi'kmaq were promised traditional hunting and fishing rights, and the written text of the treaty obliged them to recognize British sovereignty

over 'Nova Scotia or Accadie'. Since formal treaties were a British innovation, only time would tell whether they were worth the paper on which they were written.

The test of Acadian neutrality and Aboriginal alliances came in 1744, with the outbreak of the War of the Austrian Succession. News of the declaration of war reached Louisbourg three weeks before it arrived in Annapolis Royal and Boston. Using this information to his advantage, Governor Jean Baptiste-Louis Le Prévost Duquesnel authorized privateers to attack New England shipping and dispatched a force against Canso. The 87 soldiers stationed there were caught off guard and surrendered almost immediately in May 1744. Encouraged by this success, Duquesnel moved against Annapolis Royal, sending an advance force of some 300 Mi'kmaq and a few Acadians, mobilized by Le Loutre, to lay siege to the poorly defended capital. Fortunately for the British, a Massachusetts force intervened. Despite the small size of the contingent, Le Loutre's army took flight, believing that it included 'a great number' of Mohawks, who had the reputation of being formidable enemies.[4] Later in the summer, Captain François Du Pont Duvivier attacked Annapolis Royal with the help of 160 Mi'kmaq and 70 Maliseet. Commander Paul Mascarene might well have been forced to surrender, but once again reinforcements arrived from Boston and assistance from France failed to materialize.

Alarmed by developments on their northeastern frontier, the New Englanders moved quickly to mount a sustained assault against Louisbourg. In the spring of 1745 a volunteer militia of 4,300 men, led by William Pepperrell and supported by a British naval squadron, landed at Gabarus Bay, about three kilometres from the fortress. Dragging their cannon over the difficult terrain, the New Englanders pounded their objective for seven weeks. Governor Louis Du Pont Duchambon, his fortified town in ruins and its inhabitants facing extreme deprivation, surrendered on 17 June. New Englanders also destroyed French installations on Île Saint-Jean, including Roma's base at Trois-Rivières. In 1746 the French tried to recapture Louisbourg, but the large expedition—54 ships carrying 7,000 men under the command of the Duc d'Anville—was dogged by bad luck and poor management. The fleet took nearly three months to reach North America, where sickness and adverse weather eventually forced it to retreat.[5]

Its navy devastated, France could do little to sustain military campaigns in North America. The force of 680 men under the Sieur de Ramezay, sent from Quebec to support the hapless Louisbourg expedition, was therefore left to its own devices. Learning that Governor Shirley of Massachusetts had sent 500 colonial militia to keep the Acadians under surveillance, de Ramezay dispatched Captain Louis Coulon de Villiers and 300 Canadiens on a classic winter guerilla campaign. They made their way overland through heavy snow to Grand Pré, where they found the New Englanders quartered in Acadian homes. Using information provided by sympathetic Acadians, the French troops surrounded the houses where the New Englanders were sleeping, killed 70 of them, and forced the rest to surrender.

The 'Massacre of Grand Pré', as the English called it, made the Acadian strategy of neutrality irrelevant: the authorities would remember the few 'treacherous informers' and 'traitors' who had helped de Villiers, not those who tried to maintain a desperate neutrality. British administrators were now convinced that the Acadians could be pressed into supplying both French and Natives with billets, intelligence, and provisions during military campaigns. Whether their compliance with French wishes was voluntary or extracted under duress was entirely immaterial.

Reprisals were temporarily averted by the Treaty of Aix-la-Chapelle in 1748, by which Britain and France agreed to return what each had captured from the other—including Louisbourg. New Englanders fiercely criticized the British government for compromising their safety in this way. Aware of their resentment, the British decided to build a fortified base on the south shore of the Nova Scotia peninsula to counter the threat posed by Louisbourg. In June 1749, Edward Cornwallis led an expedition of more than 2,500 British soldiers, settlers, and labourers to the shores of Chebucto Bay. The founding of Halifax was Britain's first serious attempt to colonize the territories acquired by the Treaty of Utrecht. As such it marked a turning point in the history of the Atlantic region, signalling a new determination on the part of the British to control Nova Scotia after nearly four decades of benign neglect.

This initiative posed a threat not only to the French but also to the Mi'kmaq and Maliseet-Passamaquoddy. The British insisted that all First Nations that had fought on the side of the French must sign separate peace treaties. While the Maliseet and Passamaquoddy seemed prepared to reconfirm the treaty of 1726, the Mi'kmaq remained defiant. They attacked the British at sea and harassed the settlers at Halifax, which had been estab-

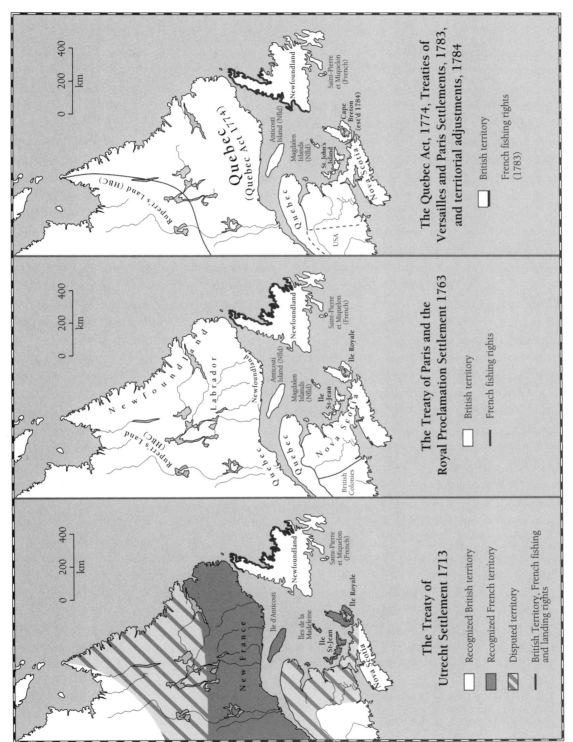

The Treaty of
Utrecht Settlement 1713

☐ Recognized British territory

■ Recognized French territory

▨ Disputed territory

— British Territory, French fishing
   and landing rights

The Treaty of Paris and the
Royal Proclamation Settlement 1763

☐ British territory

— French fishing rights

The Quebec Act, 1774, Treaties of
Versailles and Paris Settlements, 1783,
and territorial adjustments, 1784

☐ British territory

☐ French fishing rights
   (1783)

Eighteenth-century treaty boundaries. Adapted from Buchner and Reid, *The Atlantic Region to Confederation*, 143.

lished on one of their favourite summer en-campment sites. Cornwallis responded not by declaring war—to do so, he reasoned, 'would be . . . to own them a free and Independent people'—but by issuing a proclamation order-ing British subjects to 'take or destroy the sav-ages commonly called Micmacks wherever they are found' and offering a reward 'to be paid upon producing such savage taken or his scalp (as is the custom of America)'. Not sur-prisingly, the Mi'kmaq resisted British policies designed to exterminate them. Diplomatic efforts were undermined by the participation of Le Loutre and Maillard, who had been instructed to do everything possible to impede British expansion.[6] Although France and Britain remained officially at peace between 1748 and 1756, authorities at Louisbourg and Quebec took steps to strengthen their military presence in the region and, not to be outdone by Cornwallis, offered bounties for English prisoners and scalps.

As hostilities escalated, the Acadians were caught in the middle, pressed by both British and French to take sides. Shortly after his arrival, Cornwallis summoned Acadian repre-sentatives to Halifax and demanded that the Acadians take an unqualified oath of alle-giance. This they refused to do, no doubt fear-ing reprisals from either the French or the Mi'kmaq, if not both. Increasingly, however, it was becoming impossible to remain neutral. In 1750 the French built Fort Beauséjour north of the Missaguash River on Chignecto Isthmus, and began urging Acadians to move to French-controlled territory, where they could establish farms to supply food to Île Royale, augment the colonial militia, and bolster French territo-rial claims. Acadians who refused to relocate

were instructed upon pain of death not to sell their produce to the British, or to assist them in any way. The golden age of Acadia had come to an abrupt and dramatic end.

A seasoned military man, Cornwallis was astonished at the audacity of the French in occupying disputed territory, inciting the Mi'kmaq to war, and mobilizing the Acadians into a fifth column. He ordered the construc-tion of Fort Edward at Piziquid (Windsor) in 1749 to keep an eye on the Minas settlements, and dispatched Lieutenant-Colonel Charles Lawrence to build a fort across the river from Beauséjour. Despite stiff opposition from French forces, Fort Lawrence was completed in 1750, but the French still had the upper hand. In response to growing pressure, Acadians and Le Loutre's Mi'kmaq allies began to move in significant numbers to the Chignecto area and to nearby Île Saint-Jean.

In 1752 Governor Peregrine Thompson Hopson, who succeeded Cornwallis, con-cluded a treaty with the Mi'kmaq to the east of Halifax, but raids, skirmishes, and reprisals continued. Other regions of North America were also drawn into military conflicts between English and French forces and their Aboriginal allies. Following clashes on the Ohio frontier in 1754, the British and aggrieved New Englanders decided to launch a four-pronged attack against the outer defences of New France: Fort Duquesne in the Ohio Valley, Fort Niagara in the Great Lakes region, Fort Frédéric on Lake Champlain, and Fort Beauséjour in Nova Scotia. The offensive proved ineffective on all fronts save one. A colonial militia force of 2,500 men com-manded by Colonel Robert Monckton cap-tured Beauséjour on 12 June 1755 after a brief

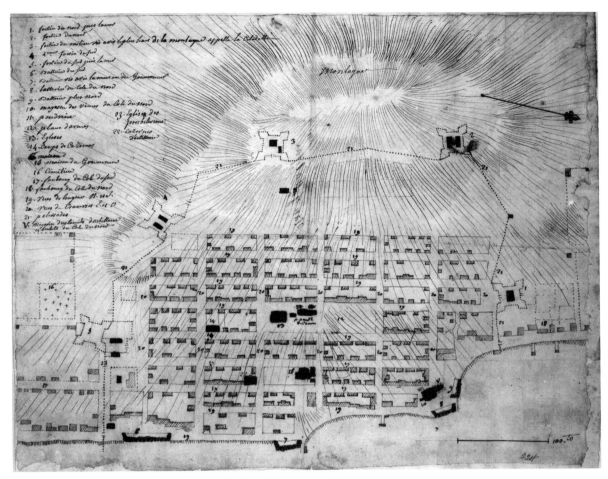

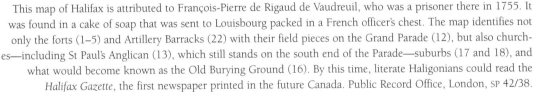

This map of Halifax is attributed to François-Pierre de Rigaud de Vaudreuil, who was a prisoner there in 1755. It was found in a cake of soap that was sent to Louisbourg packed in a French officer's chest. The map identifies not only the forts (1–5) and Artillery Barracks (22) with their field pieces on the Grand Parade (12), but also churches—including St Paul's Anglican (13), which still stands on the south end of the Parade—suburbs (17 and 18), and what would become known as the Old Burying Ground (16). By this time, literate Haligonians could read the *Halifax Gazette*, the first newspaper printed in the future Canada. Public Record Office, London, SP 42/38.

siege. With only 160 regular soldiers and 300 colonial militia, the French commander's position was hopeless.

Before the campaign against Beauséjour, British authorities had made plans to remove the Acadians from the Chignecto region. When it was discovered that as many as 300 Acadians were inside the fort and presumably helping to defend it, the fate of the entire Acadian population hung in the balance. In July 1755 Governor Charles Lawrence offered Acadian delegates one last chance to take an unqualified oath of allegiance. When they refused, Lawrence and his council decided to

'View of Fort Cumberland in Nova Scotia taken from the French 1755, from a View taken on the Spot by Capt. J[ohn] Hamilton of His Majesty's 40th Reg't.' NAC, C-2707.

solve the problem of the 'neutral French' once and for all. Military commanders at Chignecto, Piziquid, and Annapolis Royal were instructed to seize Acadian men and boys, along with their boats, so they could not escape. The Acadians were to be deported to the other British colonies in North America, taking only what they could carry.

Waiting for transports sent from Boston, the Acadians watched in horror as soldiers burned their homes, barns, churches, and crops, and seized their cattle to pay the costs of what was by any measure an expensive military exercise. The sorrows of the deportation did not end there. Since authorities in the receiving colonies had not been informed of the deportation, they offered little assistance, and some even refused to accept their quota of refugees. Despite the obvious logistical problems and human misery associated with the deportation of 1755, expulsions continued until the Seven Years' War ended in 1763. In all, over 11,000 Acadians were removed from Nova Scotia, Île Royale, and Île St-Jean. Of the rest, those who were not held prisoner either escaped to Quebec or managed to hide out until the hostilities ended. Many of the deportees died of disease and misadventure. Of the 3,100 Acadians shipped from Île St-Jean in 1758, for example, 679 drowned at sea and another 970 died from various causes before reaching their destinations.[7]

Letter from Charles Lawrence concerning the expulsion of the Acadians, 11 August 1755. NAC, MG 53, No. 71 2–4.

The Acadian diaspora had a remarkable reach. It took some to Louisiana, where their descendants, the Cajuns, still live; to Canada, where they quickly integrated into the colonial population; to the Îles de la Madeleine, St Pierre and Miquelon, the West Indies, Great Britain, France, and even the Falkland Islands. Those who went to France felt like strangers and asked to be returned to North America. When the war ended, some of them got their wish. In 1764 Acadians who agreed to take an oath of allegiance were permitted to settle in their former homeland—but not, for the most part, in the areas where they had lived. Their farms, cleared and ready for settlement, had already been taken up by new immigrants.

While cruel in the extreme, the expulsion of the Acadians did have the military impact that Lawrence had hoped for. The French food-supply problem reached crisis proportions. In Louisbourg, the authorities were besieged by destitute Aboriginal allies and Acadian refugees, who added greatly to the pressure on their limited resources. Thus, even before warfare officially resumed in 1756, the French had lost the first round. 'Maybe more than any other single factor,' Stephen E. Patterson suggests, 'the supply problem spelled doom to French power in the region.'[8]

Newfoundland's experience between 1713 and the Seven Years' War was very different from Nova Scotia's. The fisheries that were the reason for the European presence in the colony were generally poor until the late 1720s, prompting the English to enter the offshore fishery for the first time. Thereafter the offshore banks became an increasingly important part of the overall fishing effort. The inshore failures may explain the fairly slow movement of the English fishery along the south coast, now abandoned by the French, where Placentia and St Pierre became the early centres. Expansion on the northeast coast, into Bonavista and Notre Dame bays—where the French claimed exclusive fishing rights but were unable to enforce them—was more vigorous, possibly because of the opportunities to diversify into furring, sealing, and salmon fishing.

Economic activity picked up in all the bays

as fish catches improved from the 1730s onward. The number of winter inhabitants reached over 7,000 in the 1750s (the summer population was more than twice as large). Of these, just under half were immigrants from southeast Ireland. Before the 1720s, Newfoundland's inhabitants had come almost exclusively from the hinterlands of the English West Country ports involved in the fishery. The arrival of the Irish reflected not only domestic economic problems, but also the fact that West Country vessels habitually stopped at Waterford for salt provisions and fishing crews.

This change in the population was noted with some concern by the British authorities, but there was little they could do about it. Indeed, it was in this period that the views of Newfoundland held by the authorities and the merchants began to diverge. The government still saw Newfoundland as a fishery and a nursery for mariners. Merchants, however, increasingly saw it as a place to make money— not just by fishing on their own account, but by supplying residents and migratory fishermen and purchasing their catches. A quasi-colonial society began to emerge on the island without any encouragement from the British government. Largely male—women made up less than a third of the population—and transient, it was composed of British merchants at the apex, planters in the middle, and servants at the bottom, and lacked a middle class in the usual sense of the term.[9]

Although hostilities during the War of the Austrian Succession had an impact on the English migratory fishery, no military campaigns were conducted on the island. The Seven Years' War (1756–63), by contrast, had important consequences for the whole Atlantic

BRITAIN'S GLORY, or the *REDUCTION* of CAPE BRETON, *In the* GALLANT ADMIRAL BOSCAWEN & GENERAL AMHERST.

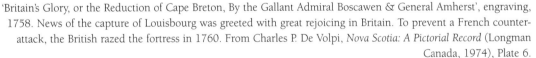

Extract of a Letter from LOUISBOURG, *dated July 30, 1758.*

'Britain's Glory, or the Reduction of Cape Breton, By the Gallant Admiral Boscawen & General Amherst', engraving, 1758. News of the capture of Louisbourg was greeted with great rejoicing in Britain. To prevent a French counterattack, the British razed the fortress in 1760. From Charles P. De Volpi, *Nova Scotia: A Pictorial Record* (Longman Canada, 1974), Plate 6.

region. In 1758 the British launched a massive attack on the fortress of Louisbourg. Governor Drucour surrendered after a seven-week siege, his army of 4,000 regular troops, colonial militia, and Aboriginal warriors overwhelmed by a force twice that size led by General Jeffrey Amherst and supported by the British navy under the command of Admiral Edward Boscawen. Amherst consolidated his victory by sending troops to Île Saint-Jean, the Gaspé, the Miramichi, and the St John River valley to round up Acadians for deportation and destroy both their settlements and those of their Native allies. To assist in these mopping-up operations, the British employed detachments of Rangers—special forces of colonial militia known for their ruthlessness. Even Amherst blanched when he learned of the bloody campaign conducted along the St John River by Rangers under Moses Hazen. 'I gave a

The church of Saint Paul and the Parade are shown in a view of Halifax drawn by Richard Short in 1759. By this time the town was basking in the glow of wartime prosperity—a glow that would dim after New France surrendered in 1760. NAC, C-4293.

Commission of Captain to Lieutenant Hazen as I thought he deserved it,' he wrote. 'I am sorry to say what I have since heard of that affair has sullied his merit with me, as I shall always disapprove of killing women and helpless children.'[10] A similarly brutal policy was carried out by General James Wolfe in the Bay of Chaleur and Gaspé.

With the collapse of French power in the region, the Mi'kmaq and Maliseet-Passamaquoddy sued for peace with the British. During 1760 and 1761, all bands sent delegates to Halifax to sign formal treaties of 'peace and friendship' with the governor and council, acknowledging 'the jurisdiction and Dominion of His Majesty George the Second over the Territories of Nova Scotia or Accadia' and agreeing to submit 'to His Majesty in the most perfect, ample, and solemn manner'. These treaties promised government-operated trading posts, but made no mention of reserved lands for hunting and fishing. Governor Belcher was instructed by the British government to draw up a proclamation forbidding encroachment on Aboriginal lands, which he obediently did, but he refused to publicize it because, as he told his superiors, 'If the proclamation had been issued at large, the

Indians might have been incited . . . to have extravagant and unwarranted demands, to the disquiet and perplexity of the New Settlements in the province.'[11]

The final chapter in the Seven Years' War took place in Newfoundland. Following the surrender of Montreal in 1760, the French devised a bizarre plan to disrupt the English bank fisheries by capturing St John's and impressing French and Irish fishermen to help them retake Île Royale. In 1762 six vessels bearing 750 soldiers under the command of Charles-Henry d'Arsac de Ternay set sail from France. They occupied St John's, Harbour Grace, Carbonear, and Trinity, and destroyed fishing premises and fishing vessels all along the coast. A hastily assembled British force, recruited from New York and Nova Scotia and led by Colonel William Amherst, recaptured St John's. It was the last Anglo-French battle to take place in North America.

In the Treaty of Paris formally ending the war, France gave up most of its North American empire to Great Britain. A major sticking point in the negotiations was the Newfoundland fisheries. The final deal renewed France's right to fish on the Treaty Shore, and ceded to it the islands of St Pierre and Miquelon, explicitly as an unfortified shelter for French migratory fishermen. The islands would serve as a minimal replacement for Île Royale, which French negotiators had fought hard to keep.

On 7 October 1763 the British government issued a proclamation outlining, in broad strokes, what it intended to do with its newly acquired territories. In the Atlantic region, Île Royale (renamed Cape Breton) and Île Saint-Jean (anglicized to the Island of St John) were placed under Nova Scotia's jurisdiction; the coast of Labrador, Anticosti Island, and the Îles de la Madeleine were placed 'under the care and inspection' of the governor of Newfoundland. In addition, the proclamation set out the Crown's policy regarding Native people. No European settlement would be permitted west of the Appalachian Mountains, and elsewhere Native people were not to be 'molested or disturbed' in the areas set aside for their hunting. All lands in the settled colonies not 'ceded or purchased by Us' were to be 'reserved to the said Indians', and no 'private person', only the 'Governor or Commander in Chief of our Colony', was authorized to buy land from Native people. Conceived with the western frontier in mind, these policies were deliberately ignored by administrators in Nova Scotia, who were slow to establish reserves and only minimally involved in land transactions with the Mi'kmaq and Maliseet. Whether the Royal Proclamation even applied in Newfoundland and Labrador is still a matter of contention.

In 1763, for the first time, all of what is now Atlantic Canada came under a single jurisdiction. The French presence was reduced to a seasonal fishery on the Newfoundland Treaty Shore and a base at St Pierre and Miquelon. With the Acadians effectively eliminated and the Aboriginal threat neutralized, the British were eager to see the region—Newfoundland and Labrador excepted—settled by Europeans, preferably English-speaking and Protestant.

CHAPTER SEVEN

Community Formation: 1749–1815

*B*etween the founding of Halifax in 1749 and the end of the Napoleonic wars in 1815, the Atlantic region was reorganized and essentially remade.[1] Most communities in the region trace their origins to this critical period, when nearly 75,000 settlers arrived in what would become Atlantic Canada. The first immigrants to what are now the Maritime Provinces were directly recruited by the British authorities, but in time more and more arrived independently. Some were refugees from the political and economic revolutions sweeping the North Atlantic world; others were attracted to the region's ability to profit from resource development and warfare. Many of the new settlers came from other parts of North America, but they shared with immigrants from Great Britain and Europe a determination to improve their lot in an unstable and rapidly changing North Atlantic world.

War continued to define boundaries and identities in the region. The Seven Years' War turned out to be only a truce in Great Britain's ongoing struggle with France. Between 1776 and 1783 the Thirteen Colonies, with the support of France, successfully defended their declaration of independence from Great

Britain, and, following the outbreak of the French Revolution in 1789, Britain became engaged in a prolonged war with France that inevitably spilled over into North America.

To support their imperial objectives of trade, settlement, and military security, extensive exploration and mapping was required. George Mitchell had already surveyed the Bay of Fundy in the 1730s. During the Seven Years' War, James Cook charted part of the Gulf of St Lawrence and helped to prepare the map that enabled Wolfe to successfully reach Quebec in 1759. When the war ended, Cook became the naval surveyor for Newfoundland, charting the island's south and west coasts and the Strait of Belle Isle. His meticulous charts were still in use a century later, as were those of his assistant Michael Lane, who completed the work begun by Britain's most famous marine surveyor.

Cook's equivalent in Nova Scotia was Joseph F.W. DesBarres, a military engineer who painstakingly charted the water around the Nova Scotia peninsula, Cape Breton, and St John's Island between 1764 and 1773. His original drawings were engraved and published in several beautifully illustrated volumes under

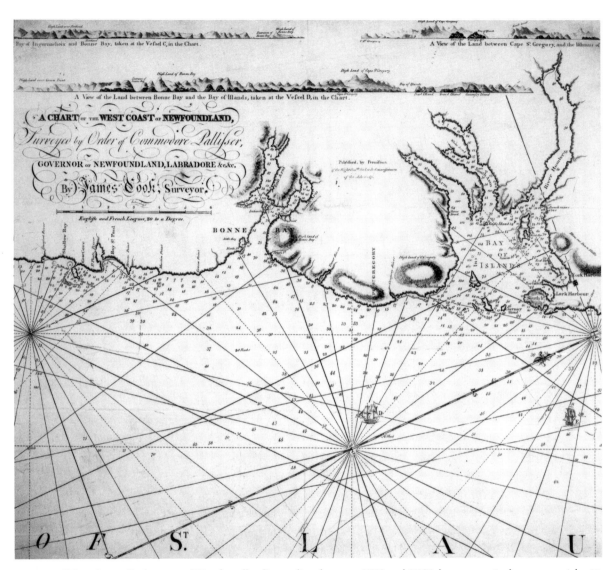

When James Cook surveyed Newfoundland's coastline, between 1763 and 1767, he was required to pay special attention to the areas used by French fishers on the French Treaty Shore, which included the island's west coast, and around St Pierre and Miquelon. This chart, based on surveys made in 1767, shows Bonne Bay and the Bay of Islands. Many placenames derive from these surveys. CNS, MUN.

the title *The Atlantic Neptune* (1774–84). A major achievement in Canadian cartographic history, DesBarres's charts, like those of Cook and Lane, remained in use for many years.

Beginning in 1764, another legendary British surveyor, Samuel Holland, carried out extensive surveys in the Atlantic region. His report on St John's Island laid out counties,

Wreckers' Den near the Pond on the Isle of Sable.

The surveyor of Sable Island, J.F.W. Desbarres, included this view of a Wreckers' Den (with Sable Island ponies in the distance) in his *Atlantic Neptune* (1777). So many ships came to grief on its shores that the island became known as the 'Graveyard of the Atlantic'. Killam Library, Dalhousie University.

parishes, and townships; fixed the site of the projected capital, which he named Charlotte-town in honour of George III's Queen; and gave a detailed account of the island's resources and climate. Holland then moved on to the Îles de la Madeleine and Cape Breton, where he drew attention to the island's deposits of coal, building stone, and gypsum. In the early 1770s he helped to map the coast from the St John River to New York, and conducted hydraulic surveys in Nova Scotia.

Northern Labrador became better known in the second half of the eighteenth century, largely through the activities of Moravian missionaries who began investigating the coast in 1765. The interior of Newfoundland, by contrast, remained largely unknown to Europeans, but was home to a dwindling number of Beothuk, and to Mi'kmaq who moved to the island in increasing numbers following the Seven Years' War. It was the Mi'kmaq who informed Cook about river systems of the island's west and south coasts, which he included on his 1770 general map, and it was concern about the Beothuk that led to exploration of the Exploits River and Red Indian Lake, beginning in 1768 with an expedition led by Lieutenant John Cartwright.

In 1749 Charles Morris was appointed Nova Scotia's first surveyor general, a post that

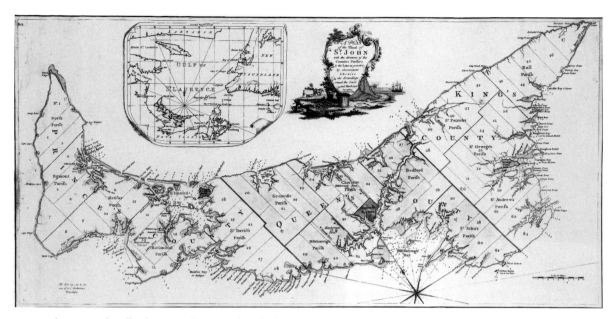

When Samuel Holland surveyed Prince Edward Island he divided it into 67 lots (or townships), three counties, and three 'royalties'. The royalties—pastures and garden plots—were set aside for the three principal communities: Georgetown, Charlottetown, and Princetown. NAC, NMC-23350.

would stay in his family until 1851. Morris played a major role in surveying the land for immigrants, who began moving to Nova Scotia in significant numbers after the founding of Halifax in 1749. Between 1750 and 1753, nearly 2,500 German- and French-speaking Protestants, recruited by the British in Europe, arrived in Nova Scotia. Some of these 'foreign Protestants' stayed in Halifax, but the majority moved on, helping to found the town of Lunenburg in 1753. With the threats posed by hostile French and Aboriginal forces uppermost in their minds, British authorities designed Lunenburg as a compact community that would be more easily defended, in the event of attack, than scattered farm settlements. The rigid grid of streets marching up the steep slope from the harbour still testifies to the clas-

sic principles that governed town planning in the eighteenth century. Despite several difficult years, the Lunenburg settlers soon became productive farmers and eventually engaged in fishing and shipbuilding as well.

Many of the disbanded soldiers and sailors who helped to build Halifax quickly moved on to Boston, but merchants and artisans, eager to profit from the vast sums of money being invested in the colony, stayed—at least for a time. The Jersey-born merchant Joshua Mauger emerged as the most powerful force in the colonial capital, making his fortune from the West Indies trade, smuggling with Louisbourg, and the sale of rum. In the early 1760s he returned to Great Britain, where, as a member of Parliament, he played an important role in determining colonial policy.

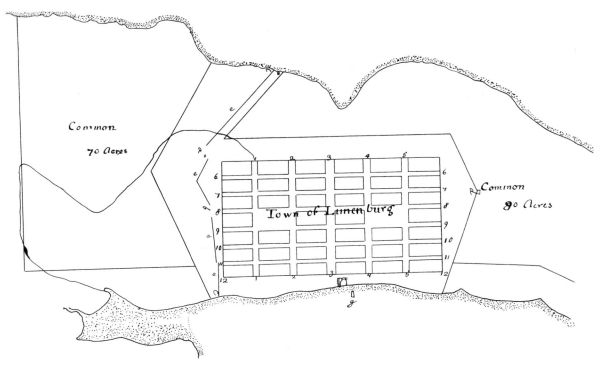

Common
70 Acres

Common
80 Acres

Town of Lunenburg

An early plan of Lunenburg as laid out by Charles Morris in 1753. The rigid grid of streets, typical of town planning in the middle of the eighteenth century, took little account of the steep slopes that rise from the water's edge. NSARM, N-9814.

The expulsion of the Acadians had drastically affected the region's agricultural output, a problem that colonial administrators were eager to rectify. Although its proximity and rapidly growing population made New England a promising source of immigrants, its inhabitants were reluctant to move to a colony where their 'rights as Englishmen' were in question. This obstacle was overcome when the Board of Trade, which was responsible for colonial policy, obliged a reluctant Governor Charles Lawrence to call Nova Scotia's first elected assembly in 1758 and offer terms of settlement that would appeal to New Englanders. According to a proclamation published early in 1759, there would be two elected assembly representatives for each settled township, a judicial system similar to the one in 'Massachusetts, Connecticut, and the other Northern Colonies', and freedom of worship for Protestant dissenters. Bona fide settlers were to receive land grants—100 free acres for each head of household, with an additional 50 for each family member and servant—that would be exempt from taxes for ten years. Assistance was even provided to help the immigrants move to their new homes.

Their concerns thus addressed, some 8,000 'Planters' from New England settled in Nova Scotia between 1759 and 1767. Creating a new New England on the south shore of Nova Scotia, in the Annapolis Valley, and in other areas formerly occupied by the Acadians, the New Englanders added a distinctly 'Yankee' flavour to the region, and, living close to their homeland, they drew freely on its resources. They recruited ministers for their Congregational churches in New England, traded fish and farm produce in Boston, and returned 'home' periodically to visit family and friends. Although most of the Planters came with little capital, they were among the most fortunate of immigrants, making impressive progress in standards of living in only one generation.

The North American settlement frontier also extended to the north shore of the Bay of Fundy. In 1762 James Simonds, James White, and William Hazen, New England merchants associated with Joshua Mauger, established trading operations in the region, eventually locating their headquarters at Portland Point, near the mouth of the St John River. They developed a flourishing trade with the local Native people, and brought in labour to exploit the area's resources of fish, timber, and limestone. When, farther up the river, a group of farmers from Essex County, Massachusetts, squatted on land occupied by Acadians and Maliseet, Mauger's intervention ensured that the newcomers prevailed. In 1765 some 20 pacifist Protestant German families from Pennsylvania settled on the Petitcodiac River, where they became the founders of Hopewell, Hillsborough, and Moncton.

After the Seven Years' War, Acadians were again permitted to settle in the Atlantic region. They carved out communities in a number of locations, especially Argyle and Clare in south-western Nova Scotia, Île M Cheticamp in Cape Breton, the noru. shore of what would later become Nev. Brunswick, and the western end of St John's Island. Scratching a hardscrabble existence from the inferior soil typical of the lands granted them, they soon turned to fishing and became an indispensable labour force for the Jersey-based fishing companies that set up operations in the Gaspé and Cape Breton following the British conquest. By 1800 the Atlantic region counted at least 8,000 Acadians (out of about 23,000 scattered throughout the North Atlantic world), and their numbers would continue to grow impressively with each generation.

In an attempt to populate the region on the cheap and at the same time promote a land-based social hierarchy, British authorities made large land grants to 'proprietors' on condition that they recruited Protestant settlers, improved their properties, and paid quitrents (taxes) to sustain the colonial administration. In a single 17-day period in 1765, over one million hectares of Nova Scotia were handed over to speculators. Two years later, in an even more spectacular display of largesse, 64 of the 67 lots on St John's Island that Samuel Holland had surveyed were granted to favourites of the king and court.

Although most of the proprietors failed to meet the conditions of their grants, a few attempted to do so. Alexander McNutt, who planned to settle thousands of Ulster Protestants from Ireland and from New Hampshire on his enormous grants, managed to bring a few hundred settlers to communities such as Londonderry (Colchester County) and New Dublin (Lunenburg County). Near

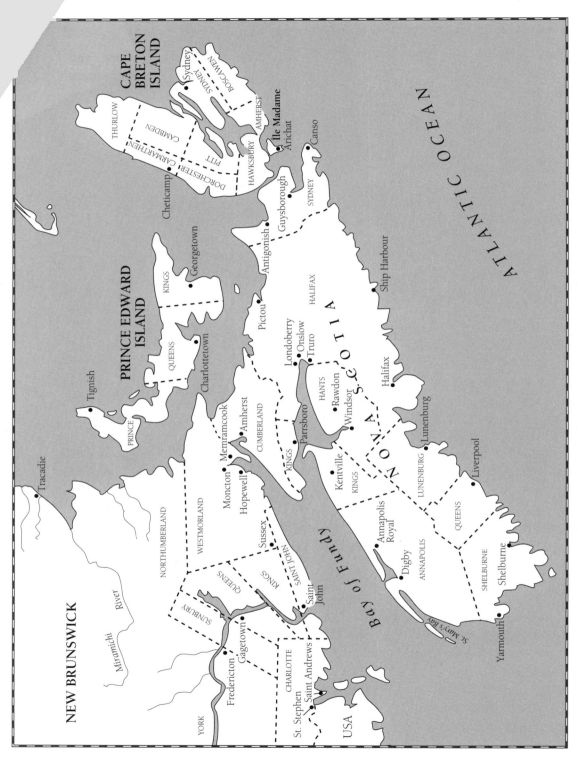

The Maritime colonies, c. 1800. Adapted from *Historical Atlas of Canada*, I (Toronto: University of Toronto Press, 1987), plates 25 and 32.

Windsor, Nova Scotia, two would-be aristo-
crats, Henry Denny Denson and J.F.W.
DesBarres, employed tenant and slave labour
to work their estates. Located on the Minas
Basin, Windsor was fast becoming not only the
country seat of the Halifax élite but a commercial centre of some importance. In 1767 it
hosted the region's first agricultural fair.

The Philadelphia plantation, granted in
1765 to 14 proprietors in what is now Pictou
County, attracted a few settlers from Pennsylvania, but the majority of its first European
inhabitants arrived on board the *Hector* in
1773—the beginning of what was to become a
substantial wave of immigration from Scotland. Always alert to lucrative trading opportunities, Scottish merchants too were drawn to
the region, specifically for its timber and fish.
In 1765, William Davidson and his associates
received a grant of 100,000 acres on the
Miramichi, where they developed a salmon
fishery and eventually branched into timber
and shipbuilding operations.

Between 1772 and 1776 roughly 1,000
people from Yorkshire, many of them Methodists, settled in the Chignecto area and elsewhere in Nova Scotia. Pushed out of England
by high rents, land enclosures, and their own
ambitions, they brought with them commercial and farming skills of a high order. Many of
them had sufficient capital to purchase their
farms outright, and quickly brought them into
efficient production.

Most of the unsettled proprietorial grants in
Nova Scotia eventually reverted to the Crown,
but this was not the case on St John's Island
(renamed after Prince Edward in 1799). By having the island proclaimed a separate colony in
1769 and controlling its administration, the

proprietors succeeded in frustrating any and all
attempts to settle 'the land question'. In this way
the colony became saddled with an absentee
landlord system that was increasingly out of
step with the system of freehold tenure favoured
in most of North America.

Despite these relatively unfavourable conditions for landholding, the island did attract
some settlers. Many of the early immigrants
were Scots, whose homeland was suffering
such severe political and economic upheaval
that emigration appeared an attractive option
even if it meant leasing rather than owning
land. The first settlers, some 80 Scots recruited
by Captain Robert Stewart for Lot 18, arrived
on the *Arabella* in 1770. They were soon followed by a group of indentured servants under
contract to grow flax on the estates of Sir James
Montgomery; Roman Catholic Highlanders
under the direction of John MacDonald of
Genaladale; Protestants from Ulster; and
Quakers from London. By 1775 the 300
Acadian and Mi'kmaq living on the island were
outnumbered four to one by the 1,200 immigrants from Great Britain.[2]

The year-round population of Newfoundland also grew, to about 10,000 in the 1770s,
but in the same way as earlier in the century:
slowly, informally, and without official encouragement. The reactionary Sir Hugh Palliser,
governor from 1764 to 1768, did what he
could to discourage permanent settlement and
support the migratory fishery. In pursuing this
policy, he focused his attention on southern
Labrador, where a state of warfare existed
between fishermen and the Inuit who travelled
south to the Strait of Belle Isle to trade whalebone and scavenge from fishing camps. Eager
to pacify the area, Palliser welcomed a pro-

An imagined depiction by Mary Spilsbury of a Moravian missionary talking to Inuit at Nain, Labrador, *c.* 1800.
NAC, C-124432.

posal from the highly disciplined Protestant sect commonly called the Moravians—officially the Unitas Fratrum (United Brethren)—to establish a mission in Labrador. In 1771 the first Moravian mission station, complete with a trading store, was built at Nain. Its presence seems to have encouraged Inuit to stay in the north, and helped to calm the situation in the Strait. Although Labrador was placed under the jurisdiction of Quebec in 1774, the governor of Newfoundland retained responsibility for the mission stations, and for supervising the fisheries there.

In 1775, growing tensions between the British government and the New England colonies led to the decision to curtail the trade conducted by Massachusetts and close the port of Boston. Most American ports retaliated by banning trade with Newfoundland. This move caused widespread hardship on the island, which had come to depend on New England for foodstuffs and shipping in the West Indies trade. Without any formal political life, Newfoundlanders showed no interest in joining the Thirteen Colonies when they declared independence from Great Britain in 1776. Throughout the American Revolutionary War, American predators made all fishing hazardous, especially offshore. Migratory activity decreased, the resident population fell, and food shortages were frequent. In the winter of 1779–80 James Balfour, an Anglican missionary in Conception Bay, reported that there was 'raging Famine, Nakedness & Sickness in these Parts. None can express the heart felt woe of Women & Children mourning for want of Food.'[3]

As in Newfoundland, political and economic development in Nova Scotia and St John's Island was not sufficiently advanced to make independence appealing—or even possible. Many people who had received land from the British Crown on exceptionally favourable terms were reluctant to support the rebellious colonies for fear the British would prevail, which seemed likely at the outset of the war. Even if there was sympathy for the rebel cause, as was certainly the case in some areas, the British military presence in colonial capitals and coastal waters served as a powerful deterrent to armed resistance. The reach of Halifax was clearly demonstrated in the fall of 1776, when Jonathan Eddy and John Allen, both from the Cumberland area, led a force of 180 men, including a few Maliseet and Acadians, against the garrison at Fort Cumberland (formerly Fort Beauséjour). The attack was easily repulsed, and no further attempt was made to dislodge imperial control in Nova Scotia.[4]

Notwithstanding the presence of the British fleet, raids by New England privateers were a fact of life throughout the region—as far north as Labrador, where George Cartwright's trading posts in Sandwich Bay were plundered in 1778. Most raids were selective, leaving all but the targeted victims unmolested, but they did little to endear the rebels to the pioneer settlers. In November 1775 Yankees even attacked Charlottetown,

A half-pay army officer, George Cartwright spent 16 years as a trader on the Labrador coast (1770–86), enthusiastically recording his experiences and observations in a detailed journal that he published in 1792. In later years Cartwright came to be known as 'Old Labrador'. CNS, MUN.

seizing provisions and carrying away the colony's acting governor. After the British defeat at Saratoga in 1777, the fighting moved to the middle colonies and people in Nova Scotia settled down to profiting from the increased military presence and the influx of Loyalist refugees. By this time, too, a religious revival, led by the itinerant preacher Henry Alline, was well under way in the colony. Many New England Planters, who had more difficulty than other settlers in deciding where their loyalties lay, responded enthusiastically to Alline's message that good Christians should pursue spiritual salvation rather than fight military battles. Alline's ministry was short—he died in 1784—but he laid the foundations of an evangelical tradition that is still strong in Nova Scotia and New Brunswick.

France joined the war on the side of the United States in 1778, and the British were eventually forced to concede defeat. In the Treaty of Paris (1783) Britain recognized the independence of the United States of America, leaving the Atlantic colonies, Quebec, and the Hudson's Bay Company territory to form what was left of 'British' North America. The Americans were allowed, in a significant concession, to continue fishing in the Gulf, on the banks, and on the Newfoundland coast outside the French Treaty Shore; they also had the 'liberty' to dry fish on the unsettled coasts of Nova Scotia, the Îles de la Madeleine, and Labrador.

In a separate treaty with Britain, France obtained concessions in Newfoundland. The boundaries of the Treaty Shore were moved to Cape St John and Cape Ray, away from the areas where the English usually fished. An appended declaration, while avoiding the word 'exclusive', in effect defined the Shore as a French fishing zone. St Pierre and Miquelon were returned to France without the deeply resented conditions imposed in 1763, although in the declaration both governments agreed that the islands would never become 'an object of jealousy'. Not surprisingly, such vague wording invited continuing dispute.

The American Revolution was a defining moment in the history of the Atlantic colonies. Not only did it create a new boundary separating them from New England; it also more than doubled their population with the arrival of over 35,000 civilian refugees and disbanded soldiers from the United States. These 'Loyalists' began moving to Nova Scotia even before hostilities were officially declared, but most of them arrived between 1782 and 1784 on ships from New York, where they had gathered under British protection in the final stages of the war. Although they had few good words for 'Nova Scarcity', the Loyalists were luckier than many refugees. The British government supplied provisions and temporary shelter, compensated some for their losses, and provided most of them with free land.

Nearly 15,000 Loyalists landed at the mouth of the St John River, engulfing the tiny population already living there and founding the city of Saint John. Both Maliseet and Acadians were pushed off their land farther up the river, the former into reserves, most of the latter to Madawaska and Memramcook. Even more Loyalists, approximately 19,000, went to peninsular Nova Scotia, half of them settling in Shelburne, which for a time became the largest city in British North America. When it failed to develop into the prosperous trading centre they had expected, the Loyalists drifted away. Some moved back to the United States when they judged it safe; others to Quebec; still others to Halifax, Saint John, and the dozens of smaller communities, including Aylesford, Digby, Gagetown, Guysborough, Rawdon, Ship Harbour, St Andrews, and Sussex Vale, established by Loyalists.

Relatively few of them settled on Cape Breton Island, though Sydney was founded as a Loyalist town. In 1784 the island was made a separate colony, largely on the strength of Abraham Cuyler's abortive scheme to attract 5,000 Loyalists from Quebec. St John's Island attracted little attention either: only some 800 Loyalists were prepared to begin new lives as

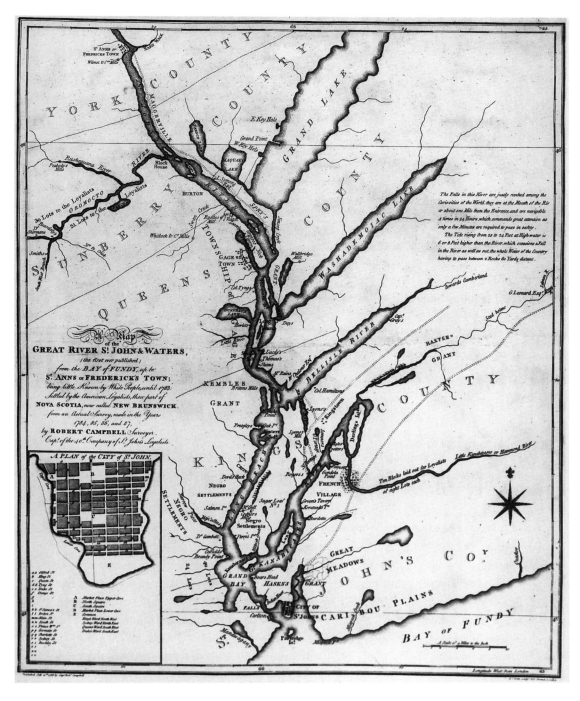

Robert Campbell, 'A Map of the Great River St John & Waters', engraved by S.I. Neele and published in London in 1788. The St John River Valley was soon to become the heart of Loyalist New Brunswick. NAC, NMC-254.

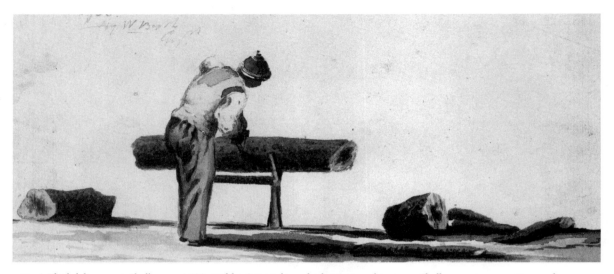

A Black labourer at Shelburne, 1788. Unlike Saint John, which continued to grow, Shelburne soon saw its population drain away, dropping from 10,000 in 1783 to 1,000 a decade later. Among the emigrants were many of Shelburne's Black Loyalists, who in 1792 left to help found Sierra Leone. NAC, C-40162.

tenant farmers on land granted to absentee proprietors. And no one was interested in what Newfoundland had to offer.

Old Nova Scotia was further truncated in 1784 when the British government was persuaded, after intensive lobbying by élite Loyalists from the St John River, to create the new colony of New Brunswick. These men hoped that the colony, which they expected to dominate, would become 'the envy of the American states', a model of order and hierarchy in contrast to the democratic anarchy that would surely engulf their neighbours to the south. Concluding that the busy mercantile town of Saint John was both too crass and too close to the American border, they choose Fredericton as the capital of what they hoped would become 'a stable agricultural society led by a landholding gentry'.[5] The pretensions of the Loyalist élite were not well received by the mass of the refugees. When 55 prominent Loyalists,

'of the most respectable Characters', as they themselves declared, petitioned for estates of 5,000 acres—nearly ten times the average grant—the wishes of the majority prevailed.[6] During the 1785 election, the inhabitants of Saint John violently protested the condescension of the government based in Fredericton.

Loyalists were also politically active in Nova Scotia, where the New Hampshire-born Sir John Wentworth was appointed lieutenant-governor in 1792. Revelling in the court-like atmosphere of Halifax social life, the Loyalist élite were enchanted by the presence of the king's son, Prince Edward Augustus, and his beautiful mistress, Madame de St Laurent, who resided in the city between 1794 and 1799. Outside provincial capitals the pioneer experience had a levelling effect, and Loyalist roots counted for little in a region where, after 1783, nearly everyone claimed to have supported the British cause.

George Heriot, 'Chief Justice Ludlow's House on the River St. John, New Brunswick', watercolour. A lawyer from Long Island, George Ludlow became New Brunswick's first Chief Justice and a member of its first legislative council. His home at 'Spring Hill', near the colonial capital of Fredericton, was typical of the rural estates built by the Loyalist elite. Photograph courtesy of the Royal Ontario Museum, © ROM.

The Loyalists represented a thick slice of North American society and greatly increased the region's cultural diversity. As well as élites with aristocratic ideals, the mix included military veterans of all ranks, farmers and tradesmen, and a wide range of ethnic groups, including African Americans, many of them former slaves who had been encouraged to leave their masters by promises of freedom if they fought in British regiments. Over 3,000 Black Loyalists moved to Nova Scotia, but they soon realized that freedom did not bring equality. Given smaller and less fertile grants than white Loyalists, they were often targets for hostility and violence during the tension-ridden early years of settlement. Nearly 1,200 Black Loyalists left the region in 1792 for the new colony of Sierra Leone—though slaves were denied that option.[7] Following the abolition of the slave trade in 1807, slavery gradually disappeared in the Atlantic region and was abolished throughout the British Empire in 1833.

In the wake of the American Revolution, the British government was eager to strengthen the Church of England as a way to bolster the authority of the Crown and reinforce a rigid

Upon his arrival in Halifax in 1794, the 27-year-old Prince Edward (later to become the Duke of Kent and the father of Queen Victoria) was struck by 'the miserable state of all the works and public buildings' in the city. He devoted considerable energy to improving this state of affairs. In addition to overhauling the city's defences, he was instrumental in the construction of three exquisite round structures: St George's Anglican Church, the Prince's Lodge Rotunda, and, shown here, the Old Town Clock. Chris Reardon.

social hierarchy. Thus in 1787 Charles Inglis, the Loyalist former rector of Trinity Church in New York, was consecrated the first bishop of Nova Scotia, with jurisdiction over all the British North American colonies, including Newfoundland and Bermuda. Inglis supported the founding of King's College in Windsor in 1789 as an exclusive institution for the sons of the Anglican élite, as well as the Provincial Academy of Arts and Sciences in Fredericton, which received its charter as the College of New Brunswick in 1800. Inglis and his clergy strenuously opposed evangelical enthusiasm, but despite all their efforts the Church of England in the Maritimes steadily lost adherents to the Baptists and Methodists. In a democratic age, the hope of personal salvation and spiritual equality that these evangelical churches offered (often through itinerant ministers) was increasingly attractive to ordinary people.

In Newfoundland, the American Revolution forced changes in customary trade patterns. Merchants began to send their own ships to the West Indies, sometimes using Bermuda shipowners as middlemen. Although it was still possible to import food from the United States after the war, so long as it was transported in British ships, Newfoundland importers increasingly looked to other sources of supply, especially in the Maritimes and the Canadas. A shipbuilding industry grew on the island, and a Newfoundland-based fleet, managed largely by merchants newly arrived from Greenock, Scotland, traded to the mainland and Caribbean. The winter population soon recovered to pre-war levels and began to grow steadily, with residents taking an increasing percentage of the total catch of cod as migratory activity declined.

The naval state remained in place in Newfoundland, with the court system becoming more elaborate over time. A supreme court was established in 1791, and civilians began to join naval officers as surrogate magistrates. A government house was built in the early 1780s. It was a practical and reasonably effective system of government. The navy even contributed to religious life, since its chaplains were active on shore as well as on board their vessels, at least among Protestants. A proclamation of 1784 established religious freedom in Newfoundland, and in the same year Father James O'Donnell arrived as prefect apostolic (he would become bishop in 1796) to organize the few Roman Catholic priests ministering to the increasing numbers of Irish. As in the Maritimes, the Anglican clergy in Newfoundland were supported by the Society for the Propagation of the Gospel. Most immigrants from England belonged to the established church, but Protestant dissenters were gaining ground. From 1766 the Reverend Laurence Coughlan preached Methodism on the north shore of Conception Bay with considerable success, and in St John's dissenters attended John Jones's Congregational 'Dissenting Church of Christ'.

Between 1783 and 1803, nearly 17,000 Highland Scots emigrated to the Maritimes, most of them settling on St John's Island, Cape Breton, and in eastern Nova Scotia. One of the most ambitious settlement schemes was sponsored by the Earl of Selkirk, who in 1803 brought 800 Highlanders to the Orwell–Point Prim area of Prince Edward Island. On the Miramichi, Fraser and Thom, a Scottish timber and shipbuilding company, recruited Scottish labourers. Scottish Highlanders tended to be Gaelic-speaking Roman Catholics, whereas Lowland Scots were more likely to be English-speaking Presbyterians, and to place strong emphasis on education. For example, it was two immigrant Presbyterian ministers, James MacGregor and Thomas McCulloch, who helped to make Pictou, Nova Scotia, a religious and educational centre.

Like Scotland, Ireland was experiencing major social and economic upheavals, including periodic famines, that contributed significantly to the stream of immigrants to the Atlantic region. While Protestant Irish quickly assimilated into the dominant culture, Roman Catholics remained distinct, separated by religion, history, and, for many, their Gaelic language. Irish Catholics swelled the population of southeastern Newfoundland outports, became tenant farmers on Prince Edward Island estates, harvested New Brunswick forests, and worked as domestic servants. In major port cities such as St John's, Halifax, and Saint John, the Irish quickly came to constitute a significant portion of the population. The desperate condition of many among them inspired their philanthropic compatriots to found a Charitable Irish Society in Halifax in 1776 and similar organizations in Saint John and St John's in 1806.

For the Mi'kmaq and Maliseet, these migrations represented yet another threat to their survival as more territory fell into private hands and competition for fish and game increased. Recognizing their vulnerability, Aboriginal leaders petitioned for land, and sometimes received it—but much of it was stolen back by white squatters who knew that the authorities would not object. In 1783 the Mi'kmaq chief John Julien obtained a licence of occupation for 20,000 acres (8,100 hectares) on the Miramichi River, but half of it was gone by 1807 when the government finally got around to establishing the Eel Ground Reserve. In Prince Edward Island the

Mi'kmaq eventually received permission from proprietor James Montgomery to live on the barren and rocky Lennox Island, but no formal Indian reserves were established.[8]

The final round of the Anglo-French struggle began in 1793 and would not end until 1815. Like the wars earlier in the century, this lengthy conflict had a profound and lasting impact on the Atlantic region. British demand for fish, foodstuffs, and timber skyrocketed, and with alternative sources of supply cut off, the Atlantic colonies found ready markets for their resources. Production was further stimulated by the Navigation Acts and the whole framework of mercantilist regulation that gave colonial producers preference in British markets over their foreign competitors. With the demand high and money pouring in to pay for defence against a possible French attack, colonials found themselves in a privileged and profitable position.

The most critical resource for an empire at war in the eighteenth century was wood, and for many years the British had reserved great stands of timber in North America to supply the Royal Navy. After 1800 these forest reserves came under intense development. Between 1805 and 1812 the exports of fir and pine timber from New Brunswick, Britain's pre-eminent 'timber colony',[9] increased more than twenty-fold. Businessmen, many of them based in Greenock, brought their capital, labour, and technology to the shores of the Miramichi and St John rivers, and shipbuilding soon emerged as a sideline of the timber trade. By 1815 New Brunswick's economy was dominated by forest-based industries.

Attempts by the United States to remain neutral and trade with both sides were met by Great Britain's insistence on a strict definition of the rights of neutral countries, which could be backed up with sea power. President Thomas Jefferson responded in 1807 with an embargo on British trade. While this hurt American exporters, it also wrought havoc with the British war effort. Britain retaliated by declaring Halifax, Shelburne, Saint John, and St Andrews to be 'free ports'—a clever manoeuvre that effectively undermined the embargo. Annoyed by the restrictions, New England shippers took advantage of the free ports to sell their cargos and buy manufactured goods from Britain as well as colonial produce. Thus the policy not only served its purpose of keeping the British army and navy supplied, but helped to make the designated ports important commercial centres in the expanding regional economy. During the war vessels from the Maritimes also began competing successfully with New Englanders in the carrying trade to the West Indies, where the sugar plantations worked by vast numbers of slaves represented a lucrative market. Halifax in particular emerged as a significant entrepôt for produce shipped under convoy to the Caribbean.

If the trade war between Great Britain and the United States benefited the Maritimes, the official conflict, known as the War of 1812, brought more economic blessings. Buffered by New England, whose leaders refused to participate in the war, the Atlantic region was spared military invasion and became the centre of a vigorous clandestine trade between the two belligerents. In addition, the British naval and military presence generated unprecedented market opportunities and increased the supply of hard currency. The war also inspired moments of great excitement. In June 1813, for example,

Painted by J.C.Schetky Esq.ʳ & On Stone by L.Haghe.   Designed by Capt.ᵗ R. H. King R. N

To Captain Sir Philip Bowes Vere Broke, Bart.ᵗ and K.C.B.

*This representation of H.M.S. SHANNON leading her PRIZE the AMERICAN FRIGATE CHESAPEAKE into HALIFAX HARBOUR, on the 6ᵗʰ June 1813
is Dedicated by his obliged and most grateful Servant R.H.King.*

London Pub.ᵈ by Smith Elder &C.ᵒ 65 Cornhill

The HMS *Shannon* leading its prize, the USS *Chesapeake*, into Halifax harbour, 6 June 1813. The inscription on this print by Captain R.H. King, RN, reads in part: 'As the ships entered the harbour, the men of war manned their yards in honour of the conquerors; the inhabitants crowded to the shore and lined the wharfs and buildings of the town. As they sailed past the assembled crowds, one burst of loud congratulations rose upon the air; but while the *Chesapeake* returned the cheering, an affecting silence distinguished the *Shannon*.' NSARM, N-2301.

Haligonians were treated to the spectacle of HMS *Shannon* arriving with the USS *Chesapeake* in tow following a brief engagement off Boston harbour. The following year, a British army under Sir John Sherbrooke occupied part of the coast of present-day Maine, providing more opportunities for commercial profit.

The war of 1812 expanded the potential for privateering, an activity that had been conducted, with more or less enthusiasm, against French shipping for nearly two decades. During the conflict with the Americans, 37 vessels from the Atlantic region engaged in privateering, recording 207 captures. Privateers

'View of Saint John, New Brunswick', 1814 by Joseph Brown Comingo (1784–1821, Canadian School). Fuelled by a vibrant timber industry during the French and Napoleonic Wars, Saint John quickly developed into the commercial capital of the Bay of Fundy region. Born in Nova Scotia, Comingo painted this watercolour in 1814. The New Brunswick Museum, Saint John, NB.

from Liverpool, Nova Scotia—a major centre for such enterprise since the American Revolution—were particularly successful in their escapades on the high seas. While historians still debate the military significance of privateering, there can be no doubt that it helped to line the pockets of ambitious merchants who bought the vessels in prize courts and sold their contents at immense profit to themselves.[10] The *Liverpool Packet*, the most successful of the privateer vessels, is reputed to have captured enemy prizes worth $1.5 mil-

lion, and greatly advanced the fortunes of its owner, Enos Collins. The communities where captures were auctioned, such as Halifax and St John's, also reaped financial rewards. On one memorable occasion, residents of St John's were able to observe 30 American prize ships roped together in the harbour.[11]

By 1815 St John's had emerged as the capital of Newfoundland, which had become a colony in all but name and constitutional status.[12] The long period of warfare all but killed the English migratory fishery, and the bye-boatmen completely disappeared. As a result, the resident fishery expanded and the permanent population increased to over 20,000. The settlers were not prosperous, but they survived by growing potatoes and fishing along an increasing stretch of the coastline. During the War of 1812, Newfoundland fish producers enjoyed a monopoly in Spain and Portugal, while continuing to supply the Italian and West Indian markets. Fish prices climbed to unprecedented levels, producing a few fortunes and attracting a wave of migrants from Ireland.

In the 1790s, for the first time, schooners from Conception Bay and other areas began to exploit the spring seal fishery. It rapidly became an important part of the local economy, and in good years a lucrative one. Labrador, which had been attached to Quebec in 1774, was returned to Newfoundland's jurisdiction in 1809. This decision reflected the necessity of providing more effective protection for the region's mercantile establishments in time of war.

As the French and Napoleonic wars came to a weary end, the demand for staples declined and prices fell, but the contours of the Atlantic regional economy had been set. Newfoundland had found its niche in the rich fisheries off its shores; New Brunswick in the timber trade and shipbuilding; Prince Edward Island in wheat, root crops, and cattle. Nova Scotia had not only developed the most diversified economy (based on farm, fish, and forest resources) but was carving a place for itself in the carrying trade to the West Indies and beyond. And in every colony, British settlers and culture prevailed.

CHAPTER EIGHT

Maturing Colonial Societies: 1815–1873

Let the Frenchman delight in his vine-covered vales,

Let the Greek toast his old classic ground;
Here's the land where the bracing North-wester prevails,

And where jolly Blue Noses abound.[1]

In the half-century following the Napoleonic Wars, the Atlantic colonies witnessed unprecedented population growth and institutional development that made them more like each other and their 'mother' country.[2] Paradoxically, as Joseph Howe's ode to 'The Blue Noses' suggests, these trends would also encourage colonials to imagine new identities and destinies for themselves. Between 1867 and 1873 the Maritimes were swept into the Dominion of Canada, a bold political experiment to create a transcontinental nation separate from the United States but still within the orbit of the British Empire. Only Newfoundland resolutely resisted the pressure to join Confederation, most of its inhabitants seeing no advantage to throwing in their lot with the distant 'Canadian wolf'.

The region's coastal parameters were more or less firmly set by nature, but the landward

boundaries were another matter. While there seemed no need to survey a line in the rough terrain separating Labrador from Lower Canada and Rupert's Land, the international boundary between New Brunswick and the United States became a source of ongoing tension in this period. During the negotiations ending the American Revolution, the Ste Croix River and some vaguely imagined 'highlands' separating the St Lawrence watershed from the waters draining into the Bay of Fundy were established as the boundary line between British and American territory. Unfortunately, the map used by the negotiators—George Mitchell's work—proved woefully inadequate in helping to determine which river was the Ste Croix and where the watershed lay. A boundary commission agreed on the location of the Ste Croix River in 1798, when the site of Champlain's ill-fated settlement on an island in the river's mouth was identified, but it was not until 1842 that the Webster-Ashburton Treaty finally put an end to wrangling over disputed territory in the Aroostook-Madawaska region on the upper St John.

The flood tide of largely British immigration, most of it to the Maritimes, continued from 1815 until the 1840s. Thereafter population growth depended on natural increase, which in the 1850s and 1860s reached impressive levels. By 1871 there were over 900,000 people living in the region, up from 200,000 in 1815. Census figures record a mature and relatively stable pre-industrial society: the ratio of men to women was nearly equal, over half the population was under the age of 18, and almost 90 per cent was native-born. Completed families were large, averaging seven children, but this statistic masked great differences in family size across class and culture.[3] Like other areas of the Western world, the Atlantic region in the second half of the nineteenth century began to reflect the impact of new values that favoured later marriages and smaller families, especially among members of the urban middle class.

As in the eighteenth century, British emigration in the first half of the nineteenth century was prompted by economic and political pressures at home. Irish (both Protestant and Catholic), Scots, English, and a few Welsh filled up unsettled areas in the Maritimes and the remoter coastlines of Newfoundland and Labrador. Following the War of 1812, 2,000 African Americans, offered their freedom if they deserted their owners to join the British cause, also moved to the Maritimes, most of them settling in Preston and Hammonds Plains in Nova Scotia and Loch Lomond, New Brunswick.

The most dramatic episode by far was the arrival of thousands of destitute Irish following the potato famine of 1845. The Maritimes received only a small percentage of the more than 300,000 Irish who came to British North America between 1846 and 1851, and many of them quickly moved on, but they nevertheless represented a challenge to the port authorities whose job it was to process the destitute and often disease-ridden refugees. As many as 30,000 entered through Partridge Island, the quarantine station at the mouth of the St John River, while others fetched up in Chatham, Charlottetown, Halifax, St Andrews, and other ports connected to the North Atlantic carrying trade. Most of the good agricultural land in the region had been long taken up and the destitute Irish had to be content to work as labourers or eke out a living in marginal and often remote farming frontiers.[4]

Clearing the land was a daunting task for most immigrants. Slashing and burning their way through the forests that impeded their progress, they often set runaway fires that devastated huge areas. Walter Johnstone, a Scottish visitor to Prince Edward Island, remarked in 1820 that the burnt woods around the settlements formed 'a scene the most ruinous, confused and disgusting the eye can possibly look upon'.[5] In 1825 a fire on the Miramichi consumed more than two million hectares of forests and took the lives of 160 people. Animals also felt the impact of the immigrants and their profligate ways. In New Brunswick moose had virtually disappeared by the 1820s, and the great auk, a large flightless bird that Cartier had observed in vast numbers on the Funk Islands off Newfoundland in the sixteenth century, had already become extinct by 1800.

With the increase of European settlement, Aboriginal peoples reached new levels of desperation. Their numbers declined dramatically in the first half of the nineteenth century as disease and poor living conditions took their toll. By mid-century New Brunswick and Nova

Clearing the land, New Denmark, New Brunswick, *c.* 1872. A new settlement arising from amidst a field of stumps must have been a familiar sight throughout much of the Atlantic region in the early nineteenth century. PANB, P5-167.

Scotia had appointed Indian commissioners and began to delineate reserves, but the story remained the same. Abraham Gesner, Indian commissioner in Nova Scotia during the 1840s, was aware of the unjust exchange that was the cause of their difficulties: 'in return for the lands for which they were the rightful owners, they have received loathsome diseases, alcoholic drink, the destruction of their game, and threatened extermination.'[6]

Gesner's comment reflected the changing attitude, at least at the official level, towards Aboriginal peoples. No longer a threat to European dominance, they became the subject of political, philanthropic, and ethnographic interest. Prince Edward Island finally

appointed an Indian commissioner in 1856 and, with the assistance of the London-based Aborigines' Protection Society, purchased Lennox Island as a reserve in 1870. Although his evangelizing efforts had little impact, the Baptist missionary Silas Rand helped to preserve the culture of the Mi'kmaq by collecting oral history and compiling a dictionary. Native crafts—quill boxes, woven baskets, brooms, and birchbark canoes, in particular—were widely sought by collectors. For those with special talents, such as Christianne Morris of Halifax, it was possible to make a decent living from the sale of their handiwork.

Despite predictions to the contrary, the Mi'kmaq and Maliseet managed to survive the

'View of the Indian Village on the River St John above Fredericton, New Brunswick, Feb. 1832.' Lieutenant John
Campbell, aide-de-camp to his father, Lieutenant-Governor Sir Archibald Campbell, painted this watercolour of the
Native community of Kingsclear, near Fredericton, in 1832. NAC, C-11076.

European presence. So too did the Innu and
Inuit, whose world—for good or ill—became
increasingly open to commercial influences
with the establishment of Hudson's Bay
Company posts in Labrador beginning in the
1830s. The fate of the Beothuk, in contrast, was
unquestionably tragic.[7] Cut off from marine
resources by the spread of European settlement
along the northeast coast of Newfoundland,
they retreated to the interior, where their living
conditions and health declined. Efforts to make
contact with the Beothuk, now that their survival was in doubt, sometimes led to disastrous
consequences. In 1819, for example, a woman
named Demasduit was captured at Red Indian

Lake. Her husband was killed in the encounter,
and the child to which she had recently given
birth was left behind to die. Two years later
Demasduit (called Mary March by her captors)
herself died of tuberculosis. In 1829 Shanawdithit, the last surviving Beothuk, suffered the
same fate. In the final year of her life she lived
in St John's under the care of William Cormack,
president of the recently established 'Boeothick
Institution', helping Cormack to develop a
Beothuk vocabulary and drawing pictures
depicting the culture of her people as she had
known it.

In contrast to the Aboriginal experience,
European society in the Atlantic region went

The *Samson* was one of three steam locomotives shipped, in pieces, from Newcastle-on-Tyne to Pictou in 1838, and was the first to be assembled for a test run in December of that year. History Collection, Nova Scotia Museum, Halifax, NSM 27.38/copy neg. N-3563.

from strength to strength, buoyed by an increasingly productive commercial economy. Following the Napoleonic Wars, a recession wreaked hardship on rich and poor alike, but by the 1820s conditions had improved. Colonial staples of fish, foodstuffs, and timber found markets in an expanding global economy, and shipbuilding, financed by British and colonial capitalists, emerged as a major industry. In 1827, under a monopoly granted by the British Crown, the General Mining Association began

developing Nova Scotia's coal resources in Cape Breton and Pictou County. The company brought in skilled miners and introduced modern technology, including steam-driven machinery and vessels, and, in 1839, a railway line, which carried coal from Albion Mines (now Stellarton) to Pictou harbour. After the abolition of the General Mining Association's monopoly in 1858, investment in coal mining increased dramatically, stimulated by rising demand in the rapidly industrializing United States.

The Farmer's Bank of Rustico. In the early 1860s, Father George-Antoine Belcourt helped his fellow Prince Edward Island Acadians to establish a school and a banking co-operative to meet the challenges of the new industrial order.

PEIPARO, 2320/20-4.

At the same time Newfoundland's resources attracted growing interest. In 1822 Cormack walked across the island—the first European known to have done so—and in 1839–40 the government sponsored the first geological surveys, carried out by James Jukes. He found little that was promising, but the development of copper mining in Notre Dame Bay prompted the government to establish a permanent Geological Survey in 1864. Under

its first director, Alexander Murray, and his assistant, James P. Howley, a systematic exploration of the island's interior began. Their optimistic reports had an important influence on public policy, raising the possibility that Newfoundland might become something more than a producer of saltfish and seal oil.

Elsewhere, natural resources were rapidly being identified and exploited. Gypsum and stone for building and grinding found markets

This dramatic painting by Fitz Hugh Lane shows the Cunard sidewheeler *Britannia* labouring through a mid-Atlantic storm on its 13-day maiden voyage from Liverpool to Halifax in 1842. On board was the novelist Charles Dickens, who found the passenger cabins cramped and uncomfortable. Courtesy, Peabody Essex Museum, Salem, MA.

both locally and in the United States. In Albert County, New Brunswick, over 230,000 tons of Albertite, a sort of solidified asphalt yielding oil and gas, were produced between 1850 and 1880. The discovery of gold on Nova Scotia's south and eastern shores stimulated a brief flurry of activity in the 1860s. By this time, the iron works at Londonderry was turning out $40,000 of products annually. The founding of banking institutions, beginning with the Bank of New Brunswick in 1820, testified to the growth of the region's economy.

Although constrained by their colonial location, the region's mercantile élite were any-thing but narrow in their ambitions. Samuel Cunard, who invested in the New Brunswick timber trade and owned estates in Prince Edward Island, inaugurated transatlantic steamship service between Great Britain and North America in 1840. Beginning with a clock-making business in St John's, Benjamin Bowring became the head of a highly successful mercantile house with links to Liverpool. The most successful entrepreneur in this period was Enos Collins; having made a fortune in trade and privateering during the French and Napoleonic Wars he went on to build a business empire based on trade and banking in Halifax.

Courtney Bay, New Brunswick, *c.* 1860. Many of the region's sailing ships were launched from this port, near East Saint John. Among them was the *Marco Polo*, famed for the speed with which it delivered its passengers and cargo to the Australian gold fields in the early 1850s. PANB. P5-360.

Although the region's economic growth was tied to the fortunes of the British Empire, there were few special privileges after the 1840s, when Great Britain abandoned most of the preferences granted to colonial trade and shipping. The dismantling of the old mercantile system helped to make the 1840s a 'decade of tribulation',[8] but the transition proved less disastrous than many had feared. Part of the reason was that Britain negotiated free trade in colonial primary products—most notably fish, farm produce, minerals, and timber—with the United States in 1854. The so-called Reciprocity Treaty

remained in place until 1866 and, together with the high demand generated by the American Civil War (1861–5), stimulated colonial production and the carrying trade. In this period, too, the region's economy became more global in its reach. Vessels built and owned in the Atlantic colonies could be found in ports all over the world, sometimes delivering products from home, more often carrying the world's freight at globally competitive prices.

The success of the shipping and shipbuilding industries between 1850 and 1880 has become the stuff of legend and a source of local pride. In this period the Maritimes and Newfoundland accounted for more than 70 per cent of the tonnage registered in British North America, which boasted the fourth largest merchant marine in the world, after Great Britain, the United States, and Norway. Ships like the *Marco Polo*, built in Saint John in 1851, broke world speed records and helped to make the region's shipbuilding skills known in international circles. Although Saint John was the largest shipbuilding centre, other communities in the sea-girt region, including St Martins, Yarmouth, Windsor, Pictou, and Charlottetown, became well-known for their output of wooden vessels. In the 1880s shipping barons in the Maritimes decided to invest their fortunes in railway and manufacturing ventures rather than in a steel and steam-driven merchant marine—a decision that led to a rapid decline in shipbuilding. Nevertheless, while it lasted, the industry helped to put the region on the map and contributed perhaps more than any other single factor to the retrospective view of the mid-nineteenth century as a 'golden age', at least for the Maritimes.[9]

The Newfoundland economy was altogether more precarious, and no memories of a golden age linger there. Nevertheless, merchants invested in larger wooden vessels, mainly to exploit the seal fishery off the island's northeast coast more effectively. Although seal skins were taken, the main object of the hunt was the seal fat that, when rendered into oil, was widely used during the nineteenth century for lighting and lubricants. At its height in the 1850s, as many as 14,000 men took part in this dangerous enterprise every spring, and sealing yielded nearly a quarter of the colony's

exports by value. In the 1860s merchants turned to steamers to increase both yields and profits, a move that centralized the industry in St John's and Conception Bay and reduced the number of men involved. Yet the industry declined as herds decreased and seal oil began to face competition from mineral and vegetable oils.[10]

By mid-century the Industrial Revolution was beginning to transform production processes. The steam-driven machinery, factory system, and conflicts between capital and labour that were the hallmarks of the industrial age required difficult adjustments for people accustomed to artisan production, kinship loyalties, and noblesse oblige. Saint John emerged as the major industrial centre, with foundry, footwear, and clothing industries all surpassing shipbuilding in value by the 1860s.[11] Halifax too developed an industrial base, specializing in food-processing industries such as brewing, distilling, and sugar-refining.

Still, most people in the region lived at one remove from industrial discipline, their lives dominated by the seasonal rhythms of domestic production based on farming, fishing, and forestry—or in many cases all three. Even though the products of the factory system were beginning to flood the market, most families continued to make their own cloth and clothing, to produce and preserve their own food, and to craft their own houses, barns, ploughs, carriages, horseshoes, furniture, soap, and candles. Milling was the most common industry in rural areas of the Maritimes. Prince Edward Island alone boasted 500 carding, fulling, grist, dressing, saw, and shingle mills in 1871.[12] Surplus produce was bartered for the imported items—

TRYON WOOLLEN MILLS ESTABLISHED 1856. REID BROS. PROPRIETORS.
NORTH TRYON, LOT 28, P.E.I.

The Tryon Woollen Mills, Lot 28, Prince Edward Island. In the mid-nineteenth century many communities in the Maritimes supported mills such as this. PEIPARO, 2320/12-14.

flour, molasses, sugar, tea, cloth, metal utensils of various kinds—that stocked the shelves of local merchants. In turn, the merchants sold the products of farm and fishery in colonial towns and cities, to the men engaged in the region's fishing, shipping, and timber trades, or to markets in Europe, the United States, and the West Indies. In many communities, especially those focused on the fisheries, survival depended on a credit system, by which mer-chants advanced supplies and paid for prod-ucts in goods rather than cash. This 'truck sys-tem' encouraged dependence, but enabled producers to participate, however minimally, in the market economy.

Despite the growing complexity of the region's economy, poverty and destitution were the lot of many people. The demand for food-stuffs outstripped supplies, and even farming families often had difficulty making ends meet.

alut 1850

City ~ Clergy *N˚ M̄ Preston*

The Reverend Mr Richard Preston, ink drawing by Dr J.P. Gilpin, *c.* 1850. An African American who fled to Nova Scotia following the War of 1812, Preston studied for the ministry in Great Britain and helped to establish the African United Baptist Association in 1854. History Collection, Nova Scotia Museum, Halifax, NSM, P176.25 copy neg. N-4442.

When crops failed, as they sometimes did in all areas of the Atlantic region, disaster threatened. The potato blight hit the colonies in the late 1840s, creating hardship almost as severe as in Ireland and prompting at least one group of settlers in St Ann's, Cape Breton, under their puritanical leader the Reverend Norman McLeod, to search for greener pastures in Waipu, New Zealand.[13] Others shipped off to the United States, where jobs in the expanding industrial and service sectors, and free homesteads on the western frontier, offered hope for a better life.

By the 1830s free land in the Atlantic colonies was largely a thing of the past. Not only recent immigrants but growing numbers of descendants of earlier settlers were therefore obliged to purchase property or take up marginal lands that yielded a meagre subsistence. Some of the poor squatted on Crown and Native reserves; others drifted to urban centres to find work.[14] Given the small size and poor quality of their original grants, it is hardly surprising that Blacks in Nova Scotia began moving to Halifax, where wage-paying jobs were more plentiful. They kept to themselves in an area on the Bedford Basin that soon became known to their white neighbours as Africville.

The Christian churches that became firmly rooted in the colonies in this period played a major role in making life more secure. Roman Catholics were granted full civil rights within the British Empire in 1829, but even before that date Catholics in the Atlantic region had gained concessions. The laws that had prevented them from voting, acquiring land, and worshipping in public were abolished in the 1780s, and the ban on their holding public office was lifted in Nova Scotia in 1823 for Lawrence Kavanagh, a Cape Breton merchant elected to the Assembly. Although Newfoundland had its own bishop as early as 1796, Maritime Catholics remained

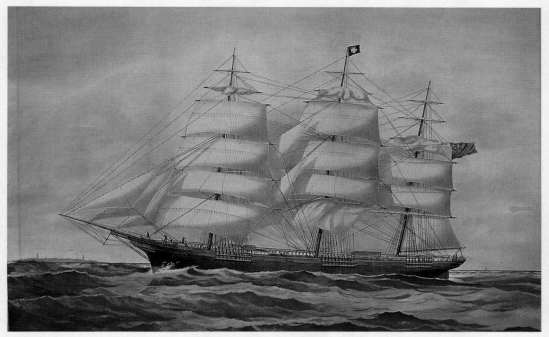

Edward John Russell, 'Governor Tilley', 1892, watercolour over graphite on wove paper. A versatile artist, Russell is best known for his marine paintings, which were widely commissioned—at prices as low as four dollars--in the age of sail. The New Brunswick Museum, Saint John, NB, 53.21.

C. Lewis, 'A Part of the Ways, Goings and Doings of the Newfoundlanders at the Seal Fishery', watercolour, 1881. These sealing vessels were owned by the firm of Bowring Brothers. Though in decline by this time, sealing has remained an important part of the Newfoundland economy. Collection of the Newfoundland Museum.

Frederic Edwin Church, 'The Ice Bergs', oil on canvas, 1861. A prominent member of the
Hudson River School of painters, Church (1826–1900) visited Newfoundland and Labrador in
1859 in search of icebergs. This painting was developed from sketches made during the trip.
Dallas Museum of Art, anonymous gift, 1979.28.

Sir W.C. Van Horne, 'Steel Mills at Sydney, Cape Breton', 1907, oil on canvas.
Between 1900 and 1905, two new steel-producing plants were built on the shores of
Sydney harbour, offering jobs by the hundreds and producing an instant city. With
their ovens, blast furnaces, and rolling mills, they dominated the Sydney skyline,
especially at night, and so impressed the railway magnate Sir William C. Van Horne
that he was moved to paint the scene. Musée des Beaux-Arts de Montréal, 1945.946.

Christianne Morris, quillwork cradle, *c.* 1868. The quillwork artistry for which the Mi'kmaq are renowned reached its height in this exquisite cradle, embellished with many characteristic symbols and motifs. Desbrisay Museum collection, Bridgewater, NS. Photo R.E. Merrick for the Nova Scotia Museum, Halifax.

Maria Morris Miller, 'Mayflower', water-colour, *c.* 1830s. A growing interest in natural history in the nineteenth century inspired the Nova Scotia artist Maria Morris and the pioneer naturalist Titus Smith to publish their book *Wildflowers of Nova Scotia* in 1839. Photo Scott Robson, History Collection, Nova Scotia Museum NSM 76.32.1.

The Roman Catholic Cathedral in St. John's, Newfoundland, engraving by A. Ruger, 1878. To the right of this imposing building are the Presentation and Mercy convents, to the left St Bonaventure's College. Consecrated in 1855, it overlooks the harbour, and represents Bishop Michael Fleming's determination to have 'a temple superior to any other on the island'. Courtesy John FitzGerald.

under the jurisdiction of Quebec until 1817, when Edmund Burke was appointed bishop of Nova Scotia. Twelve years later, his jurisdiction was divided and separate bishops were appointed for New Brunswick and Prince Edward Island. These administrative changes marked the beginning of a reinvigorated Catholic church that ministered to a growing constituency. By the mid-nineteenth century, over 40 per cent of the populations of Newfoundland and Prince Edward Island, a third of New Brunswickers, and a quarter of Nova Scotians were Roman Catholics.

Although the evangelical churches generally took the lead in seeking converts and promoting moral rectitude, all churches were

Facing above. Robert Harris, 'A Meeting of the School Trustees', oil on canvas, 1885. Only seven years old when his family migrated from Wales to Prince Edward Island, Harris (1849-1919) became one of Canada's best-known artists. His fine portrait work won him a commission to paint the Fathers of Confederation, which he completed in 1884. Scenes similar to the one depicted here must have been played out in many communities following the introduction of publicly funded schooling. National Gallery of Canada, Ottawa. Purchased 1886, #6.

Facing below. James Henry Holman, 'The Woodburn Family', oil on canvas. Holman (b. 1821), who came to Saint John from London, England, as a child, is considered to be the region's best portrait artist. Trained by his father in house, sign, and decorative painting, he began producing portraits in the 1850s, just as photography was becoming popular. In the 1860s he found work retouching and colouring photographs for the Notman Studios in his hometown, and eventually moved to their studios in Boston. The New Brunswick Museum, Saint John, NB, A69.29.

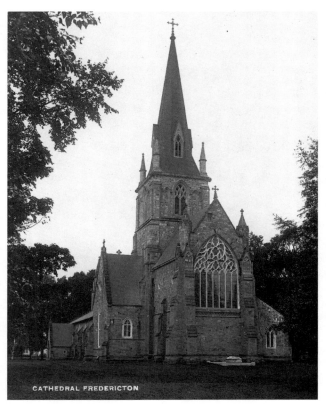

CATHEDRAL FREDERICTON

In the mid-nineteenth century, churches were the most prominent public buildings in most colonial communities. Christ Church Cathedral in Fredericton, consecrated in 1853, is an excellent example of the English Gothic Revival style favoured by the Anglican Bishop of New Brunswick, John Medley, who also developed more modest designs in the same style for rural parishes throughout the Maritimes. PANB, P11-39.

swept up in the reforming spirit of the age. The temperance movement became popular in the 1830s, and most denominations supported initiatives to found academies, Sunday schools, charity schools, orphanages, hospitals, and shelters. Eager to spread the gospel to lost souls near and far, evangelicals took the lead in establishing home and foreign missions. The Maritime Baptists sent Richard Burpee to India

in 1845, and in the following year the Presbyterian Church of Nova Scotia sponsored John Geddie's mission to the Hebrides. Major religious denominations either published or supported newspapers sympathetic to their views. In St John's, for instance, *The Public Ledger* represented a Protestant perspective, while *The Newfoundlander* reflected Roman Catholic viewpoints. The first French-language newspaper in the region, the *Moniteur Acadien*, founded by Israël J.-D. Landry in 1867 in Shediac, New Brunswick, was closely aligned with the Roman Catholic hierarchy.

Concerned by growing sectarian tensions, reformers were eager to effect a revolution in education by creating a system of uniform, non-denominational, state-supported schools. In all the Atlantic colonies their efforts were opposed by Roman Catholic leaders, and linguistic minorities, such as the Acadians, who feared the homogenizing tendencies of a 'common school' system that in practice was dominated by English-speaking Protestants. Each colony worked out its own compromise on the education issue. To a greater or lesser extent, all the Maritime colonies incorporated existing Catholic schools into their public education systems. In Newfoundland, however, efforts to introduce non-denominational public education in the 1830s were opposed by the Anglican hierarchy as much as the Roman Catholic. A denominational system developed there that would remain in place until the 1990s.

Denominationalism prevailed in higher education throughout the region. The Anglican exclusiveness imposed at King's College in Windsor and the College of New Brunswick in Fredericton inspired other denominations to establish their own institutions. Between 1838 and 1873, the foundations were laid for seven denominational colleges in the Maritimes: Acadia (Baptist); Mount Allison (Methodist); St Mary's, St Dunstan's, St Francis Xavier, Collège St-Joseph, and Mount Saint Vincent (Roman Catholic). Dalhousie College, founded in 1818 as a non-denominational institution, became effectively Presbyterian when it finally began to offer classes in the 1860s. Prince of Wales College, established in Charlottetown in 1860, served a primarily Protestant student population.

Although clerics preached spiritual equality, church practices perpetuated worldly notions of hierarchy and prejudice. Many churches rented their pews, permitting the rich to sit closer to the pulpit. In some churches women were relegated to separate sections. People of colour were almost always set apart. Never fully accepted by their co-religionists, Black Baptists and Methodists formed separate churches and associations. Protestants and Catholics each formed (or imported) their own organizations, of which the Protestant Orange Order was one of the most successful. Conflicts between Protestants and Catholics in the Maritimes became particularly violent during the late 1840s. On 12 July 1847, a battle between three hundred Irish Catholics and an equal number of Protestants in Woodstock, New Brunswick, resulted in ten deaths. Two years later, another bloody confrontation rocked the Catholic enclave of York Point in Saint John.

Violence was not confined to religious rivalries; it punctuated all aspects of colonial life. Men still occasionally challenged each other to duels. At election time, voting was conducted orally, often with the result that polling stations became scenes of violence and intimi-

dation. Wife-beating was still legally sanctioned, and the 'spare the rod and spoil the child' philosophy was the foundation of disciplinary policy both at home and at school. Cock fights and bear-baiting were popular pastimes. In Newfoundland, mummering—a traditional folk practice associated with Christmas—became so menacing that in 1861 laws were passed making it illegal for people in St John's to appear in public masked or otherwise disguised. Seaport towns were renowned for the violent and illegal activities that flourished along their waterfronts where an underworld of crimps (procurers of crewmen for sailing vessels), prostitutes, and unsavoury boardinghouse-keepers took advantage of the sailors in port. Like the British soldiers who continued to be stationed in the region's major cities until mid-century, or the men confined throughout the long winters to remote lumber camps, sailors on board ship lived in an all-male environment, under repressive and often harsh conditions.[15] Because colonial courts were likely to side with captains, sailors were notorious for undertaking various forms of resistance ranging from absence without leave to desertion, insubordination, and even mutiny.

Middle-class citizens expressed growing concern about violence, and made concerted efforts to control it. City councils or magistrates in unincorporated areas appointed marshals and constables to keep the peace, swore in special deputies during emergencies, and in extreme cases called on the military stationed in the colonial capitals for help. By mid-century, full-time police forces were beginning to emerge in the larger urban areas. Legislation, backed by force, was imposed to control any workers who dared to use strikes or intimida-

The opening of the Academy of Music, Saint John, May 1872. In the mid-nineteenth century, the performing arts flourished in Saint John. Inaugurated with a 'musical convention' of artists from New York, Boston, and Bangor, the hall burned down only three years later in the Great Fire of June 1877, which also destroyed the Dramatic Lyceum (opened in 1857). Until a new Opera House was opened in 1891, live performances were held in the city's Mechanics' Institute, which had been a centre of artistic and intellectual activities since 1840. Sketch by E.J. Russell. The New Brunswick Museum, Saint John, NB.

tion to improve their wages and working conditions. By encouraging self-discipline, public schooling, and church attendance, reformers hoped to create a society in which the values of peaceful coexistence and civic virtue would be internalized, and force would no longer be required to maintain social control.

Yet colonial life was not all conflict and drudgery. In rural areas 'bees' and 'frolics' brought people together in communal bonhomie, and everywhere Sundays offered relief from weekday routines. Significant events on the Christian calendar, such as Christmas and Easter, as well as saints' days, provided opportunities for holidays and celebrations. In cities and towns, regimental bands, choral recitals, and singing schools flourished. Although organized sports were only in their infancy, racing, yachting, rowing, curling, and cricket clubs were springing up in urban centres. Hockey, also called 'hurley' or 'shinny', was popular in Nova Scotia, though one commentator in 1864 argued that such a rowdy and dangerous game 'ought to be sternly forbidden'.[16] In St John's an annual regatta on Quidi Vidi Lake, begun in 1826, was a highlight of the summer season.

Educated people in the Atlantic region were full participants in the intellectual awakening that swept the Western world in the nineteenth century. In a matter of weeks, ideas percolating in Boston, New York, Edinburgh, and London became topics of debate among colonial newspaper editors, college professors, and urban élites. Ambitious young colonials travelled to Great Britain and the United States for their education and returned home to practice or teach their newfound knowledge. In the 1830s Mechanics' Institutes, founded in Scotland to disseminate scientific education among the artisan class, took root in the colonies, offering a broad range of literary, dramatic, and artistic activities.

Literacy was highly prized. In all the colonies, newspaper editors emerged as influential political figures, often because they championed progressive causes. Other people too took up writing, whether for literary glory or simply to make a living. In 1824 Julia Catherine Beckwith, who lived in Fredericton, became the first native-born British North American novelist with the publication of the little-read *St Ursula's Convent*, written when she was only 17 years old. The Reverend R.T.S. Lowell's novel

The New Priest in Conception Bay (1858)—the first to be set in a Newfoundland outport—captured a distinctive lifestyle and dialect. The most successful colonial writer was Judge Thomas Chandler Haliburton, who made an international reputation with his series recounting the adventures of the clock-peddling Yankee salesman Sam Slick. Before turning his hand to satire, Haliburton had written a two-volume history of Nova Scotia, published in 1829. By that time, the Reverend Lewis Anspach's *History of the Island of Newfoundland* (1819) and Peter Fischer's *First History of New Brunswick* (1825) had already appeared.

These pioneering works reflected a cultural maturity that also expressed itself in practical ways. In 1818 John Young, a Scottish merchant in Halifax, wrote a series of letters, under the name 'Agricola', encouraging scientific methods in agriculture. His efforts, together with financial assistance from the government, resulted in the establishment of numerous agricultural societies in Nova Scotia. This fashion spread throughout the region, and by 1842 a society was founded in Newfoundland to encourage more effective use of the island's thin, acidic soils. Meanwhile, colonial inventors such as Charles Fenerty and Abraham Gesner were devising methods of making paper out of wood and kerosene from petroleum.

At mid-century developments in transportation and communication further reduced the time it took for ideas to penetrate the Atlantic region. By the late 1840s, the telegraph was beginning to link the colonies both to each other and to cities in the United States. The successful laying of an underwater telegraph cable between Great Britain and Heart's

'Landing the Cable at Heart's Content Bay, Newfoundland', *London Illustrated News*, 8 Sept. 1866. The first successful transatlantic submarine cable was landed from the *Great Eastern,* then the world's largest ship, at Heart's Content on 27 July 1866. In exchanging greetings, Queen Victoria and US President Andrew Johnson inaugurated a communications revolution.

Content, Newfoundland, in 1866 dramatically reduced the time it took for information to arrive from Europe. Meanwhile railways, the wonder of the age, were promising not only to overcome the limits of land-based travel and bring prosperity to those communities fortunate enough to lie near them, but also to transform colonial politics.

In the wake of the American Revolution, the British government had deliberately imposed on its remaining American colonies constitutions designed to limit the democratic tendencies of elected assemblies. Power was weighted towards appointed elements—the governor, his council, and the judiciary. Assemblies, where they existed, were relatively powerless talking-shops, but their consent was needed to pass legislation relating to money bills. Deadlocks between elected and appointed

bodies were common. Although considered the birthright of all self-respecting Britons, representative government was denied to Cape Breton until the island was reunited with the mainland in 1820. Thereafter, with two seats in the Nova Scotia assembly, the island had representative government at least in theory, but little political clout.

After the Napoleonic Wars, business and professional élites in St John's, led by Dr William Carson and Patrick Morris, began to argue that Newfoundland should be formally recognized as a colony with representative government, security of land tenure, and the full range of British civil rights. The necessity of such reforms was driven home by a notorious incident in 1820, when two Conception Bay fishermen, convicted for contempt by surrogate magistrates, were flogged and had their premises seized for debt. With support from the reformers, the fishermen sued the magistrates for assault and false imprisonment. Their case was unsuccessful, but the scandal stimulated the movement for change. In 1824–5, circuit courts were instituted and Newfoundland was declared a Crown colony. Sir Thomas Cochrane was appointed the colony's first civil governor in 1825, but it was not until 1832 that representative government was established. Religious and ethnic divisions characterized Newfoundland politics in the early years of representative government, and electoral violence erupted in some districts. In an attempt to calm the situation and prevent legislative deadlocks, the Colonial Office instituted an experimental constitution that amalgamated the assembly and council in 1842.

Meanwhile, the Atlantic colonies too were beginning to demand not just representative but

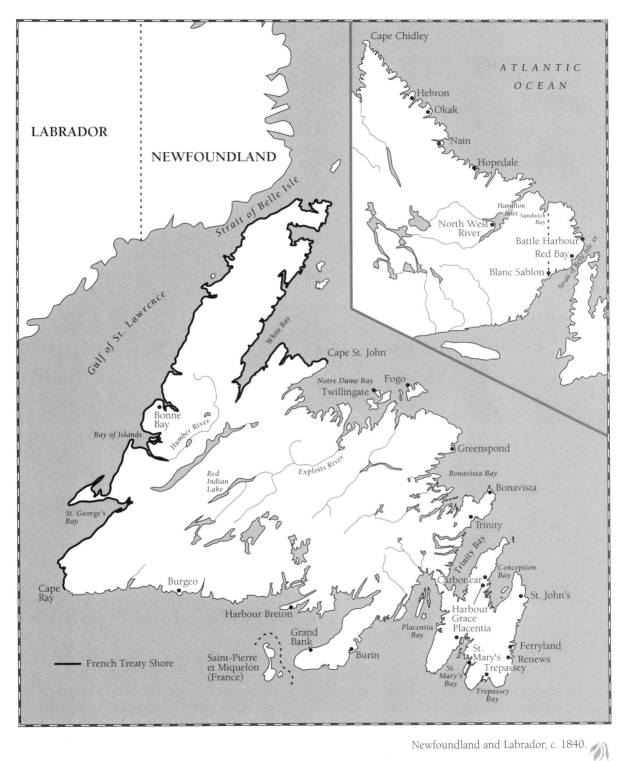

LABRADOR

NEWFOUNDLAND

Strait of Belle Isle

Gulf of St. Lawrence

White Bay

Cape St. John

Bonne Bay

Bay of Islands

Humber River

Red Indian Lake

Exploits River

Notre Dame Bay
Twillingate
Fogo

Greenspond

Bonavista Bay
Bonavista

Trinity

St. George's Bay

Trinity Bay
Carbonear
Conception Bay
St. John's

Cape Ray

Burgeo

Harbour Breton

Grand Bank

Saint-Pierre et Miquelon (France)

Burin

Harbour Grace
Placentia

Placentia Bay

St. Mary's
Trepassey

St. Mary's Bay

Ferryland
Renews

Trepassey Bay

—— French Treaty Shore

Cape Chidley

ATLANTIC OCEAN

Hebron

Okak

Nain

Hopedale

Hamilton Inlet *Sandwich Bay*

North West River

Battle Harbour
Red Bay

Blanc Sablon

Strait of Belle Isle

Newfoundland and Labrador, *c.* 1840.

'responsible' government, in which the executive would be composed of members of the majority party in the assembly, to which it would be directly responsible. The most eloquent advocate for this democratic reform was Nova Scotia's Joseph Howe, who in his famous letters to the Colonial Secretary, Lord John Russell, in 1840 insisted that 'every poor boy in Nova Scotia' should have 'the same rights to honours and emoluments as he would have if he lived in Great Britain or the United States'. In Prince Edward Island William Cooper, the leader of the movement to escheat (take back) the lands granted to absentee proprietors, won an overwhelming election victory in 1838, but was refused even a hearing from Russell, who would have nothing to do with undermining property rights. In New Brunswick, revenues from the sale, leasing, and licensing of Crown lands dominated political debate. Charles Simonds, a powerful Saint John timber baron and leader of the reform cause, managed to extract two important concessions from the Colonial Office in 1837: control over Crown land revenues (as long as the salaries of appointed administrators were guaranteed) and consultation with elected representatives in the appointment of the governor's executive councillors.

Britain's resistance to responsible government in settler colonies collapsed following its adoption of free trade. In 1847 Nova Scotia's Lieutenant-Governor, Sir John Harvey, was instructed to choose advisers from the party that had a majority in the assembly. Reformers were victorious in an election held later that year, and on 2 February 1848 a Liberal government under the leadership of James Boyle Uniacke became the first 'responsible' administration in the British Empire. By 1855 all the remaining Atlantic colonies had followed Nova Scotia's lead. Nevertheless, this milestone in the region's political history did not mean that the colonies were fully independent: the Colonial Office still kept a watchful eye over defence, external affairs, legal matters, and constitutional amendment.

Although the colonial franchise was quite wide, extending to men of modest means, for all practical purposes political power was concentrated in the hands of commercial and professional élites. Most of these men were conservative in their political outlook and wanted little to do with the radical liberal and socialist ideas that by mid-century were being debated in Great Britain and the United States. Women, no matter what their property status, were disqualified from voting in all the colonies, along with Native people, landless labourers, wards of the state, and relief recipients. Labrador, inhabited primarily by Inuit and Innu, was entirely ignored in the debate over political rights, as were the inhabitants of the Newfoundland French Treaty Shore.

Despite—or perhaps because of—the closed circle in which it operated, responsible government in the early years was a messy and muddled affair. Administrations were often unstable, with 'loose fish' crossing the floor when they differed from their party on issues great or small. Bureaucratic processes were embryonic, patronage appointments commonplace, and alliances based on religious affiliation—all to the detriment of good government. Governors continued to meddle, even though, like the British monarch, they were supposed to stand apart from the daily routine of political life and follow the recommendations of their executive advisers.

CONVENTION AT CHARLOTTETOWN, PRINCE EDWARD ISLAND.
OF DELEGATES FROM THE LEGISLATURES OF CANADA, NEW BRUNSWICK, NOVA SCOTIA, AND PRINCE EDWARD ISLAND, TO TAKE INTO CONSIDERATION THE UNION OF THE BRITISH NORTH AMERICAN COLONIES,—SEPTEMBER 1, 1864.

1. Col. the Hon. John Hamilton Gray, M. P. P., Prince Edward Island,—CHAIRMAN OF CONVENTION.
2. The Hon. John A. McDonald, M. P. P., *Attorney General, Canada West.*
3. The Hon. George E. Cartier, M. P. P., *Attorney General, Canada East.*
4. The Hon. Thomas D'Arcy Magee, M. P. P., *Minister of Agriculture, Canada.*
5. The Hon. Wm. A. Henry, M. P. P., *Attorney General, Nova Scotia.*

6. The Hon. Wm. H. Steeves, M. E. C., New Brunswick.
7. The Hon. John M. Johnson, M. P. P., *Attorney General, New Brunswick.*
8. The Hon. Samuel Leonard Tilley, M. P. P., *Provincial Secretary, New Brunswick.*
9. The Hon. Robert Dickey, M. L. C., Nova Scotia.
10. Lt. Col. The Hon. John Hamilton Gray, M. P. P., New Brunswick.

11. The Hon. Edward Palmer, M. L. C., *Attorney General, Prince Edward Island.*
12. The Hon. Edward Botsford Chandler, M. L. C., New Brunswick.
13. The Hon. H. L. Langevin, M. P. P., *Solicitor General, Canada East.*
14. The Hon. Charles Tupper, M. P. P., *Provincial Secretary, Nova Scotia.*
15. The Hon. A. J. Galt, M. P. P., *Finance Minister, Canada.*

16. The Hon. Adams G. Archibald, M. P. P., Nova Scotia.
17. The Hon. Andrew G. McDonald, M. L. C., Prince Edward Island.
18. The Hon. Wm. Campbell, M. L. C. *Commissioner of Crown Land, Canada.*
19. The Hon. Wm. McDougall, M. P. P. *Provincial Secretary, Canada.*
20. The Hon. Wm H. Pope, M. P. P., *Colonial Secretary, Prince Edward Island.*

21. The Hon. Jonathan McCully, M. L. C., Nova Scotia.
22. The Hon. George Coles, M. P. P., Prince Edward Island.
23. The Hon. George Brown, M. P. P., *President Executive Council, Canada.*
24. Major Bernard, *Secretary to the Attorney General, Canada West.*
25. Mr. Charles Drinkwater, *Private Secretary to the Attorney General, Canada West.*
26. William H. Lee, *Clerk Ex. Council, Canada.*

PHOTOGRAPHED BY G. P. ROBERTS, St. John, N. B.

The delegates to the Charlottetown Conference, September 1864. NAC, C-733.

These difficulties notwithstanding, the rituals of responsible government took root with surprising speed. By the 1860s political parties had emerged in all the colonies, borrowing the names (and often the programs) of their Liberal and Conservative counterparts in Great Britain, and colonial leaders had begun to move beyond religious and ethnic allegiances to define new community goals. With political visions increasingly defined by industrial progress, public works, and material well-being, politicians even found themselves discussing a plan for colonial union.

Discouraged by the parochial nature of provincial politics, Nova Scotia's Conservative Premier Charles Tupper inadvertently started the process of Confederation by promoting the idea of Maritime Union. Early in 1864 the issue was debated in the Nova Scotia assembly, which agreed to send delegates to a conference on the subject. Although New Brunswick supported this initiative, Prince Edward Island ignored it. The idea of Maritime Union would almost certainly have remained dormant but for the fact that politicians in the United Canadas were seeking solutions to the political deadlock in their own legislature. On hearing of the developments in the 'Lower provinces', they sought permission to attend the proposed conference. It took place in Charlottetown early in September 1864, and quickly expanded into a discussion of the Canadian proposal for a federation of all of British North America. A month later, the delegates reassembled in Quebec to hammer out a detailed agreement. Joined by two representatives from Newfoundland, the delegates produced 69 resolutions, which became the basis of the British North America Act.

Since legislative union was unacceptable to most of the delegates, the Confederation agreement envisaged a federal system with national and provincial levels of jurisdiction. Representatives to the federal House of Commons were to be elected on the basis of population, giving the United Canadas (Ontario and Quebec), with their far greater numbers, overwhelming control. The appointed Senate was designed to provide a regional counter-balance, but was dominated by the Canadas because the Atlantic delegates failed to insist on equal provincial representation, settling instead for equal *regional* representation—the Maritimes, Quebec, and Ontario—with four additional seats for Newfoundland. Coupled with the agreement that senators would be appointed for life by the federal government, this structure ensured that 'the Senate would have no moral authority to challenge the gov-

erning party in the House of Commons and limited its effectiveness as the guardian of regional interests.'[17]

The federal government was assigned the most significant powers, including control over interprovincial trade and transportation; foreign policy and defence; criminal law; Indian affairs; currency and banking; and the fisheries. It also controlled all the major sources of taxation. The provinces had jurisdiction over commerce within their borders, natural resources, civil law, municipal administration, education, and social services. Agriculture and immigration would be joint responsibilities.

It is highly unlikely that internal pressures alone would have produced a Confederation agreement. External forces were also critical, especially the threat posed by the United States. As the civil war came to an end, Secretary of State William Seward began making noises to the effect that it was the manifest destiny of the United States to control the whole continent. The situation of the British North American colonies was further complicated by the Fenian Brotherhood, whose leaders concocted a scheme to launch an invasion from American soil—a clever way, they thought, of provoking a war between Great Britain and the United States that might give Ireland a better chance of achieving independence.

Neither the colonies nor Great Britain wanted a war with the United States. Indeed, the Colonial Office strongly supported the idea of British North American union as a way of reducing imperial responsibilities, especially military commitments, in North America. To compound what was developing into a full-scale military crisis, the United States served notice that it would terminate the Reciprocity Treaty in 1866, causing consternation among those who relied on American markets. Confederation, it was thought, might promote increased interprovincial trade and improve military protection. If nothing else, it would facilitate plans for an intercolonial railway linking the region's ice-free ports with the St Lawrence colonies, a project supported in both the Canadas and the Maritimes.

Since none of the leaders who attended the 1864 conferences had an electoral mandate to enter a political union, they were obliged either to call elections or to have the confederation agreement endorsed by their legislatures. The Quebec resolutions passed easily through the legislature of the United Canadas, but the Atlantic colonies were less enthusiastic. In Prince Edward Island, Conservative Premier John Hamilton Gray shelved the issue. Neither his party nor the electorate saw any merit in a scheme that gave the island five seats in the Commons and did nothing to resolve the 'land question', which had returned to the top of the political agenda as a result of agitation led by the newly formed Tenant League.[18] Premier Hugh Hoyles of Newfoundland also found little support for Confederation either in his party or in the colony at large. Only 5 per cent of the island's trade was with British North America, and talk of railway building and military preparedness intensified well-founded fears that Newfoundland would be saddled with taxes from which it would receive little benefit. Moreover, among those of Irish descent, Confederation conjured up memories of the hated union of Great Britain and Ireland in 1801, and invoked fears that newly won rights with respect to

schools and political patronage would be jeopardized. So contentious was the issue in Nova Scotia, where Joseph Howe became the spokesman for the anti-confederate cause, that Tupper was forced to delay introducing the Quebec resolutions into the legislature. New Brunswick's Premier Samuel Leonard Tilley took a more direct route. In March 1865 he led his badly divided party to a resounding electoral defeat at the hands of anti-confederates led by Albert J. Smith.

Strong forces intervened, some intentionally, others fortuitously, to put the Confederation movement back on track. In New Brunswick, Smith's anti-confederate government broke into warring factions and the lieutenant-governor, in a high-handed manoeuvre, forced another election in May 1866. This time Tilley, promising major revisions to the Quebec agreement, won a convincing victory (33–41). Support from Roman Catholic bishops and timber merchants, money from the Canadians and their Grand Trunk railway allies, and a timely invasion by the Fenians helped to effect this reversal of fortunes. In April 1866, Tupper and the lieutenant-governor together twisted enough arms to ensure passage of a resolution in the Nova Scotia legislature authorizing continued discussion of British North American union. The final negotiations were held in London in the fall of 1866. Although no substantive changes were made to the constitutional arrangements forged in Quebec in 1864, Tupper managed to secure a clause in the British North America Act guaranteeing the building of an intercolonial railroad. With little debate, the Act passed in the British Parliament in March 1867, and on 1 July 1867 the Dominion of Canada, made up of Ontario, Quebec, New Brunswick, and Nova Scotia, came into being.

Although they may not have liked the final deal, New Brunswickers were forced to concede that they had been consulted on the issue. Nova Scotians, in contrast, had good reason to feel they had been hoodwinked into joining a union that was not in their best interests. Neither the province's voters nor their elected representatives had given their approval to the proposals that ultimately became the basis for Confederation. Commercial elements in the colony were particularly wary of a political structure initiated by 'Upper Canadians' who might pursue trade and tariff policies that would cripple their prospects. In the elections held in 1867, Nova Scotians returned a strong anti-confederate contingent to the provincial assembly (36–38), and only Tupper survived a contest that elected 18 anti-confederates to the 19 seats available to the province in the House of Commons. So determined were separatist forces to dissolve the union that some of them even saw union with the United States as preferable to Confederation, and formed an Annexation League to promote this alternative.

Nova Scotia's opposition to Confederation represented more than wounded local pride. As constituted in 1867, the Dominion of Canada was little more than the United Canadas writ large, and was designed to serve the needs of the larger colony. The capital of the new nation was Ottawa, the former capital of the United Canadas, and the civil service was Canadian in structure and personnel. The introduction, during the first sitting of the House of Commons, of policies such as an increase in tariffs only confirmed the fears of Nova Scotia's mercantile interests. The financial arrangements established by the British North America Act were particularly disadvantageous for Nova Scotia. In absorbing the revenues from customs duties, Ottawa took away the chief source of funds for colonial administrations and offered the less populous colonies a per capita grant formula that proved inadequate to fund their provincial responsibilities.[19]

Such feelings prompted Howe and the other anti-confederates to demand repeal of the hated union, but there was little support for the idea in London. As annexation sentiment in the province increased, Howe—ever loyal to Great Britain—agreed to an accommodation that gave seats in the federal cabinet to two anti-confederates, and promised the province a ten-year bridging subsidy of about $800,000, with additional compensation for those public buildings that were transferred to federal control. Largely because of the lingering separatist sentiment in Nova Scotia, Prime Minister John A. Macdonald immediately authorized construction of the Intercolonial Railway and, as a member of the British delegation that met with American representatives to settle a variety of issues, promoted a new reciprocity treaty. Protectionists in the United States were too strong to be moved, but Macdonald did manage to ensure that the Treaty of Washington (1871) provided free entry for Canadian fish into the American market, as well as compensation, determined by arbitration, for American access to Canadian inshore waters—terms that also applied to Newfoundland. Anti-confederate feeling in Nova Scotia diminished, but the province's continuing financial problems and the difficulties faced by both the primary and the commercial sectors guaranteed that it could easily be rekindled.

Meanwhile, Macdonald made efforts to induce Newfoundland and Prince Edward Island into Confederation. Despite widespread opposition to the idea, Confederation remained on the political agenda of Newfoundland's Conservative premier, Frederic Carter. In the months preceding the 1869 election, he persuaded the assembly to accept draft terms for union more generous than those proposed in the Quebec resolutions. Canada was prepared to offer a special annual grant of $175,000 for the surrender of its Crown lands, an agreement that no export tax would be levied on Newfoundland fish, and a promise that Newfoundlanders would not be drafted into the Canadian militia. With no overwhelming debt and little tangible to be gained from union, Newfoundlanders were not impressed. Anti-confederate forces, led by the eloquent and persuasive merchant Charles Fox Bennett, won two-thirds of the seats in the assembly. Most Newfoundlanders, it seems, were convinced that their country had the resources to support an independent future.

By contrast, in 1873 Prince Edward Islanders joined Confederation. Island politics in the years since the Quebec Conference had been dominated by the activities of the militant Tenant League, debates over the funding of denominational schools, and the problem of debts incurred when the Conservatives under James Pope embarked on a railway-building orgy in the early 1870s. Pope, who supported Confederation, argued that the only answer to the debt and land problems was to let Ottawa come to the rescue. Macdonald agreed not only to assume the railway debt and buy out

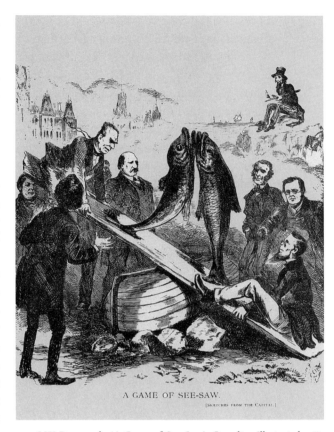

A GAME OF SEE-SAW.
[SKETCHES FROM THE CAPITAL.]

J.W. Bengough, 'A Game of See-Saw', *Canadian Illustrated News*, 4 May 1872. In the 1872 election, Maritime opposition to Confederation was sufficiently muted to give the federal Conservatives a large majority of seats. One reason, this cartoon suggests, was Macdonald's success in gaining entry to American markets for Canadian fish. Courtesy of Chinook Multimedia, Edmonton.

the remaining absentee proprietors, but also to establish year-round communications with the mainland and concede the six House of Commons seats that Islanders demanded.

The debate over Confederation in the Atlantic region had been defined to a considerable degree by economic considerations. At the risk of oversimplification, one might say that anti-confederates tended to look east and south—to the North Atlantic, Britain, the oceanic trades, and the promising US market. By contrast, supporters of Confederation looked westward, seeing the future in economic integration with the central provinces and expansion to the Pacific. They recognized the need to adjust to a changing world, one in which Britain had abandoned imperial protectionism for free trade, reduced its defence commitments, and accepted colonial demands for responsible government. These departures coincided with the spread of new technologies, based on coal, iron, and steel, that threatened the traditional reliance on wood and wind. In a time of flux, it seemed to many people in the Maritimes that political consolidation made sense. Newfoundlanders took much longer to accept that their future was as a North American, not a North Atlantic country.

CHAPTER NINE

Industrial Challenges: 1873–1914

*I*f the three Maritime provinces and Newfoundland had chosen separate political destinies, they nevertheless followed parallel paths in the late nineteenth century. While the Maritimes were obliged to work out their position within a federal state dominated by Ontario and Quebec, Newfoundland had to deal with an imperial government that hoped the colony would soon see the error of its ways. For both Newfoundland and the Maritimes, relations with Ottawa and London were characterized by ambivalence and frustration. Although Maritimers became increasingly conscious of being Canadians, at the same time they joined Newfoundlanders in celebrating their membership in the ever-expanding Empire on which, as imperial enthusiasts were fond of saying, 'the sun never set.' At a more fundamental level, people everywhere in the Atlantic region were forced to adjust to the demands of the new industrial order that was restructuring all aspects of their society.

Across the region, the last three decades of the nineteenth century were characterized by the decline or realignment of older industries and the aggressive pursuit of new ones. In the 1870s agriculture was the most important activity in the Maritimes, but markets both at home and abroad were vulnerable to competition. Farmers reacted to falling prices by abandoning marginal lands and specializing their crops. Orchards proliferated in the Annapolis Valley, which exported apples in increasing volume to Great Britain. Potatoes became an important crop in Prince Edward Island and the St John River Valley, and livestock and dairy farming expanded throughout the Maritimes. At the end of the century, fox farming became another significant rural pursuit, particularly on Prince Edward Island. However, further development was hampered by the relatively small amount of high-quality acreage available—especially in Newfoundland—and the mass exodus of people from the rural areas. Between 1891 and 1911 the Maritimes lost 20,000 farmers, with the result that the crisis in rural life became a growing cause for concern.

The forest industry, centrally important to the New Brunswick economy, was badly damaged by the decline in the British market both

John Gothard Baker, 'When Do We Eat?', 1934, oil on canvas. In the 1890s, Prince Edward Islanders Charles Dalton and Robert Oulton experimented with breeding silver foxes in captivity. Their eventual success set off such a boom that by 1902 there were 300 fox farms on the island, catering to an ever-expanding fashion industry. Collection of Confederation Centre Art Gallery and Museum, Charlottetown, Prince Edward Island, CAG 77.30.

for lumber and wooden ships. During the 1870s Saint John lost 29 per cent of its total population. A disastrous fire in June 1877, which caused losses estimated at $27 million, was a further blow. Lumbering gradually recovered, the construction industry expanded and, after the turn of the century, pulp and paper production accelerated. By contrast, shipbuilding and ship-owning gradually declined into insignificance. With iron (later steel) hulls and steam taking over the marine world, wooden sailing ships were confined to the coastal trades, fishing, and some long-distance freight routes. As Caribbean markets contracted with the decline of the West Indian sugar industry, the Maritimes traded increasingly with Central Canada and the United States, but without government encouragement and protection there was little incentive either to build iron or steel vessels or to maintain a sizeable merchant marine. Although locally built cargo schooners remained in use until the 1940s, small-vessel

Sinclair Mill, Newcastle, New Brunswick, 1895. With the expansion of construction in the late nineteenth century, lumber mills such as this one found a steady demand for their products both at home and abroad. PANB, P6-182.

fleets in the region slowly declined except in Newfoundland, where the fleet continued to expand until 1919.[1]

The swarm of small Newfoundland schooners reflected that colony's reliance on the cod and seal fisheries, as well as the absence of reasonable road and rail connections until the turn of the century. In the 1880s the fishery represented about 67 per cent of goods production—compared to 13 per cent

in the Maritimes—and employed roughly 85 per cent of the workforce.[2] The Newfoundland economy was therefore vulnerable to falling international prices for salt cod and seal oil.

By mid-century the Maritimes had expanded the range of their fisheries to include Labrador and the offshore banks. Stimulated by government support, and with vessels often crewed by Newfoundlanders, the fishery expanded until the 1880s, when the end of rec-

'Making' fish at The Battery, near the entrance to St John's harbour, *c.* 1900. As this picture suggests, women played an important role in the production of saltfish. PANL, F 50-6.

iprocity with the United States, together with generally poor market conditions, led to numerous bankruptcies, including that of Charles Robin and Company, the largest inshore cod firm in the Maritimes. Nevertheless, if saltfish production declined, bank fishing continued to be an important industry, centred in Lunenburg and adjacent ports. As inshore fishermen came to rely less on cod, they turned to the catching—and often canning—of lobster, oysters, salmon, and sardines. Newfoundlanders remained tied to the increasingly difficult markets in the Caribbean and

southern Europe, but Maritimers were well-placed to meet an increasing North American demand for fresh fish.

Coal, found in abundance in Cape Breton, northeastern Nova Scotia, and, to a lesser extent, southern New Brunswick, was the key component in the efforts of Maritime élites to promote industrialization. In addition to supplying the Canadian and New England markets, Maritimers hoped that a convenient and cheap coal supply would give their industries a competitive advantage. The success of this strategy depended on the completion of a rail-

A famous photograph of a small boy with two prize codfish at Battle Harbour, Labrador, *c.* 1900. PANL, VA 212-18.

way to the St Lawrence heartland and the imposition of a protective tariff. For this reason many Maritimers were enthusiastic supporters of the National Policy tariff introduced by the federal Minister of Finance, Samuel Leonard Tilley, in 1879. By this time the Intercolonial Railway linked Halifax and Saint John to Lévis, giving the Maritimes the access they had long desired to Central Canadian markets. Extensions to Sydney and Yarmouth were in place by 1891.

Protected by tariffs, Maritime entrepreneurs embarked on a binge of industrial investment,

hoping to capture a national market. There were two zones of development: the southern ports such as Halifax, Saint John, and Yarmouth, where imported cotton, spices, and sugar were processed for sale elsewhere, and the northern corridor defined by the Intercolonial line, where manufacturing was based on coal, iron, and steel. By 1885 the Maritimes supported eight cotton mills, three sugar refineries, two confectionaries, two rope works, and a glass factory. At the same time the foundations were being laid for an iron and steel industry. The Nova Scotia Steel and Coal Company,

Workers at the Intercolonial Railway shop in Moncton. Completed from Halifax to Lévis in 1876, the Intercolonial helped to make Moncton, the railway's eastern headquarters, a major distribution and manufacturing centre. Moncton Museum Collection.

established at New Glasgow in 1882, was, for a while, the country's leading producer of iron and steel products, and in 1900 it consolidated operations at Sydney Mines using Newfoundland iron ore. In the same year the Dominion Steel Company—closely associated with the Dominion Coal Company at Glace Bay—began construction of a large primary steel mill at Sydney. Meanwhile, small rolling mills were established in Halifax and Saint John, as well as Amherst, where in 1893 J. Rhodes, Curry and Company built the first railway cars manufactured in Canada. In other strategically located towns such as Moncton, Truro, Windsor, and Yarmouth, factories produced textiles, foundry goods, furniture, and processed foods. On the surface, at least, it looked as though the Maritimes were doing well in their transition to an industrial economy.

Even so, Maritime factories tended to be smaller and less efficient than those in Central Canada, which meant comparatively lower pay for workers and lower profits for owners. The decline was not evident in all sectors, or all provinces, throughout the period, but the general trend was clear. Although the gross value of production increased significantly in all sectors between 1880 and 1910—mining ahead of all the others, with an increase of almost 410 per cent, fishing at the bottom with 33 per cent, the total overall at 91 per cent—regional capital, financial and human, fled elsewhere.[3] Handicapped by a relatively small local market, managerial inexperience, and a recession running from the 1870s to the 1890s, the region failed to keep up with faster growing areas of North America. Increasingly reluctant to prop up regional enterprises, Maritime

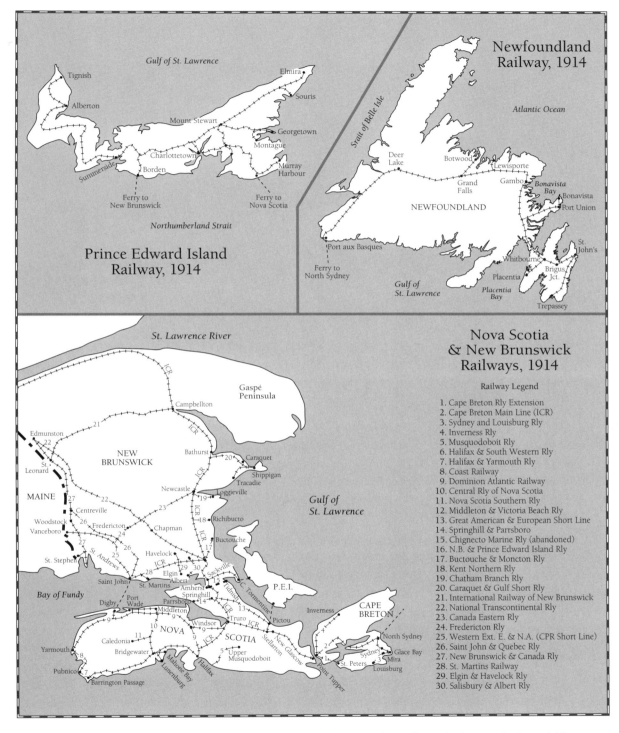

Newfoundland Railway, 1914

Gulf of St. Lawrence

Strait of Belle Isle

Atlantic Ocean

Deer Lake
Botwood
Lewisporte
Grand Falls
Gambo
Bonavista Bay
Bonavista
NEWFOUNDLAND
Port Union

Port aux Basques

Ferry to North Sydney

Gulf of St. Lawrence

St. John's
Whitbourne
Brigus Jct.
Placentia
Placentia Bay
Trepassey

Prince Edward Island Railway, 1914

Gulf of St. Lawrence

Tignish
Alberton
Elmira
Souris
Mount Stewart
Georgetown
Montague
Charlottetown
Summerside
Borden
Murray Harbour

Ferry to New Brunswick

Ferry to Nova Scotia

Northumberland Strait

Nova Scotia & New Brunswick Railways, 1914

Railway Legend

1. Cape Breton Rly Extension
2. Cape Breton Main Line (ICR)
3. Sydney and Louisburg Rly
4. Inverness Rly
5. Musquodoboit Rly
6. Halifax & South Western Rly
7. Halifax & Yarmouth Rly
8. Coast Railway
9. Dominion Atlantic Railway
10. Central Rly of Nova Scotia
11. Nova Scotia Southern Rly
12. Middleton & Victoria Beach Rly
13. Great American & European Short Line
14. Springhill & Parrsboro
15. Chignecto Marine Rly (abandoned)
16. N.B. & Prince Edward Island Rly
17. Buctouche & Moncton Rly
18. Kent Northern Rly
19. Chatham Branch Rly
20. Caraquet & Gulf Short Rly
21. International Railway of New Brunswick
22. National Transcontinental Rly
23. Canada Eastern Rly
24. Fredericton Rly
25. Western Ext. E. & N.A. (CPR Short Line)
26. Saint John & Quebec Rly
27. New Brunswick & Canada Rly
28. St. Martins Railway
29. Elgin & Havelock Rly
30. Salisbury & Albert Rly

St. Lawrence River

Gaspé Peninsula

Campbellton

NEW BRUNSWICK

Edmunston
St. Leonard
MAINE
Centreville
Woodstock
Vanceboro
Fredericton
St. Stephen
St. Andrews
Saint John
St. Martins
Bay of Fundy
Digby
Port Wade
Parrsboro
Springhill
Amherst
Middleton
Windsor
Caledonia
Bridgewater
NOVA SCOTIA
Yarmouth
Pubnico
Barrington Passage
Mahone Bay
Lunenburg
Halifax
Truro
Stellarton
New Glasgow
Pictou
Upper Musquodoboit
Point Tupper
Inverness
CAPE BRETON
North Sydney
Sydney
Glace Bay
St. Peters
Mira
Louisburg
Bathurst
Caraquet
Shippigan
Tracadie
Loggieville
Newcastle
Richibucto
Buctouche
Havelock
Elgin
Albert
Sackville
C. Tormentine
P.E.I.
Chapman
Chatham

ICR

Railways in the Atlantic region, 1914. Adapted from Shirley E. Woods, *Cinders and Saltwater: The Story of Atlantic Canada's Railways* (Halifax: Nimbus, 1992).

The Newfoundland Railway was constructed between 1881 and 1897, and in 1898 the island was connected to Cape Breton by regular ferry service from Port aux Basques. This linkage marked a significant step in Newfoundland's gradual shift in its orientation, away from the Atlantic towards Canada. CNS, MUN.

banks looked for better investment opportunities elsewhere. Eventually the Bank of Nova Scotia shifted its headquarters to Toronto, and the Royal—formerly the Merchants Bank of Halifax—to Montreal. By 1910, takeovers had reduced the number of regional banks to three and forced the closure of small community ventures such as the Farmers' Bank of Rustico.

Centralization in banking mirrored industrial concentration. To 'rationalize' production and protect their profits, Central Canadian interests took over the Maritimes' cotton mills. Diamond Glass of Montreal bought the three

glassworks at Trenton and eventually closed them. It was the same story in coal, sugar, and cordage. By 1895, only confectionary and manufacturing related to iron, steel, and local staples remained under regional control.[4] Small manufacturers and traditional trades vulnerable to the marketing, through branch businesses, of goods produced elsewhere, also faced eclipse. With the completion of nationwide railway systems, mail-order companies—such as the one established by Timothy Eaton in Toronto—extended their reach into the remotest corners of the nation.

Newfoundlanders were similarly caught up in dreams of new industries and diversification, with results not unlike those experienced in the Maritimes. Realizing that political independence required a stronger and more diversified economy, the government led by Sir William Whiteway in the late 1870s and early 1880s adopted a local version of the National Policy, trumpeted as the 'Policy of Progress'. Its centrepiece was a railway across the island—the first track was laid in 1882—that, like the Canadian Pacific Railway, was designed to link the east and west coasts and stimulate the development of land-based industries. Tariff policy was adjusted to protect small manufacturers in St John's. Convinced by Geological Survey reports that the island contained valuable natural resources in abundance, railway boosters predicted rapid growth in agriculture, forest industries, and mining.

Another dimension of this policy was a determined attempt to gain unrestricted access to the resources of the French Treaty Shore. France had long claimed that its citizens possessed the exclusive right to fish between Cape St John and Cape Ray, and that settlement on that coast—and by implication economic development—was illegal because it would interfere with the fishery. As a result, the growing numbers of settlers on the Shore were not represented in the Newfoundland legislature, had no local government, and were denied Crown land grants as well as mining and timber licences. Although France's shore fishery was declining as its bank fishery, based at St Pierre, rapidly expanded, it was reluctant to give up or even modify its pretensions. For its part, the British government was wary of precipitating a diplomatic crisis. Whiteway succeeded in extending the authority of the colonial government to the Shore, with some important limitations, but effective development did not get under way until after 1904, when eighteenth-century treaties were replaced by a new agreement that allowed French fishermen to use the sea but not the land within the same limits.

In the short term, at least, the Policy of Progress failed to achieve any significant change in the island's economy. Railway-building created work, but elsewhere waged employment was scarce. Nor was Newfoundland safe from the economic imperialism of Central Canada. In 1890 the railway project was taken over by the Montreal-based contractor Robert G. Reid, who had close links with the CPR and the Bank of Montreal, which became banker to the Newfoundland government after the crash of the colony's two private banks in 1894. As a result Newfoundland, like the Maritime provinces, lost control of its financial institutions, and its currency became tied to the Canadian dollar. In the same period mainland steel companies took over the huge deposits of iron ore at Bell Island in Conception Bay, shipping it to their blast furnaces in Cape Breton.

As the structures and values of the age of industry took root in the region, people moved in ever increasing numbers from country to town, and from the Atlantic region to other parts of North America. The Maritimes had begun to suffer net migration loss in the 1860s, which reached a peak in the 1880s but continued at a significant rate until the 1930s. Population growth, which had reached 13.5 per cent between 1871 and 1881, dropped to 1.2 per cent between 1881 and 1891, and 1.5

COAXING NEWFOUNDLAND INTO CONFEDERATION.

J.W. Bengough, 'Coaxing Newfoundland into Confederation', *Grip*, 29 October 1887. During the 1880s and 1890s the Canadian government made several futile attempts to bring Newfoundland into the federation. Chinook Multimedia, Edmonton.

per cent from 1891 to 1901. Between 1891 and 1925 the population of Prince Edward Island declined in absolute terms, from 109,000 to 86,000. In all, more than half a million people left the Maritimes between 1881 and 1931. Women were more likely to emigrate than men, young people more likely than the middle-aged, anglophones more likely than francophones but no group could resist the lure of distant opportunities.[5] So great was the economic and social impact of the exodus that the historian Judith Fingard concludes it 'may have resulted in the decapitation of Maritime society.'[6] The haemorrhage

was not quite as severe in Newfoundland, but the trends were similar. Net migration loss began in the 1880s—a decade in which the colony's population grew by only 3 per cent—and districts on the southeastern Avalon declined in absolute numbers.[7]

Because out-migration was so significant in this period, historians have tended to pay less attention to immigration, which continued to have an impact on many communities. Coal-mining and industrial work attracted newcomers from Great Britain, continental Europe, the United States, and the West Indies, many of them skilled labourers eager to try their luck in North America. Immigrant entrepreneurs appeared throughout the region, exerting enormous influence in communities as diverse as New France in western Nova Scotia and Nordin on the Miramichi, both of which experienced brief periods of expansion as a result of the growing demand for lumber. In cities such as Saint John, Moncton, Halifax, Yarmouth, Sydney, and St John's, sizeable Jewish communities emerged. By 1914 there were well over 3,000 Jews in Atlantic Canada—a sixfold increase over 1871. Often shunned by their neighbours, Jews and other ethnic minorities tended to focus their energies in the retail trades and service industries, which were open to all comers. Even rural communities often found their overwhelmingly British and French stock leavened by the presence of a Lebanese or Jewish merchant prepared to endure social isolation in order to make a living. Following the completion of the Canadian Pacific Railway, Chinese workers drifted eastward as far as St John's in search of opportunities that were usually confined to laundries and restaurants—although in the early 1900s the owners of the Bell Island mines hired Chinese men to do shore work for the island's fisheries.[8] The head taxes imposed by both Canada and Newfoundland on Chinese immigrants were only the most blatant of a continuum of policies that discriminated against racial minorities.

The Native people of the Maritimes, meanwhile, not only faced a declining market for their crafts but were, for all practical purposes, barred from industrial ventures by local prejudice, lack of capital, and the rigid provisions of the Indian Act. Under the BNA Act Mi'kmaq and Maliseet living on reserves—like all 'Status Indians'—fell under the jurisdiction of the federal government. The Indian Act of 1876 consolidated policies across Canada with little concern for regional and cultural differences. Based on the notion that Native people were incapable of integrating into 'civilized' society, the Act insisted on close supervision of 'Status Indians'. As a result, Native people had virtually no opportunity to engage in the sorts of economic activity required to improve living conditions on the reserves, which continued to present a stark contrast to surrounding communities. Denied the right to vote or drink alcohol, Indians also risked losing their status if they pursued higher education or took up a profession. Native women who married white men automatically lost their Indian status. The Act had the effect of freezing the Mi'kmaq and Maliseet in patriarchal and pre-industrial social and economic arrangements, making their integration into the larger Maritime society highly unlikely.

In Newfoundland there were no more than 200 Mi'kmaq during this period, most of them concentrated at Conne River on the island's south coast, where they made a living working as guides or mail carriers, trapping, fishing, hunting caribou, and selling basketry. For most of the nineteenth century they had the island's interior largely to themselves, but the situation changed for the worse in the 1890s with the building of the railway. The subsequent development of forest industries depleted the fur-bearing species on which Native trappers depended, and white 'sport' hunters decimated the caribou herds.

The Labrador caribou population declined as well. This caused serious hardship for the Innu, who also relied heavily on trapping furs

Ice boats waiting to cross the Northumberland Strait. Until the twentieth century, when ferries became powerful enough to negotiate the ice in Northumberland Strait, winter crossings were often perilous. Sometimes passengers and crew were left stranded for days. From 1827 to 1918, small iceboats such as these were used to carry mail to and from the mainland. PEIPARO, 2353/225.

for trade at North West River and Davis Inlet. By the 1890s, white and mixed-blood settlers living in Hamilton Inlet were encroaching on Innu hunting territory, which led to some angry confrontations. The Inuit population of about 1,000 was assumed to be on the way, if not to extinction, then to complete absorption by the white settlers. Since the 1860s their relative isolation had been broken by the arrival of up to 1,200 Newfoundland fishing schooners each summer. Diet, clothing, and housing all began to change, and the formerly diversified economy came to concentrate on fishing for cod and char. As contacts with whites increased, Inuit proved highly sus-

ceptible to the diseases they introduced, as well as those brought back by local people who had been taken away to exhibitions in the United States and Europe.

The region's economic difficulties in this period encouraged political fractiousness. Because provincial subsidies from Ottawa were inadequate, Maritime governments were forced into reliance on lumber and coal royalties, which in turn encouraged resource depletion and generous concessions to businesses. There were frequent demands for better terms from Ottawa, and Prince Edward Islanders were particularly incensed at the federal government's failure to provide 'efficient and continuous communication' between the island and the mainland as promised by the Confederation agreement. After embarrassing Ottawa by appealing directly to the imperial government, islanders got a better ferry, although there was considerable support for a fixed link in the form of a tunnel.

In Nova Scotia, widespread frustration with federal policies and continuing economic difficulties fuelled a revival of anti-Confederation sentiment. In 1886 the province's Liberal Premier W.S. Fielding introduced a motion in the legislature calling for Maritime union as a preliminary to secession from Canada. But other Maritime governments were reluctant to support such a measure. What would be the goal of such a union? The handy majority of Nova Scotia's seats won by Macdonald's Conservative government in the 1887 election indicated that province's repudiation of secession. As a fallback position, Fielding took up the cause of provincial rights within Confederation and free trade with the United States, policies that had the support of a number of provinces with Liberal premiers as well as the federal Liberal party under its new leader, Wilfrid Laurier.

That idea of closer ties with the United States was also popular in Newfoundland, where fish exporters, facing heavy French and Norwegian competition in Europe, were looking for new markets. Asserting its rights within the Empire, the Newfoundland government requested and received permission to open talks with the American government. Late in 1890, Newfoundland's representative, Robert Bond, and the American Secretary of State, James Blaine, concluded a draft reciprocity treaty that was received with surprise in

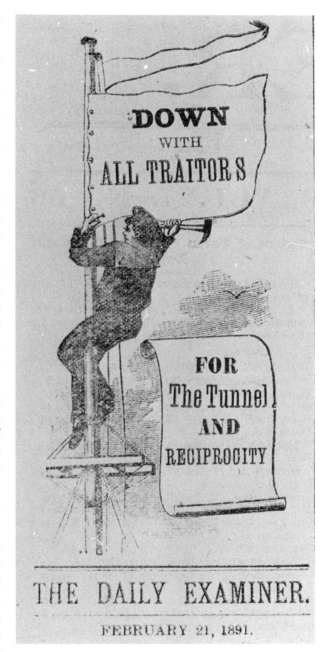

The masthead of the Charlottetown *Daily Examiner*, 21 February 1891, supporting a fixed link for Prince Edward Island and reciprocity with the United States. PEIPARO, 2755/151.

London, consternation in Ottawa, and outrage in Halifax. If Newfoundland was allowed to gain advantages outside Confederation that Nova Scotia could not obtain within it, secession might well become more than just a threat. The treaty was swiftly killed by London. Humiliated and angry, Newfoundland retaliated by imposing extra duties on imports from Canada and refusing to issue bait licences to Nova Scotian fishermen. Canada countered with similar measures.

The crisis eventually blew over, and the two sides met in Halifax in 1892 to discuss their differences. Nothing was resolved. The Newfoundlanders refused to talk about Confederation, and the Canadians maintained their objections to a separate Newfoundland reciprocity treaty. Since London and the courts had already ruled that Newfoundland could not discriminate against other British subjects, Canadians could be sure that their interests would always prevail. Bond—now the premier—tried again in 1902. On that occasion, a draft treaty was effectively rejected by the United States Senate, precipitating sanctions against American vessels purchasing herring in Newfoundland waters, and thus a serious dispute over the definition of the inshore rights still enjoyed by Americans. The dispute was eventually settled, largely in favour of Canada and Newfoundland, in an important arbitration at The Hague in 1909.

As in the past, political divisions prompted by economic questions were complicated by differences of class, ethnicity, and religion. Labour unrest, a product of urbanization, industrialization, and new political ideas, became increasingly common. The centre of organized labour activity was the Nova Scotia coal fields, where increasingly repressive and unsafe corporate practices led to the formation of Canada's first industrial union, the Provincial Workmen's Association, in 1879. A relatively conservative organization, the PWA sought to protect and enhance the position of miners as skilled tradesmen. It lobbied the provincial government on safety and other general issues, such as workmen's compensation, with considerable success, but it did not challenge the industry's structure, nor did it promote collective bargaining. As a result, coal strikes were never province-wide, but remained restricted to individual fields: Pictou in 1886–7, Springhill in 1890 and 1897, Joggins in 1896. Nevertheless, Nova Scotia's miners were responsible for some of the most protracted strikes in Canada in the late nineteenth century. Violent strikes also occurred in Saint John and on the Halifax waterfront in this period, but the labour movement was decentralized and scattered, and its overall impact limited.

If strikes reflected growing class divisions, debates over education revealed other cleavages. Efforts to impose a public school system in New Brunswick, where Roman Catholics (mostly Irish and Acadian) made up a third of the population, provoked a major crisis. Under the Common Schools Act of 1871, the provincial government insisted on a fully non-sectarian system in which all vestiges of religion would be prohibited. Outraged, Catholics refused to pay school assessments and appealed to Ottawa to disallow the act. The federal government declined to intervene on the grounds that education was a provincial responsibility, and the courts ruled the act to be constitutional. Thus fortified, the provincial

Coal miners, Caledonia Colliery, Glace Bay, Cape Breton, *c.* 1903. Shown here with their lunch pails and lamps, young boys constituted a significant proportion of mine workers at the turn of the century. Beaton Institute, University College of Cape Breton.

government went to the polls in 1874 'shouting "The Ticket, the Whole Ticket, and Nothing but the Ticket!" and whispering "No Popery".'[9] Victorious, it then began legal actions against those who refused to pay school assessments, a process that included seizing the horses and carriage belonging to Bishop Sweeney of Saint John. Resistance was especially fierce among the Acadian population. Since only one Acadian child in six received any schooling, and few attended for more than five or six years, Acadians saw little reason to pay taxes to support schools of any kind, let alone schools that excluded Catholic

teachings. Tensions culminated in the Caraquet riots of 1875, which resulted in two deaths and, finally, compromise. Where their numbers warranted, Roman Catholics could be taught by members of religious orders and receive religious instruction after school hours.

The dispute had not been about language—all three provinces insisted on the use of English in schools—and it was more anti-Irish than anti-French. Nevertheless, it had the effect of creating an increasingly self-conscious Acadian community, numbering about 90,000 scattered over the three provinces in the 1870s, half of them in New Brunswick.

The original Acadian flag, 1884, conceived by Father Marcel-François Richard. Photo Léo Blanchard, Musée acadien, Université de Moncton.

Longfellow's poem *Evangeline* (1847), a love story set against the background of the Deportation, began to circulate in French translation during the 1860s. Adopted for use in the Collège St-Joseph at Memramcook, the poem seemed to the Acadian élite to represent 'the poetic distillation of their history, the true legend of their past'.[10] It became, in effect, a unifying narrative at a time when Acadians were trying to establish a collective identity. At national conventions held in 1881, 1884, and 1890, Acadians resisted pressure to adopt Québécois symbols. The Feast of the Assumption rather than Saint Jean-Baptiste became

their national holiday, and the Acadian anthem ('Ave Maris Stella'), motto ('L'union fait la force'), and flag (the tricolour with the Marian star) all expressed a distinctive identity. Several Acadian newspapers were launched, and in 1890 a new college (Sainte-Anne) was established at Pointe de l'Église in Nova Scotia.

More reluctant than anglophones to leave the region, the Acadians also had a high fertility rate, and as a result their numbers increased both absolutely and as a percentage of the Maritime population. In New Brunswick, which lost 76,000 people to the United States during the last two decades of the century, Acadians made up 24 per cent of the population by 1901, and had replaced the Irish as the largest Roman Catholic group. Not surprisingly, it was in that province that the issue of cultural uniformity, a sensitive issue throughout Canada, surfaced in the Maritimes. In 1890, at a time when a revived cult of Loyalism with strong imperial overtones was spreading among Protestant New Brunswickers, Herman H. Pitts, editor of the influential weekly *New Brunswick Reporter and Fredericton Advertiser*, used a schools dispute in Bathurst to launch a determined campaign in favour of 'equal rights'. As in Ontario, where the same euphemism was adopted, the real goal was to end 'concessions' to Roman Catholics and francophones, and to promote an evangelical Protestant reform agenda that included prohibition, sabbatarianism, political reform, and—eventually—limited female suffrage. In 1892, in a no-holds-barred campaign, Pitts defeated Liberal Premier Andrew Blair in his own constituency. While Pitts was briefly the man of the hour, he failed to sustain the support of the electorate, who opted for accommodation and consensus over confrontation in the 1895 provincial election.[11]

The reform crusade that swept the region at the turn of the century was a mix of religion, imperialism, and faith in progress. Rooted in cities and churches—including the Salvation Army, which had arrived in the region in the mid-1880s—it addressed many of the problems associated with industrial development. Although temperance was a long-established preoccupation, reformers were equally concerned with public health, urban renewal, women's and children's rights, social and economic justice, and moral uplift. Increasingly

they looked to the state to enact various aspects of their program—a prospect not always welcomed by political leaders, understanding as they did the divisive nature of many reform issues. The essence of the new 'social gospel' was spelled out by the Reverend H.R. Grant, a leading Nova Scotian prohibitionist, in 1907: 'Public affairs, the social and political business of the country, must be brought under the Commandments and the Sermon on the Mount.'[12]

Under pressure from reformers, the Maritime provinces and Ottawa passed a number of controversial measures. By 1914 it was hard to get a drink legally anywhere in the Maritimes, though the illegal sale of liquor continued unabated. Sundays, always sober for evangelicals, were now regulated by the Lord's Day Act, passed by the federal government in 1907. Although children continued to work long hours on the farms and in the fisheries, laws prohibited their employment in mines and factories and increasingly required their attendance in schools. Concern for the plight of neglected and delinquent children led reformers to push for the creation of juvenile courts and specialized institutions designed to meet the needs of young people; church-sponsored orphanages were established in Newfoundland during the 1880s and 1890s, for instance, and the Maritime Home for Girls opened in Truro in 1914. Although male legislators in the region were prepared to pass laws giving married women more rights relating to child custody and marital property, and even conceded the municipal franchise in the Maritimes, they stopped short of granting women the right to vote at the provincial level. In 1893 the Nova Scotia legislature passed, by a narrow margin, a motion for female suffrage, but it was quashed in committee by Attorney-General J.W. Longley, who was appalled by the prospect of Nova Scotia's leading the nation in such a controversial measure. The Woman's Christian Temperance Union (WCTU) presented a suffrage petition to the Newfoundland legislature in 1891, but motions in support were defeated in both of the two following sessions.[13]

Anxious as reformers were to bring the force of law and state regulation to bear on the problems they identified, they did not hesitate to establish voluntary organizations to achieve their ends. In Halifax, the Society for the Prevention of Cruelty to Animals, founded in 1867, expanded its scope to include children in the 1870s, and Children's Aid Societies were established in the first decade of the twentieth century. Beginning in the 1850s, Young Men's and Young Women's Christian Associations took root in the region with the aim of protecting young people from the temptations of modern urban life. Branches of the WCTU were widely supported, as were the women's missionary aid societies founded by most Protestant churches. In St John's, the Cowan Mission (1903) provided care for sick and elderly women, while the Methodist Jost Mission (1905) in Halifax reached out to working-class women in the city's north end. The churches' commitment to social action prompted interest in closer co-operation, and there was talk of church union among evangelicals. At the same time the Nova Scotia government endeavoured to unite the province's several small church-sponsored colleges into one non-denominational university. Both objectives proved elusive.

Efforts at progressive reform in the Maritimes not only paralleled similar movements elsewhere in Canada, the United States, and Britain, but sometimes marched in the vanguard. In 1875, for example, Mount Allison became the first university in the British Empire to grant a degree to a woman— Grace Annie Lockhart. The region's universities were slower to admit minorities of either gender. In 1896 James Robinson Johnston became the first African Nova Scotian to earn a law degree from Dalhousie University, but few Blacks had the financial resources to pursue higher education. Nova Scotia took the lead in establishing specialized educational institutions with the founding of the Victoria School of Art and Design in 1887, the Nova Scotia Agricultural College in 1905, and the Nova Scotia Technical College in 1907. These and other institutions served all the Maritime provinces, as well as Newfoundland.

Because of its location, the Atlantic region made headlines in the field of communications in this period. Guglielmo Marconi picked up the first transatlantic radio signal on top of Signal Hill, St John's, in 1901, and a year later his Wireless Telegraph Company began operating a transatlantic radio link from Glace Bay, Nova Scotia. At his summer home in Cape Breton, Alexander Graham Bell, along with his colleagues J.A.D. McCurdy and F.W. Baldwin, experimented with aeroplanes and hydrofoil boats. Their *Silver Dart*, which took off from the ice of the Bras d'Or Lakes in February 1909 with McCurdy in the cockpit, is reputed to be the first controlled flight by a British subject in the British Empire, while their 'hydrodome' set water speed records during the First World War.

On 23 February 1909, when John A.D. McCurdy took off from the ice on Baddeck Bay and flew the *Silver Dart* a distance of half a mile, he earned the distinction of making the first powered flight in the British Empire. Parks Canada, Alexander Graham Bell National Historic Site, Baddeck, NS.

Close economic and ethnic ties with Great Britain ensured that many people in the Atlantic region would be swept up in the rising tide of imperial sentiment in the late nineteenth century. Militiamen and nurses volunteered their services for the Boer War, between the British and the Afrikaners in South Africa (1899–1902); schoolchildren participated in Empire Day activities; and portraits of Queen Victoria, who celebrated her diamond jubilee in 1897, could be found in many homes. Newfoundlanders took advantage of the 400th anniversary of Cabot's voyage to trumpet their pride in belonging to Britain's 'first and most ancient and most loyal colony . . . the foundation of her future greatness'.[14] New Brunswick-born George Parkin became a leader of the Imperial Federation Movement, which called for the colonies to pursue closer political, economic, and military ties with Great Britain. Parkin—the self-described 'wandering evangelist of Empire'—travelled extensively in support of imperial federation, which he believed would enable Great Britain to extend its reforming influence around the world.

In Newfoundland, although the progressive impulse had an impact, the churches remained generally conservative on social issues. Church leaders reacted with caution and some hostility to the arrival in 1892 of Dr Wilfred Grenfell, a personification of teetotal, muscular Christian Socialism. Despite the fact that he had trained as a doctor in London's notorious East End slums, Grenfell claimed to

Celebrations marking the 300th anniversary of Champlain's arrival in Saint John, 1904. This re-enactment was only one manifestation of the interest in Atlantic Canada's history that developed around the beginning of the twentieth century. PANB, 560.

be appalled by the social conditions that he found in northern Newfoundland and along the Labrador coast. He set about trying to improve them through the Grenfell Mission— later the International Grenfell Association— and in the process managed to offend both church leaders, whom he accused of failing to provide adequate schooling, and members of the mercantile establishment, whom he accused of exploiting the fishermen and their families. Colonial politicians, whom he

believed to be corrupt and incompetent, were castigated for providing inadequate services, particularly hospitals, in rural areas. Making no secret of his views when touring the lecture circuit in North America and Britain, he caused further offence. There can be no doubt, however, that Grenfell's ceaseless energy and activism, as well as his copious writings, made Newfoundland and Labrador much better known, led to improved medical care, and stimulated the emergence of a Newfoundland

Dr Wilfred Grenfell treating patients aboard the hospital ship *Strathcona*. The motto printed on his kit is 'Lend a
Hand'. The *Strathcona* allowed Grenfell and his staff to travel extensively in northern Newfoundland and Labrador.
Sir Wilfred Thomason Grenfell Historical Society.

public health movement, which became primarily concerned with the serious tuberculosis epidemic. Similar anti-TB campaigns began in the Maritimes where TB death rates were lower but still serious.

Much of Grenfell's support came from New England, where philanthropy joined with a fashionable enthusiasm for the Arctic and the northern wilderness, fuelled by the exploits of Robert Peary and Frederick Cook. Labrador (and, to a lesser extent, Newfoundland) was appealingly remote yet still accessible, attracting expeditions mounted by American anthropologists and amateur explorers. It was also of

increasing interest to investors, and to the governments of Newfoundland and Canada. During the 1890s, the remarkable pioneering surveys carried out by A.P. Low on behalf of the Geological Survey of Canada established the approximate extent of the central Labrador iron ore deposits, and confirmed the hydro-electric potential of the Grand (Churchill) Falls and the Hamilton (Churchill) River.

It was a grant of timber concessions on the Hamilton River to a Nova Scotia company in 1902 that raised the question of ownership. Did the colony own, as it claimed, everything inland as far as the height of land, or just a coastal strip? All sides sent for lawyers. Newfoundland realized that Labrador might be a huge asset, something more than a place to fish and trade furs; Canada was anxious to avoid a repetition of the Alaska boundary decision; and Quebec saw Labrador as a former part of New France. The Judicial Committee of the Privy Council was asked to determine where the boundary lay. The decision was slow in coming.

The global recession that had begun in the 1870s lifted in the late 1890s, but the boom that followed brought only limited benefits to the Atlantic region. As the Canadian west filled up with immigrants, Montreal and Toronto increased their metropolitan dominance, while the Maritime provinces fell even further behind. The exceptions to the general economic trend were Cape Breton and Pictou county, which at the turn of the twentieth century emerged as major centres of coal and steel production. Attracting immigrants from Europe and the United States, Sydney's population doubled between 1901 and 1911. Newfoundland profited in that the Bell Island iron ore mines began working to capacity, and men looking for jobs could find them in Cape Breton—now easily accessible with the completion of the trans-island railway in 1897 and the establishment of a regular ferry service between Port-aux-Basques and North Sydney the next year.

The most significant development in Newfoundland was the opening in 1909 of the Atlantic region's first pulp and paper mill, at Grand Falls. Awarded extraordinarily generous concessions by the Newfoundland government, the English newspaper tycoons Harold and Alfred Harmsworth not only built the first settlement of any size in the island's interior but effectively created a new staple industry. It soon became the ambition of many Newfoundlanders to land 'a Grand Falls job'.

Continuing industrial growth brought further takeovers. In Amherst, one of Canada's busiest manufacturing towns, the firm of Rhodes, Curry was amalgamated with two Montreal businesses in 1909—the deal masterminded by New Brunswick's Max Aitken—and closed down twelve years later. Toronto and Montreal interests took over Dominion Coal and Dominion Steel in 1909, added the Cumberland Coal and Rail Company at Springhill, and formed the Dominion Steel and Coal Company. The takeover precipitated one of the most bitter strikes of the period. Disillusioned with the Provincial Workmen's Association, Glace Bay miners under the leadership of James B. McLachlan joined the United Mine Workers of America. The company refused recognition, brought in strikebreakers—Newfoundlanders among them—protected by troops obligingly provided by the federal government, and gradually wore the union down. Between 1901 and 1914 the Maritimes suffered 411 strikes—evidence of an expanding industrial workforce that under the influence of syndicalism was becoming more class-conscious and increasingly aware that industrial giants were waging their competitive battles on the backs of workers. Those employers had no particular attachment or loyalty to the region, and were prepared to use any weapons at their disposal to fight unions and strikers, safe in the knowledge that they could count on the support of all levels of government.[15]

No such violent or dramatic actions took place elsewhere in the region, but there is evi-

Street railway strike, Saint John, 1914. In this period battles between labour and capital often led to violence and destruction of property. PANB, P338-200.

dence of a considerable labour militancy in St John's and on Bell Island, where one strike in 1900 went on for six weeks. In 1902, three thousand sealers refused to board the steamers in St John's harbour until the owners agreed to improvements in pay and conditions. Six years later, William Coaker founded the Fishermen's Protective Union at Herring Neck in Notre Dame Bay. Taking his populist cue from Canadian farmers' movements, Coaker sought economic, social, and political reforms that would ensure fair treatment for rural workers—hence the FPU's motto, *suum cuique* ('to each his own'). Except in predominantly Roman Catholic districts, which obeyed a conservative church hierarchy opposed to class-

based politics, the response was immediate and impressive. The FPU not only established a trading company and a newspaper, but eventually built its own town, Port Union, Bonavista Bay. It ran candidates in the 1913 election and became the official opposition in all but name, with an ambitious reform program ranging from government control of fish grading and marketing to non-denominational night schools.

The values of the industrial age were reflected in the wider regional culture. In sports, increasing competition, codification of the rules of play, and commercialization paralleled trends in the marketplace, while urbanization and improvements in transportation encouraged the

Skating behind the college at Caraquet, New Brunswick. Hockey became an increasingly popular sport in the Maritimes in the second half of the nineteenth century. PANB, P38-109, Père Joseph Courtois.

development of various sports leagues and clubs. By the end of the nineteenth century, people of all classes and cultures and both genders were taking up everything from boating and bicycling—the new rage of the 1890s—to hockey and hunting. Baseball emerged as the most popular sport in the Maritimes; amateur teams sprouted on school and community playgrounds, and professional teams, many of them on tour from the United States, drew large crowds. Although scandals occasionally erupted over gambling and game fixing, they did not dampen fans' enthusiasm for long. Horse-racing was popular in Prince Edward Island, which by the 1880s supported more than two dozen race tracks. Many Maritimers made their sporting

reputations south of the border. In 1905, Nat Butler, a native of Halifax who began his career in bicycle racing in Boston, broke all records at the Winter Velodrome in Paris in 1905. Two African Nova Scotian boxers, George Dixon and Sam Longford, won acclaim both at home and in the United States for their success in the ring.

As the exodus from rural areas continued, writers in and outside the region often romanticized what appeared to be a vanishing way of life. Bliss Carman and Charles G.D. Roberts, two of the so-called Confederation poets, celebrated the sea and landscape of their Maritime boyhoods. Yet the most successful writers in this period by far were two women: Nova Scotia's Margaret Marshall Saunders and Prince

Edward Island's Lucy Maud Montgomery, both of whom launched international careers with their first novels, *Beautiful Joe* (1894) and *Anne of Green Gables* (1908). In these and subsequent works, both writers tapped into the growing demand for fiction that sentimentalized rural life and the values they believed it represented. Journalists and boosters of various kinds, especially those connected with railroads and the emerging tourism industry, conjured up images of Nova Scotia as 'a gently rolling and fertile land filled with Old World Charm'[16] and drew on the legend of Evangeline—the subject of Canada's first feature film, in 1913—to promote an idyllic Acadia. On Prince Edward Island too, rural charms were central to a growing tourist industry, and elsewhere fishing and hunting were heavily stressed. Once regarded as backward bumpkins, rural people came to be seen as stalwart, picturesque 'folk', living enviably simple lives.[17]

The stereotype of the quaint but hardy Newfoundlander also became firmly fixed in this period. As the novelist Norman Duncan celebrated the people of the northern outports,[18] Newfoundland man of letters Moses Harvey suggested that visitors to St John's might visit the nearby village of Quidi Vidi and 'enjoy a chat with the sturdy fishermen and their wives', whose 'insular peculiarities, linguistic oddities, and quaint views of things' would surely be of interest. With an apparently straight face, the Reid Newfoundland Company assured potential tourists that 'no people in the world maintain a more comfortable and contented existence than the Newfoundland fisherman.'[19]

The loss of life in the Newfoundland seal fishery in the spring of 1914 was the highest in

Nova Scotia's Margaret Marshall Saunders (1861–1947) became a widely acclaimed author with the publication of *Beautiful Joe* (1894), reputedly the first book by a Canadian to sell a million copies. Courtesy of the Acadia University Archives.

Lucy Maud Montgomery (1874–1942) became one of North America's most popular authors following the publication of *Anne of Green Gables* in 1908. PEIPARO 3110-1.

the history of that dangerous industry. Loaded with pelts taken in the Gulf, the SS *Southern Cross* sank with its crew of 173 men in a storm somewhere off Trepassey Bay. Off the northeast coast, the crew of the SS *Newfoundland* was left on the ice for 53 hours during a blizzard. Seventy-eight men died of exposure or drowning, their bodies brought back to St John's 'stacked like cordwood'. That fall, on 4 October, the 'First Five Hundred' volunteers to join the Newfoundland Regiment left for Europe on the SS *Florizel*; 80 per cent of them were killed or wounded.

In St John's as in Halifax, Saint John, Sydney, Charlottetown, and other centres, news of the outbreak of war was greeted with an innocent patriotic enthusiasm. Had anyone known what the long-term consequences of the war would be, the excitement might well have been muted. Instead, Maritimers and Newfoundlanders looked forward to harnessing to the war effort the economies they had worked to develop over the previous forty years. They gladly sent their sons, and even a few daughters, overseas. Disillusionment was not long in coming.

CHAPTER TEN

The Crisis Years: 1914–1949

$\mathcal{B}$etween the outbreak of the First World War and the entry of Newfoundland into Confederation, the people of the Atlantic region faced what must have seemed an endless series of crises. The First World War, itself a catastrophe of unparalleled proportions, brought devastation to the city of Halifax in 1917, and was followed by a worldwide influenza epidemic that took almost as many lives as the battlefields of Europe. In the 1920s while most other areas of North America experienced a boom, the industrial economy in the Maritimes collapsed and, with few exceptions, primary industries throughout the region languished. Pitched battles between labour and capital racked industrial Cape Breton in the 1920s, while the continuing exodus of people highlighted the intensity of the economic crisis. Out-migration finally ceased in the 1930s, but only because the rest of North America began to share many of the problems that had been endemic to the Atlantic region for more than a decade. Although, with Ottawa's help, provincial governments in the Maritimes managed to survive the Great Depression of the 1930s, Newfoundland, facing bankruptcy,

reverted to a status equivalent to that of a Crown colony in 1934. The Second World War brought prosperity, but at the same time consolidated the region's disparity in relation to the rest of the continent. Small wonder that some people began to think of the pre-industrial era as a golden age.

When Great Britain declared war against Germany in August 1914, Canada and Newfoundland, as members of the British Empire, were automatically involved. Militia regiments were called out in the Maritime provinces, and in Halifax army headquarters staff began a recruitment campaign, first to bring the regiments up to strength, and then to provide additional volunteers for the army. With 'pulpit, press, and schoolroom . . . commandeered', the war effort soon became all-consuming.[1] Voluntary enlistment rates in the Maritimes were higher than in Quebec and Saskatchewan, but lower than in other provinces. In Newfoundland similar proportions volunteered, but the numbers of those who actually served were reduced by appallingly high rates of medical rejection.[2] The native-born and those living in rural areas were

The *Cacouna* at the Marine Wharf, Charlottetown, August 1914. This vessel transported islanders to the mainland for war service. PEIPARO, 2320/104-8.

least likely to volunteer in Canada and Newfoundland alike, and the rate was further reduced in the Maritimes by the importance of war-related industries such as coal mining, steel production, and agriculture. Including those compelled to enlist under conscription, implemented in Canada in 1917 and the following year in Newfoundland, some 72,500 men from the Atlantic region joined the allied army. Others served at sea, in the air force, or in the forestry corps. About 300 women from the Maritimes and 43 from Newfoundland went overseas as nurses. Among those travelling with the First Canadian Division in October 1914 were 101 volunteer nurses—the first women to be full-fledged members of the Canadian Expeditionary Force—under the direction of Pictou County's Margaret MacDonald.

By 1916 the difficulty in filling the escalating demand for soldiers gave visible minorities, who were initially not welcome as recruits, a chance to enlist for overseas service. Mi'kmaq were for the most part integrated into existing units, but most Blacks were hived off into the No. 2 Construction Battalion, which was placed under the command of white officers and attached to the Canadian Forestry Corps, to produce lumber for the trenches and coal mines.

Of the soldiers who went overseas, about 14 per cent of Canadians and 26 per cent of Newfoundlanders died.[3] In communities throughout the Atlantic region, war memorials testify to the toll exacted by the conflict. A great blow was inflicted on the newly formed Newfoundland Regiment at Beaumont Hamel

Although the No. 2 Construction Battalion included Blacks from across Canada, as well as 145 African Americans who crossed the border to participate in the war, the majority of its rank and file came from the Maritimes. Courtesy of the Black Cultural Centre for Nova Scotia.

on 1 July 1916, the first day of the Battle of the Somme. The official report listed 233 dead, 386 wounded, and 91 missing out of a total of 801 men. In time, this battle came to represent for Newfoundland what Vimy Ridge does for Canada. The anniversary is still observed each year, and the battlefield is preserved as a memorial park.

The Newfoundland Regiment was raised by the Newfoundland Patriotic Association, founded in August 1914 by Governor Sir Walter Davidson in consultation with the prime

minister, Sir Edward Morris. Largely composed of prominent men from St John's, the NPA functioned as the unofficial war ministry for three years, with a wide range of responsibilities.[4] Its creation reflected both the absence of a militia—and hence of a militia department—and a desire to place the war effort above political and denominational rivalries.

Women throughout the region, schooled for generations in voluntarism, did much to support the war effort. In Newfoundland, a Women's Patriotic Association was formed at

The Newfoundland Regiment, D Company, on the march near St John's, 1915. PANL, E-22-45.

the outset of the war under the presidency of Lady Davidson. With branches throughout Newfoundland and Labrador, it recruited 15,000 members within a few months. By 1916, women and children of both sexes had produced, among other 'comforts', some 62,685 pairs of socks—an astonishing number, which achieved legendary status abroad. The WPA not only collaborated with the Red Cross but worked on health care and general welfare issues and raised money for a range of war-related causes.[5] Women in the Maritimes engaged in similar war-work, often through the Red Cross and the Saint John Ambulance. In Halifax, a busy port throughout the war, women's volunteer services were stretched to the limit.[6]

The demands on everyone in the Halifax area increased dramatically on 6 December 1917, when the French munitions ship *Mont Blanc*, loaded with TNT, and the Belgian relief ship *Imo* collided in the harbour. The resulting

Probably taken in 1915, this photograph shows some of the socks knitted by the women (and children) of Newfoundland for the men of the Newfoundland Regiment. One soldier received a pair knitted by his own mother.
CNS, MUN.

explosion, the largest man-made blast before Hiroshima, levelled the city's North End, killing over 1,600 people and injuring 9,000.[7] As word of the tragedy spread, help poured in from around the world. That Massachusetts and Newfoundland were among the most generous contributors to the devastated city testified to the close family ties connecting these Atlantic coast communities.

The horror of the explosion brought the war closer to home, and contributed significantly to a growing mood of disillusionment. The mounting death rate overseas, rampant inflation, food regulation, and a series of tawdry scandals further dampened the enthusiasm that had initially characterized the war effort. When, in 1917, the Conservative Prime Minister Robert Borden formed a Union government with the badly split Liberals and imposed compulsory military service on men

After the Halifax Explosion, December 1917. This photograph of women travelling downtown from Africville reveals the extent of the devastation along the waterfront. City of Toronto Archives, SC 244-2451.

between the ages of twenty and thirty-five, class and cultural divisions deepened. Even the granting of suffrage to female relatives of men serving overseas was seen as a crudely calculated effort to win votes in the election of December 1917, although it would turn out to represent a major step in women's political emancipation.[8]

The imposition of conscription provoked widespread opposition in the Maritimes. As the evidence of profiteering mounted and the gap between rich and poor widened, labour unrest increased, along with calls for the conscription of wealth as well as of manpower. Farmers became disenchanted when the government refused to honour its promise to exempt their sons from the draft. Although

Acadians were not as uniformly opposed to the war as their neighbours in Quebec, they resented the anti-francophone tone of the conscription debate and the heavy-handed tactics used against 'deserters': in New Brunswick, for example, one Acadian resister was seriously wounded, and 26 others were taken to Saint John under military escort.

In Newfoundland the same factors led to a full-blown crisis when Prime Minister Morris manoeuvred the three political parties into a National Government and then promptly departed for London and a peerage, leaving his successors to introduce conscription. As unpopular in Newfoundland as in the Maritimes, conscription created tensions between urban and outport districts. In 1917 the Newfoundland Patriotic Association was replaced by an official militia department and, as on the mainland, taxes on individuals and corporations made their first appearance. So too did prohibition, which was already more or less in place everywhere in the region except Halifax. When Ottawa imposed nation-wide prohibition in 1918, social reformers in the Maritimes thought they had finally achieved their long-sought goal.

Social unrest and cultural tensions emerged against a background of general economic prosperity. As many factories converted to munitions manufacturing, the steel industry expanded. Fisheries and agriculture did well, and lumbermen diversified into the supply of pit props to British coal mines. Although these gains were offset by inflation, rising freight rates, and a shortage of shipping capacity, the region's economic performance during the war, coupled with overblown expectations encouraged by government propaganda, seemed to justify optimism. But these were, as Ian McKay writes, the 'last years of abundant hope'.[9] In 1920 the post-war recession hit the region with a vengeance. It is scarcely an exaggeration to say that the Great Depression started nine years early in the Maritimes and Newfoundland.

Throughout the region, as around the world, the end of the war coincided with the devastating Spanish influenza epidemic. The impact was particularly fierce in Labrador, where the infection was introduced by the Moravian mission ship *Harmony*. As many as a third of the Inuit in the mission area died between November 1918 and January 1919. Worst affected was the settlement of Okak: out of a population of 263, only 56 women and

The Moravian mission station at Okak, Labrador, before the devastating influenza epidemic of 1918–19 led to its abandonment. CNS, MUN.

children survived. One observer described the appalling scene:

> When the Harmony left Okak, people were beginning to fall sick. . . . Crews went off to their sealing places only to fall sick and die. . . . the dogs played havoc with the corpses. At Sillutalik 36 persons died, but only 18 remained to be buried. The only visible remains of the others were a few bare skulls and a few shankbones lying around in the houses.[10]

Recoiling from the tragedy, and facing persistent economic difficulties, the Moravians gradually reduced their activities in Labrador, closing some stations and handing over their trading stores to the Hudson's Bay Company in 1926.

In the 1920s the region's economic weaknesses were tragically exposed. The fishing industry encountered severe market problems in the Caribbean and Europe, while the United States raised tariffs and revoked permission for

Canadians to land fish in American ports: 1921 was said to be the worst year in four decades for the Atlantic fishery. Maritime lumber mills were swamped by heavy competition from western producers. Although the pulp and paper sector grew during the 1920s, this expansion did not translate into large numbers of jobs. As a result of the shipping shortages during the war, the coal industry had lost its central Canadian markets; reduced tariff protection and competition from oil and electricity made it difficult to restore them. Steel manufacturers found themselves overextended, and readjustment to peacetime production was not easy. Farmers also were hurt by falling prices, and young people continued to drift to the cities.

The recession was accompanied by a new wave of labour unrest that had been gathering strength since 1916, and that now included discontented veterans. Union membership had grown dramatically during the war, and the unions themselves became more militant, radical, and inclusive. The United Mineworkers of America, led by the legendary J.B. McLachlan, organized more than 13,000 coal workers in New Brunswick and Nova Scotia. Following the war a massive wave of strikes erupted, including general strikes on the Miramichi and in Amherst, where workers feared—with good reason—the town's economic collapse.[11] The Newfoundland Industrial Workers' Association forcefully articulated workers' grievances and in 1918 mounted a successful strike against the Reid Newfoundland Company. In Nova Scotia, members of the newly formed Labour Party entered a loose alliance with alienated farmers to win eleven seats in the 1920 provincial election, making the Farmer-

Labour coalition the official opposition to the reigning Liberals, who had held office since 1882. In the election later that year in New Brunswick, where the farmers had started to organize earlier, the United Farmers did equally well. In Prince Edward Island, where farming was the primary occupation of most voters, the two traditional parties continued to dominate the scene.

The recession blunted the force of labour's thrust for reform, but Cape Breton remained a battlefield. In 1921 the Nova Scotia Steel and Coal Corporation and the Dominion Iron and Steel Corporation merged to become the British Empire Steel and Coal Corporation, with headquarters in Montreal. The following year, BESCO announced a 37.5 per cent wage cut for miners. Already hit by plant closures and short time, the UMW local called for 'the complete overthrow of the capitalist system', elected 'Red Dan' Livingstone as secretary-treasurer, and went on strike. Spooked by the emergence of local bolshevism, authorities called in hundreds of soldiers and special police. The troops returned in 1923 during a steelworkers' strike. An unprovoked mounted charge through the Whitney Pier district of Sydney led coal miners to walk out in sympathy, and Livingstone and McLachlan were arrested for seditious libel. A bitter and protracted strike by coal miners in 1925 resulted in the death of one of the protesters on 11 June. By this time all workers in the coal and steel industries had suffered severe wage cuts, and BESCO was on the edge of bankruptcy. It was cold comfort that a provincial royal commission, chaired by the British lawyer-industrialist Sir Andrew Rae Duncan, criticized the company for bad faith and intransigence, and found the size of the original wage

Lawren S. Harris, 'Glace Bay'. A member of the Group of Seven, Harris visited Cape Breton in 1921. This stark
image of a miner's family appeared on the cover of the July 1925 issue of the *Canadian Forum*, which included an
article on the strike-bound island. NAC, C-110249.

cut unjustified. Since neither the commission nor the provincial government was prepared to consider genuinely radical solutions, the tensions continued.

At the root of industrial Cape Breton's problems were economic forces over which the region had little control. All across the Maritimes, employment in manufacturing plummeted as plants closed down and pro-

duction centralized in the St Lawrence heartland. Between 1919 and 1921 the workforce in manufacturing declined by 42 per cent; in iron and steel, by an astonishing 85 per cent. Pictou County and Amherst were particularly hard hit.[12] De-industrialization mainly affected manufacturing industries, but employment fell significantly in the primary sectors of fishing and lumbering as well. The exodus from the

Maritimes resumed in the 1920s, with as many as 150,000 people leaving for the United States and other parts of Canada.[13]

Economic collapse was compounded by constitutional problems.[14] As a result of depopulation, the Maritimes lost representation in the House of Commons to the point that, in 1914, it was finally agreed—at Prince Edward Island's insistence—that no province could have fewer members of Parliament than senators. The rise of western Canada and the dominance of Ontario and Quebec underlined the region's minority status and its increasing political marginalization. Federal leaders responded to the demands of the west and the centre, tending to dismiss the Maritime provinces as backward and its leaders as chronic grumblers with little real ground for complaint. Unable—sometimes unwilling—to counter hostile and unsympathetic federal policies and attitudes, Maritime members of Parliament exerted almost no influence on national policy.

By the 1920s, Maritimers harboured a long roster of grievances against an unresponsive federal government. There was general agreement that all three provinces were the victims of extreme parsimony in federal subsidies, especially in the light of the generous financial terms granted to the Prairie provinces when they entered Confederation. Maritimers believed they deserved additional compensation to make up for the huge chunks of the former Hudson's Bay Company territory awarded to Manitoba, Ontario, and Quebec. But Ottawa showed no signs of moving on these issues. Nor was it prepared to continue subsidizing the Intercolonial Railway as a regional carrier with low freight rates in order to encourage

industries in the Maritimes. Instead, responding to western lobbying, Ottawa moved inexorably against the Intercolonial between 1917 and 1922, integrating it with other lines into the Canadian National Railway system and allowing freight rate increases of between 140 and 216 per cent. Coupled with tariff changes that favoured Central Canada and the West at the expense of the Maritimes, this assault made it abundantly clear where federal priorities lay.[15]

A pervasive sense of grievance finally provoked a political response in the form of the Maritime Rights movement. A genuinely regional phenomenon that sought redress from the federal centre, the movement was dominated by professionals and businessmen—the Maritime Provinces Board of Trade played a conspicuous role—but it received widespread support from people of all classes and cultures. Farmers were among the strongest proponents of dramatic action. They had found it impossible to work with the western farmers' movement, which had its own regional agenda, but they shared the westerners' outrage at the declining power of rural areas. In Nova Scotia the Conservatives, led by E.N. Rhodes and fighting under the banner of Maritime Rights, won 40 out of 43 seats in a provincial election held in June 1925. Conservative premiers J.M.B. Baxter of New Brunswick and J.D. Stewart of Prince Edward Island were quick to climb on board the Maritime Rights bandwagon, though the frugal islanders, who believed in minimal government and usually enjoyed a budget surplus, never adopted Maritime Rights with the same enthusiasm as others in the region.

Maritime Rights campaigners made sufficient noise for even an unsympathetic Mackenzie King to take notice. Needing support from the Maritime members in the House of Commons to sustain his minority government, he reluctantly appointed a royal commission on Maritime Claims, chaired by the ubiquitous Sir Andrew Duncan. In a carefully worded report released in 1926, the Commission recommended increased subsidies, lower freight rates, development of the harbours at Saint John and Halifax, a steel industry subsidy, and improved ferry service to Prince Edward Island—Duncan had been convinced of the need for the latter by his trip to Charlottetown—but avoided discussion of tariffs and special grants to ensure that the level of services in the Maritime provinces would not fall behind those in the rest of the country. Well-received in the Maritimes, the report met with heavy opposition in Ottawa. The result was a compromise that, according to E.R. Forbes, 'changed Duncan's program for Maritime rehabilitation into a plan for Maritime pacification . . . to be achieved with the fewest possible concessions.'[16] And it worked. Leaders gratefully accepted what they were granted—most notably freight rate concessions—and the movement petered out.

Newfoundland had no federal government to blame for its problems, but it experienced much the same post-war dilemma as the Maritimes. As a result of the wartime boom, many businesses had become overextended and found themselves squeezed by falling export prices, rising costs, and worried bankers. The recession brought serious losses to fish exporters, and between 1921 and 1923 some 242 businesses declared bankruptcy. Saddled with a substantially increased public

Let's Keep It At The Masthead!

Donald McRitchie, 'Let's Keep It at the Masthead', *Halifax Herald*, 2 May 1925. This cartoon captured the spirit of the Maritime Rights movement that helped to define issues in both provincial and federal elections in Nova Scotia in 1925 and 1926.

debt because of the war effort, administrations had difficulty responding to the mounting crisis. In 1919 the National Government collapsed, to be replaced by a Liberal-Fishermen's Protective Union alliance led by Richard Squires. As unemployment worsened and emigration increased to between 1,000 and 1,500

From 1923 to 1931 the Toronto-born nurse Mona Wilson served as Chief Red Cross Public Health Nurse in Prince Edward Island. In the absence of a provincial health department, she and her small staff were responsible for the entire island's public health needs. When the province finally established a Department of Health, in 1931, Wilson was appointed Provincial Director of Public Nursing, a position she held until her retirement in 1961, except during the Second World War, when she served as the Red Cross Assistant Commissioner for Newfoundland. In the first half of the twentieth century, nurses played a particularly important role in delivering health services in a region that could not afford the social services available in wealthier parts of North America. PEIPARO Acc 3652.

people annually,[17] there were demonstrations in St John's and, in 1921, mob scenes at the House of Assembly.

The government's first response to chaos in the European markets was an attempt to regulate fish exports and improve quality—the FPU program long advocated by William Coaker, now minister of fisheries. This unprecedented government intervention was resisted by many merchants, who eventually managed to scuttle the entire scheme. Coming after his controversial support for conscription, this failure marked the beginning of the end of Coaker's and the FPU's influence. In the short term, however, Coaker became involved with the development of a pulp and paper mill on the Humber River, a mega-project that seemed to promise a better solution to economic difficulties than the expensive government relief projects that were driving the debt ever higher.

The Humber scheme was the brainchild of the Reids, builders and operators of the Newfoundland Railway, who had also given notice that they wanted to get out of the transportation business. In the end, the government took over the dilapidated railway—yet another financial burden—and helped to arrange financing for the Corner Brook mill development, where construction began in 1923. Moving quickly to take the credit, Squires won a snap election. His opponents then detonated a major scandal: Squires, they claimed, had taken kickbacks from the mining companies on Bell Island, and had turned the Board of Liquor Control into a covert bootlegging operation, with the profits from 'private' sales going into his political account. The charges were largely substantiated by an independent inquiry. With Squires temporarily knocked out of public life, the St John's-based Conservatives took over, promising clean, stable, business-like government.

By the mid-1920s the worst of the recession was over, Maritime claims had been put on the agenda, and external trade had improved somewhat. Potatoes, apples, fox farming, fresh and frozen fish, and pulp and paper production all showed gains. A piece of good fortune for Newfoundland came in 1927, when the Judicial Committee of the Privy Council ruled that the western boundary between Newfoundland and Canada in the Labrador peninsula should, for the most part, follow the height of land. This bonanza meant little in the short term, however. Although Newfoundland was prepared to sell it, neither Canada nor Quebec

was interested in buying. For the moment Labrador remained a potential rather than an actual asset, its location too remote for effective development of its resources. The Newfoundland government provided only minimal services, content to leave the Inuit under the care of the Moravian mission, the whites and Métis to the Grenfell Association, and the Innu largely to their own devices.

Elsewhere in the region a significant growth industry was the illicit liquor trade—an unexpected but potentially lucrative result of prohibition, which remained in place following the war and became law in the United States in 1919. With the fisheries languishing, it was all too tempting to make a living as a 'rumrunner', supplying an ever-growing local and international demand. Typically, liquor was imported through St Pierre and Miquelon and then taken on to the Maritimes and the United States. At home bootleggers began to make a tidy income, a point not lost on provincial administrations looking to finance social services such as mother's allowances and old-age pensions, and improved roads to accommodate the growing numbers of automobiles. Although prohibition was abandoned in favour of government-controlled liquor sales in Newfoundland in 1925, New Brunswick in 1927, and Nova Scotia in 1929, the trade to the United States continued unabated until 1933, when the American Congress too gave up on prohibition.[18] Only Prince Edward Island held out until after the Second World War. The island rejected daylight savings time as well, an innovation also precipitated by the war and favoured in urban industrial settings.

Although the Atlantic region failed to attract a large proportion of the immigrants streaming into North America in the first three decades of the twentieth century, the trickle of newcomers was continuous and had a significant impact. Great Britain remained the major source of immigration, but the region's social fabric was also enriched by newcomers from continental Europe, the Middle East, and elsewhere. Between the 1860s and 1920s 'home children'—orphaned and abandoned youngsters from London, Edinburgh, and other large British cities—were adopted in the region. Their lot was often a hard one, as was that of West Indian labourers recruited to work in the Cape Breton coal mines during the First World War. In the 1920s new immigrant facilities were established at Pier 21 in Halifax, which processed more than a million immigrants before it closed in 1971. Most of the newcomers, recognizing the lack of opportunity in the region, quickly moved on.

Amid the difficulties of the 1920s, there was an upsurge of romantic interest in the region's heritage and folklore. The myth of the Maritimes' 'golden age' became even more firmly embedded with the publication of F.W. Wallace's *Wooden Ships and Iron Men* in 1924, which reflected a shift in interest from the rural idyll of Evangeline to the hardy mariners and fishing folk of the sea-bound coast. Billed by 1929 as 'Canada's Ocean Playground', Nova Scotia led the trend towards the invention of local traditions. The *Bluenose*, designed as a banking schooner and racer, was launched at Lunenburg in March 1921. Defeated only once in races for the International Fishermen's Trophy sponsored by the *Halifax Herald*, the schooner entered local—eventually national—mythology as an enormously potent symbol, and has been depicted on the Canadian dime since 1937. In the same period Nova Scotia's cultural élite discovered Peggy's Cove, conveniently near Halifax, which rapidly became 'the region's primary symbolic landscape', epitomizing the hardiness, simplicity, and virtues associated with the seafaring life, as well as the physical beauty of Nova Scotia's South Shore.[19] Yet such romanticization masked deep-seated problems in coastal communities, where in the 1920s fishermen feared the introduction of large numbers of steam trawlers to supply fresh-fish plants.

Invented traditions were part and parcel of a developing tourist industry, which received major government investment in this period. The Newfoundland government erected the Newfoundland Hotel in St John's and created a Tourist and Publicity Commission that, in addition to the usual promotion of hunting and scenery, began to trumpet what is now known as heritage tourism.[20] It was following the example of Nova Scotia, where in the 1930s motoring tourists were encouraged to visit the newly constructed Cabot Trail or experience the delights of Champlain's 'Order of Good Cheer', introduced at a reconstructed Port-Royal. Under the Liberal premiership of Angus L. Macdonald, Nova Scotians were also urged to remember their Scottish heritage, now an official subject of study at the Gaelic College founded at St Ann's in 1939. It was not long before 'tartanism', complete with bagpipes, kilts, and clan insignia, trumped all other local identities in the province.

If there had been optimism in the air in the late 1920s, it was dashed by the onset of the Depression. Prices fell, markets collapsed, and unemployment climbed even higher. The resulting social problems were accentuated by the fact that emigration to the United States—

'Making the Jib Fast' aboard the *Effie M. Morrisey*, December 1912. Frederick William Wallace took this picture while researching the lives of men who made their living in the sea trades for his book *Wooden Ships and Iron Men*. Published in 1924, this book helped to idealize sailors and fishermen in the Maritimes. From the collection of Frederick William Wallace, Maritime Museum of the Atlantic, Halifax, NS.

and to Canada, in the case of Newfoundland—no longer served as a safety valve: the borders were closed to all newcomers looking for work. By 1931, 19 per cent of Maritime wage earners were unemployed. Although this figure was only slightly above the national average,[21] Maritime governments had fewer resources than most other provinces with which to join in the cost-shared relief programs established by Ottawa.

The strain on all levels of government was extreme. By 1931 Guysborough County in Nova Scotia was virtually bankrupt, a fate soon shared by counties in northern New Brunswick. Provincial governments were also in difficulty. Personal income per capita had fallen to 71 per cent of the Canadian average by 1933, revenues stagnated, and borrowing drove debt charges up to more than 30 per cent of revenue in Nova Scotia and more than 50 per cent in New Brunswick, where the government was on the verge of bankruptcy by the end of the decade. In 1933, 12 per cent of Maritimers were on direct relief, usually paid at miserable rates and sometimes cut off in the summer. Many others looked to charities, the churches, and the Red Cross. As for the elderly, strictly means-tested pensions, introduced between 1933 and 1936 at rates 20 to 40 per cent below the national average, were a convenient way to reduce relief rolls. Everywhere, the poor were subjected to investigations to establish whether or not they were 'deserving'. Even before the 1930s Depression descended, a St John's newspaper had offered a wry commentary on the 'social uplifters' who made the lives of the poor worse by their condescending ways:

> *The Social Uplifters, those eminent sifters*
> *Of merit and poor people's needs,*
> *Went down to the slums to regenerate bums*
> *And do meritorious deeds.*
> *We washed them, we dressed them, with*
> *libraries blessed them,*
> *We prayed with those ignorant mobs;*
> *And the wretches were hateful, and vilely*
> *ungrateful,*
> *And said what they wanted was jobs.*[22]

The Depression precipitated the final scenes in the drama of Newfoundland under responsible government. Squires had returned to power in Newfoundland in 1928. Four years later, revenue had fallen by 21 per cent, but expenditures had risen 7 per cent and the debt by 23 per cent, to the point that servicing it now absorbed more than 60 per cent of revenue. These bald figures represent an escalating crisis—low prices, reduced fish catches, rising urban unemployment, a quarter of the population on the dole (which was centrally administered), and the necessity of borrowing to maintain the basic operations of the state,

even after swingeing cuts in public expenditure. When bank loans became ever more difficult to arrange, another futile attempt was made to sell Labrador for $110 million. The atmosphere was especially tense in St John's, where Squires's opponents, sensing blood, organized a march on the legislature. It turned into a violent riot from which Squires was lucky to escape unharmed, and his party was virtually wiped out in the ensuing general election. Having assessed the financial situation, the new Conservative government suggested what Squires had consistently refused: a partial default on debt payments. There seemed to be no other alternative.

Alarm bells rang in London and Ottawa, where the possibility of default by a member of the Commonwealth was viewed with horror. Newfoundland was presented with an offer that it was not allowed to refuse: Canada and Britain would assist with the debt payments on condition that a jointly appointed royal commission would be called in to advise on what to do in the longer term. Chaired by Lord Amulree, the Commission reported in October 1933. The primary blame for the debt crisis was placed not on the Depression, structural economic problems, or the cost of the war and the railway, but on 'persistent extravagance and neglect of proper financial principles', 'greed, graft and corruption', and general incompetence, among other shortcomings. Its central recommendation, devised by the Whitehall bureaucracy, was that the Newfoundland debt should be rescheduled and guaranteed by the British government. In return, the colony would surrender responsible government and be administered by a British-appointed commission until it was again 'self-supporting'.

Crowds outside the Colonial Building, St John's, April 1932. In the midst of severe economic depression, accusations of corruption levelled against Newfoundland's Prime Minister, Sir Richard Squires, precipitated this demonstration, which later turned into a violent riot. PANL A19-23.

Weary of persistent economic problems, disillusioned with the political élite, fearful of further violence and unrest, Newfoundlanders threw in the towel. There were very few dissenting voices. The legislature voted itself out of existence, and the Commission of Government took office in February 1934. Though welcomed at the time, the surrender of responsible government soon came to be seen—as it is still—as a humiliation, and the analysis in the Amulree report as unfair. Confederation with Canada might have proved

less of an indignity, but there was little support for it on the island, and none in Ottawa. Once R.B. Bennett understood that Britain would intervene, his government made it clear that Newfoundland was not Canada's problem.

To help rehabilitate those most devastated by the Depression, two strategies were adopted across the region: land settlement and co-operatives. The back-to-the-land movement encouraged the unemployed and their families to become self-sufficient farmers. The program had only limited success in Nova Scotia, where

In the early twentieth century the co-operative movement helped to bring many rural people into the market econo-my. Women in the Cheticamp area of Nova Scotia became famous for their hooked rugs, which found a ready mar-ket among collectors. Here Mrs Joseph Chaisson displays a rug produced for Lilian Burke, an entrepreneur from the United States who in the 1920s turned Acadian home crafts into an industry. NSARM N-4387, Clara Dennis Collection 1981-541.

some 600 vacant farms were made available, mainly to unemployed miners. Not surpris-ingly, since they had few farming skills, many of the settlers drifted away. There was greater enthusiasm and success in New Brunswick, where the government opened new areas for pioneer settlement and provided some minimal assistance. Acadians took particular advantage of the scheme, creating a number of new settle-ments in the northern counties of New Brunswick. With most people already on the land, Prince Edward Island simply had to con-tinue attempting to do more with less. The increased popularity of catching skunks, whose snouts fetched 50 cents each, testified to the hardships that many Islanders faced during the Depression. In Newfoundland, the Commis-sion government created eight land settle-ments, relocating about 365 families. It was an

expensive undertaking, and the results were—as elsewhere—disappointing.[23]

More successful were the co-operative self-help schemes promoted by the Extension Department of St Francis Xavier, under the direction of Father Moses Coady. The Antigonish Movement, as it came to be known, focused on adult education and co-operatives to accomplish goals ranging from marketing fish to building houses. Although co-operatives were not new to the Maritimes, the Antigonish Movement provided a new impetus for them, especially in areas where the Roman Catholic church was strong. By the end of 1939, Antigonish claimed involvement in 2,390 study clubs and 140 credit unions spread throughout the three Maritime provinces. When the Newfoundland government estab-lished a division of co-operatives in the mid-

1930s, it was staffed by Antigonish alumni. Although the division achieved considerable early success in St John's and on the island's west coast, another Commission initiative was less well-received: an insistence that dole recipients use brown flour as part of a drive against beriberi (a disease caused by thiamine deficiency). A banner carried by the unemployed in St John's in 1935 read, 'We work for our cash; we want money not cattle feed.'[24]

Positive as these initiatives may have been, there was little that governments in the region could do to alleviate the misery experienced by thousands during the inter-war years. Although radical solutions were mooted by new political parties, both of the left and of the right, they failed to take hold in the region. It was not for lack of trying. The Communist Party, though banned by Ottawa in 1932, drew some support in the region, while the social-democratic Canadian Commonwealth Federation (CCF) elected members both provincially and federally in industrial Cape Breton within a decade of its founding in 1932. The upstart Reconstruction Party, which split from the Conservatives, attracted followers in eastern Nova Scotia in the 1935 federal election. Even the Ku Klux Klan reared its ugly head to scapegoat Blacks and other minorities in those difficult times.

To counter the misery and mean-spiritedness that characterized the period, people often found solace in the mass consumer culture that had begun to transform North American society in the 1920s. Under the magic spell of radio, movies, mail-order catalogues, glossy magazines, cars, and modern conveniences, older values based on self-discipline, self-denial, duty, and religiosity

began to give way to self-fulfilment and secular pleasures.[25] Although Atlantic Canadians were on the periphery of this revolution in values, they were no less attracted to them than people elsewhere. They lacked only the economic wherewithal to insist that they too should have 'a chicken in every pot and a car in every garage', or at least indoor plumbing to replace the outdoor privy.

The economic situation did not significantly improve in the Atlantic region—or anywhere else—until the outbreak of war against Nazi Germany and its allies in September 1939. The relative prosperity brought by the war would prove superficial and temporary, but—while it lasted—was a significant and welcome release from hardship. Unemployment virtually disappeared as men and women joined the armed forces and took up jobs in war-related industries. Rates of enlistment in the Maritimes were high, and about 12,000 Newfoundlanders joined either the British or Canadian forces or the Forestry Unit. Many people migrated to industrial jobs in Central Canada; others found jobs locally, often created by the construction or expansion of military installations in places such as Sydney, Summerside, Chatham, Debert, Greenwood, and Cornwallis. The drift from country to city, especially Saint John and Halifax, intensified, and other Maritime towns experienced significant growth as well—though not until the federal government finally began to invest in Maritime industries and bring them into the war effort.

Despite the presence of four Maritime ministers in Mackenzie King's wartime cabinet, Ottawa was slow to incorporate the region into its industrial strategy. The department of

The Royals Baseball Club of Saint John, 1921. Baseball teams in the region reflected the cultural divisions that characterized Maritime society. In addition to the all-Black Royals, Saint John also supported separate teams for conductors, spinners, dyers, longshoremen (North and South Wharf), and individual religious denominations. PANB, P338-2.

Munitions and Supply, under its hard-driving minister, C.D. Howe, essentially viewed the Maritimes as peripheral, and deliberately encouraged the expansion of heavy industry in Central Canada, even though, from a military and strategic point of view, significant investment in the Maritimes would have made a great deal of sense. It was not until 1941–2, following a chorus of protest, that some encouragement and contracts were given to regional industries. DOSCO began to produce steel plate, for example, while Nova Scotian coal production increased, ships were built at Pictou, and urgently needed ship repair facilities were expanded. By this time, however, it was difficult for the Maritimes to respond to the new demands for their services, since federal policies had helped create a labour shortage.

The Crisis Years: 1914–1949

King George VI and Queen Elizabeth, Doaktown, New Brunswick, summer 1939. Visiting Canada and
Newfoundland to generate support for the imminent war with Germany, the royal couple were greeted by enthusiastic crowds at every stop on their tour. PANB, P54-74.

Montreal therefore remained the major repair centre, despite its inaccessibility to ocean-going vessels for half the year and the danger posed by German U-boats in the St Lawrence.[26]

The strains caused by the war were particularly acute in Halifax, which by 1945 had to accommodate nearly 100,000 military personnel, plus their dependents and a variety of camp followers. A chronic housing shortage developed, hospital facilities were overstretched, and supplies of food and fuel were inadequate. Although churches and voluntary organizations did what they could to alleviate these problems, tensions mounted, especially since recreational facilities—very few of which

had liquor licences—were in similarly sort supply. Tensions came to a head in May 1945 when, following the announcement of the end of the war in Europe, the city erupted in two days of rioting and looting.

Newfoundland fared better than the Maritimes in wartime investment. Canada, which was responsible for the colony's defence, spent more there than in all three Maritime provinces combined. New facilities for the RCAF at Gander and Torbay (now St John's airport), and a huge airfield at Goose Bay in Labrador, were designed to accommodate the Atlantic Ferry Command—which moved some 12,000 planes from North

Jack Weldon Humphrey, 'Men Working in Plate Shop, Saint John Dry Dock, 1944', gouache over pencil on paper. In 1944, the New Brunswick-born artist received permission to document Canada's war effort in the Saint John Drydock and Shipbuilding Company's plate shop. Humphrey's images are among the few that captured industrial activity outside Central Canada. NAC, C-133332.

America to Britain during the war—and to provide air cover for the convoys sailing to and from mainland ports such as Halifax and Sydney. Convoys were protected as well by corvettes based in St John's, where substantial new naval facilities were built. That U-boats presented a genuine threat was demonstrated in 1942, when four iron-ore carriers were destroyed at Bell Island and the Gulf ferry *Caribou* was sunk with the loss of 137 lives. In addition to navy and air personnel, there were 6,000 Canadian troops stationed in New-

foundland and Labrador by 1943. This level of involvement reflected both Newfoundland's wartime strategic importance and Canada's sensitivity to American interests in the area. Under the Leased Bases Agreement of 1940–1, the United States built three bases—at St John's, Stephenville, and Argentia—which they occupied under rent-free 99-year leases. Nearly 11,000 Americans were stationed in the colony, and approximately 20,000 New-foundlanders found work in base construction. With Canadian and American bases

Bedford Basin, on the inner reaches of Halifax harbour, offered shelter to merchant ships and their naval escorts assembling for the dangerous voyage across the north Atlantic during the Second World War. Department of National Defence photograph.

serving as showcases for North American culture and values, the war marked a watershed in the history of Newfoundland and Labrador, turning the colony towards the mainland as British influences receded.

The socio-economic impact of the war on Newfoundland and Labrador was profound. Household incomes increased, living standards and public health improved, and the government could even afford to lend money to Britain. Relations between military and civilian populations were generally good, and many local women married Canadian and American servicemen. Volunteers provided help and entertainment for the servicemen who crowded St John's, and the town became known as 'a warm and outgoing place, the home of hospitable and friendly people.'[27]

War brides arriving in Canada at Pier 21. Many of the nearly 48,000 war brides and their 22,000 children arrived in Canada through Pier 21. While they were destined for communities all across Canada, many of them found homes in the Maritimes. NAC, PA-47114.

While the war thus had positive aspects for Newfoundland, this was less true of the Maritimes. It has been forcefully argued that the war intensified regional disparity, disrupted the Maritime economy, and actually harmed local industry by encouraging new competition from Central Canada.[28] This was well understood at the time, as the reconstruction reports commissioned by each province demonstrate. Nevertheless, there was hope that another slump of the kind that had fol-

lowed the First World War could be avoided. The recommendations of the Rowell-Sirois Royal Commission on Dominion-Provincial Relations (1940), which emphasized equalization payments and national standards in basic services, reflected a new approach both to federalism and to the poverty that existed side-by-side with the wealth created by the industrial system. During the war Ottawa began seriously considering a national policy that would incorporate state welfare measures. Unemployment insurance was introduced in 1940 to cover industrial workers. In 1944 family allowances became the first of a series of universal programs that by 1951 would include old age pensions. Although there were plans to help poorer provinces, these were opposed not only by the political leaders of Ontario and Quebec but, surprisingly, by the once and future premier of Nova Scotia, Angus L. Macdonald.

He was by no means the only politician of an older generation who disliked the federal tendency to centralization and was suspicious of 'state socialism'. Another was F. Gordon Bradley; in many ways an old-fashioned liberal, he nevertheless decided in 1946 to join his acquaintance Joseph Smallwood, who had a strong labour background, in an effort to make their country a Canadian province. Both were determined that Newfoundland should never again suffer as it had in the 1930s. At the end of the war, the British government announced that Newfoundlanders and Labradorians (the latter granted the franchise for the first time) would elect a national convention to recommend the constitutional options to be placed on a referendum ballot. Bradley and Smallwood were determined that one of those options should be Confederation. They knew they could rely on the discreet support of the British government, whose leaders wanted an end to the Commission system, and the Canadian government, which had finally been persuaded that taking on Newfoundland and Labrador made sense even if the financial outlay would be considerable and ongoing. Although Ottawa was less than enthusiastic about acquiring another Maritime province, strategic and economic considerations—after

'Shall We Say Grace?' This cartoon from *The Confederate,* 20 May 1948, draws on memories of the Great Depression to emphasize the message that the wealthy élites supported a return to responsible government, which (allegedly) had only brought misery to the common people in the past.

all, Labrador would be part of the package—made the prospect palatable.

The Newfoundland National Convention sat from September 1946 to January 1948. It discussed the country's condition and prospects, sent delegations to London and Ottawa, and became steadily more polarized into confederate and anti-confederate camps. The government radio station, VONF, broadcast the debates, which were closely followed. Finally, after days of passionate discussion, the Convention recommended that the choice

Gordon Higgins of the Responsible Government League escorts an elderly voter to a polling station in St John's.
CNS, MUN.

should be between continued Commission government and a return to responsible government. Although Smallwood's motion to add Confederation to the ballot was defeated, the British government was determined to transfer Newfoundland to Canada if at all possible, and decided to overrule the Convention: the voters would have three options.

The referendum campaign that followed was bitterly divisive. St John's and the Avalon Peninsula, populated mostly by Roman Catholics with Irish roots, formed the anti-confederate heartland. The rest of the island and Labrador, predominantly Protestant, tended to favour the confederates, whose leaders emphasized the fact that many members of the mercantile upper class opposed them. The first referendum eliminated continued Commission government as an option. The second, held on 22 July 1948, saw a confederate majority of 4.6 per cent over responsible government. In numerical terms this was a narrow margin, but geographically the confederates won every district off the Avalon Peninsula, including Labrador; had the referendum been an election, they would have been credited with a landslide. The result reflected the significant changes that had occurred in Newfoundland and Labrador since the early 1930s, as well as genuine uncertainty about the wisdom of returning to independence. It was also, of course, a response to the social programs offered by post-war federalism, which lay at the centre of the confederate promises. Newfoundlanders had great hopes and expectations for their future in Confederation.[29]

During the negotiation of the terms of union, difficulties arose over fisheries administration—Newfoundland had to place its main industry under federal control, which caused some justifiable shaking of heads—and financial arrangements. The final deal included a special 12-year transitional grant and a federal undertaking, in Term 29, to establish a royal commission within eight years to determine what additional assistance might be needed to maintain adequate public services without imposing higher taxes than the Maritime provinces. The terms of union were settled by the end of 1948, and Newfoundland became a Canadian province on 31 March 1949. Small-

wood, a triumphant outsider, was appointed the province's first premier, and Bradley became its first representative in the federal cabinet. The ceremonies were subdued.

A significant omission from the terms of union was any reference to Native people. Newfoundland had never had an equivalent to the Canadian Indian Act, and neither reserves nor treaties existed. Applying the act to Newfoundland and Labrador would be retrograde, it was argued: better to place Native people under the jurisdiction of the new province, with the federal government providing special grants. In the end the grants given were not to individuals but to designated communities, and it is arguable that the federal government evaded its legal responsibilities. This policy certainly saved Ottawa a considerable amount of money, but it worked to the advantage of neither Native people nor the province—even though the latter was complicit in its adoption.

In 1949, then, 'Atlantic Canada' was born. The term was convenient, but misleading: in fact, there was no effective regional identity, and the four provinces often followed separate and at times conflicting agendas. Although cushioned now by a kinder, gentler federalism, optimistic about the future, and part of a prosperous country, the region had to accept that the centralization of political and economic power was irreversible.

CHAPTER ELEVEN

The Real Golden Age?
1949–1989

*I*n his influential book *Age of Extremes*, the historian Eric Hobsbawm argues that the three decades following the Second World War were a 'golden age' of 'extraordinary economic growth and social transformation, which probably changed human society more profoundly than any other period of comparable brevity'.[1] By any standard the mid-twentieth century was extraordinary. Two world wars and the 1930s Depression encouraged people everywhere to create a better world, while the Cold War competition between capitalism and communism forced policy-makers on both sides to demonstrate the superiority of their respective systems. In Canada, the federal government's commitment to economic planning, social welfare, and human rights created a receptive environment for efforts by Atlantic Canadians to pursue regional development. Social and economic transformation was indeed the result. The new golden age began turning to bronze with the 'oil crisis' of the early 1970s, but it left a legacy in Atlantic Canada of interregional co-operation, institutional development, and claims to entitlement that still inform pubic policy.[2] It also inspired a rich outpouring of

scholarship, art, literature, and music that expressed an emerging regional culture.

The Canadian welfare state, which offered a level of security difficult to imagine in an earlier era, helped to legitimize Confederation in Atlantic Canada, but it was not the only stimulus to pan-Canadian feeling. With the St Lawrence heartland experiencing unprecedented growth in the 1950s and 1960s, and the West coming into its own in the 1970s and 1980s, Atlantic Canadians were drawn to jobs in those regions rather than the 'Boston states'. The Trans-Canada Highway and two national airlines made it relatively easy for those who left to keep in touch with the folks 'down home'. The transcontinental television networks— CBC/Radio Canada and CTV—introduced in this period also served as 'Canadianizing' influences. Although these networks often relied heavily on American programming, until the 1980s Canadians everywhere watched the same few channels and shared a common cultural experience. The centennial of Confederation in 1967 was celebrated just as enthusiastically in Atlantic Canada as anywhere else in the country.

By that time, the idea of regional development had also taken root in Canada, spurred by what were increasingly being described as 'third world' conditions in the Atlantic provinces. Trends long associated with the region—low incomes, high unemployment rates, mass out-migration—continued unabated after the Second World War and galvanized the region's political leaders to action. Their task was a challenging one. With a per capita income 24 per cent below the national average in 1945, the Maritimes sank to 33 per cent in 1955. Newfoundland was the nation's poorest province, with a per capita income only 55 per cent of the Canadian average.[3]

Premier 'Joey' Smallwood was the most articulate and persistent spokesman for regional development. Presiding over what he himself described as a 'democratic dictatorship', he enlisted the aid of a Latvian economist, Alfred Valdmanis, to attract European investment. When Valdmanis proved to be a crook and many of the 'new industries' he promoted—including a chocolate factory at Harbour Grace—unsustainable, Smallwood, undaunted, turned to American promoters. 'Uncle Ottawa', Smallwood's term for the federal government, was not let off the hook. Three years before the deadline provided under Term 29 for a review of the province's financial position in Confederation, Smallwood began building his case for a generous and permanent federal grant. He also lured J.W. Pickersgill, former assistant of prime ministers King and St Laurent, to the riding of Bonavista-Twillingate in 1953. Well-placed to manipulate the levers of federal power, Pickersgill gave Newfoundland a powerful voice in Ottawa.

Maritime premiers were no less eager than Smallwood to enlist federal support for regional development. Following his victory at the polls in New Brunswick in September 1952, Progressive Conservative Premier Hugh John Flemming began an aggressive campaign to develop 'power for industry'. When the St Laurent government—already committed to mass capital infusions to build and maintain the St Lawrence Seaway—refused to provide assistance for the Beechwood power project on the St John River, Flemming was outraged. Prince Edward Island's Liberal Premier Alexander Matheson was similarly offended when the federal minister of finance insisted that the province return $1.4 million mistakenly paid out in per capita grants. Having had his fill of federal politics during his wartime stint in Ottawa, Nova Scotia's Premier Angus L. Macdonald was suspicious of federal schemes of any kind, but his death in April 1954 opened the way for a more interventionist approach under Robert Stanfield, who led a Progressive Conservative government from 1956 to 1967.

Private interests played a critical role in defining the post-war version of regional protest. In 1951 the Maritime Provinces Board of Trade, an organization with more than a hundred affiliates and nearly 8,000 members, established an office in Moncton as a vehicle for encouraging regional co-operation. The Board sponsored a meeting with Atlantic premiers in September 1953 and inspired the creation of the Atlantic Provinces Economic Council to spearhead development efforts. Ottawa's decision in 1955 to appoint a Royal Commission on Canada's Economic Prospects, chaired by Walter Gordon, played into the regional agenda and led to a flurry of research in support of 23 submissions from Atlantic Canada. In July 1956, the Atlantic premiers held the first of what would become annual conferences to discuss mutual interests. To keep up the momentum, APEC sponsored a three-day seminar, held at the University of New Brunswick in September 1956, on the economy of the Atlantic region. In his address, the historian W.S. MacNutt caught the growing spirit of regional purpose by pointing out parallels with Quebec in the Atlantic region's economic 'conquest' by Canada.[4]

Blessed with treasury surpluses in the 1950s, the federal government began looking for ways to accommodate what MacNutt described as the 'Atlantic Revolution'.[5] In 1956 Ottawa announced plans for equalization payments to the poorer provinces and, the following year, offered the Atlantic region concessions on freight rates and power development. At Pickersgill's insistence, the cabinet agreed to include fishery workers under the terms of the Unemployment Insurance program.[6] The preliminary report of the Gordon Commission, released in January 1957, singled out the Atlantic provinces as deserving of 'positive and comprehensive' attention.

The Progressive Conservatives, under their new leader John Diefenbaker, also showed a new sensitivity to regional concerns. During the 1957 election campaign, Progressive Conservative candidates from the region developed a series of 'Atlantic Resolutions' that drew heavily on the Gordon Commission's recommendations. Their wish list included a national resource development program, decentralization of industry, federal aid to power development, freight rate adjust-

ment, a capital projects program, special 'adjustment grants', and a Canadian coast guard.[7] The politics of regionalism quickly paid dividends when Diefenbaker squeaked to victory with an eight-seat margin. For the first time in Canadian history, cabinet ministers from the Atlantic and Western provinces outnumbered those from Quebec and Ontario, and several policies dear to the hearts of Atlantic ministers were implemented before Canadians headed to the polls in March 1958. With a $25-million Atlantic Provinces Adjustment Grant, a $29.5-million loan to the Beechwood power development, subventions for coal, and aid to thermal power development, 25 Progressive Conservatives from the region were smiling on election night when the Diefenbaker government won by a landslide.

The only province that failed to give the Conservatives a majority was Newfoundland. Having thrown in his lot with the federal Liberal party, Smallwood was reluctant to desert it, and had generally stood at one remove from the 'Atlantic front', hoping that the special status of his province as the youngest member of Confederation would serve him better than the politics of regionalism. But his strategy backfired. In May 1958 the McNair Royal Commission, appointed to determine what compensation Newfoundland should get under Term 29, recommended an annual grant of $8 million, rather than the $15 million for which the province had asked. A bitter confrontation between Smallwood and the federal government ensued, and was compounded when Diefenbaker attacked Smallwood's belligerent suppression of a loggers' strike in central Newfoundland.

Whether united or divided, the Atlantic

Robert Chambers, 'The Order of Good Cheer—circa 1960', *Atlantic Advocate*, September 1960. This cartoon reflects the optimism that circulated in the region as the 'Atlantic Revolution', led by the region's premiers, got under way. With permission from the Chambers family.

provinces benefited from a succession of minority governments between 1962 and 1968 that enabled them to wrest concessions from Ottawa. In the dying days of the Diefenbaker administration, the Atlantic Development Board was established to orchestrate invest-

Malcolm Rogers' house, moored off the beach at Dover, Bonavista Bay, waiting for the high tide so it can be hauled ashore. It had been floated from Fox Island as part of Newfoundland's outport resettlement program in the 1960s. B. Brooks, NAC, PA-154123.

ment in the region. The Liberals under Lester Pearson enlarged its functions and endowed it with money. Other federal programs, such as Roads to Resources and the Agriculture and Rural Development Agreement, were tailored to meet the region's needs. After Pierre Elliott Trudeau roared to power in 1968 with a majority drawn from Ontario and Quebec, his gov-ernment replaced the ADB with the Department of Regional Economic Expansion, which applied regional development principles to the entire nation. During its lifetime—DREE was rolled into the Department of Regional Industrial Expansion (DRIE) in 1982—the pro-portion of regional funding spent in Atlantic Canada dropped from 53 to 32 per cent, while the Atlantic share of total spending in DRIE in 1984–5 was only 16.1 per cent.[8] Nevertheless, federal largesse remained an essential element of the region's economic strategies. Local direction over development funding was restored with the creation of the Atlantic Canada Opportunities Agency in 1986.

Spurred by infusions of federal money, provincial administrations in Atlantic Canada embarked on ambitious programs. Development agencies were created to lure industrial investment, while planners in the recesses of the civil service worked feverishly to devise blueprints for social change. Faced with rising expectations and demands for government services, in 1954 the Smallwood government began encouraging people to leave the remote outports, a policy that was further advanced by a joint federal-provincial resettlement program in 1965. Approximately 30,000 people relocated, and 250 communities disappeared between 1954 and 1970. The results were mixed. Those who moved enjoyed better public services, but 'growth centres' often failed to provide the expected jobs, and leaving a deeply rooted way of life proved wrenching for many. Perhaps the most controversial issue of the Smallwood era, resettlement remains a potent reminder of the costs associated with modernization, and the image of a house being floated to its new location a reminder of a lost world.

In New Brunswick, Louis J. Robichaud became the region's first Acadian premier when he led his Liberal party to victory in 1960. Robichaud ensured that a majority of his cabinet members were francophones and set out to improve conditions in the poor, rural municipalities where most Acadians lived. While his 'Program of Equal Opportunity' brought howls of a 'French takeover' from many anglophones, it transformed New Brunswick's political landscape. The centralization of health and educational services, the establishment of a francophone university in Moncton in 1963, and the decision in 1969 to declare New Brunswick a bilingual province—the only one in Canada—underscored the growing power of the province's Acadian minority. Robichaud lost the 1970 election to the Progressive Conservatives under Richard Hatfield, but the new political and cultural realities were in New Brunswick to stay.[9]

Prince Edward Island also bought into the Atlantic Revolution. In 1969 Liberal Premier Alexander Campbell agreed to a 15-year Comprehensive Development Plan that promised an investment of $725 million to help restructure farming and fishing activities, improve infrastructure, and diversify the economy, most notably in the area of tourism. Although there had been some interest in building a causeway to the mainland, this controversial—and costly—initiative was once again shelved by a federal government whose attention, by 1969, was increasingly focused on Quebec.

In Nova Scotia, economic planning was fuelled in large measure by the collapse of the coal industry. Oil and gas were becoming the preferred fuels, and the region's steel industry, which had absorbed much of its coal, was also in crisis. Taking its cue from the recommendations of the 1960 Royal Commission on Coal chaired by Chief Justice Ivan Rand, the federal government embarked on a program to develop alternative industries on Cape Breton Island, where the hardship was most acute. Money was pumped into Cape Breton

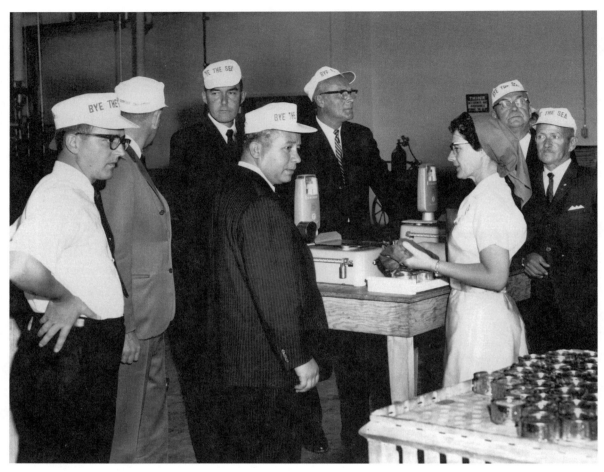

Louis Robichaud at a fish plant in New Brunswick in the 1960s. It was during his premiership that rural areas of the province began to feel the impact of government policies designed to modernize primary industries such as the fisheries. Centre d'études acadiennes, Université de Moncton.

Highlands National Park and the restoration of the fortress of Louisbourg, but these initiatives absorbed only a fraction of the miners and steel workers facing unemployment. Cape Bretoners left in droves for jobs on the mainland, their departure made much easier by the completion of a causeway across the strait in 1955. To ease the human disaster and avoid the political repercussions that would result from the closure of the Dominion Steel and Coal Company, Ottawa created the Cape Breton Development Corporation in 1967, which purchased and ran the mines, and the provincial government established the Sydney Steel Corporation to buy the steel mill.

In their eagerness to support economic development, political leaders made the region notorious as a breeding ground for 'white ele-

Premier Richard Hatfield's efforts to industrialize New Brunswick included the production of the Bricklin sports car. Despite its gull-wing doors, the Bricklin never got off the ground, but before it was scrapped taxpayers had sunk nearly $20 million into the project. PANB, P282-4.

phants'. Clairtone Sound and the Point Tupper Heavy Water plant were serious embarrassments for the Stanfield government, and Hatfield's playboy image—he was sometimes seen cavorting in New York's trendiest hot spots—was tarnished when the Bricklin gull-wing sports car on which he had pinned his industrial hopes proved unviable. Throughout the region, government-assisted food- and fish-processing operations appeared and disappeared with unnerving regularity. Smallwood, ever a gambler on the next big project, fell victim to a succession of dubious entrepreneurs. Indeed, his decision to back John Shaheen's scheme to build an oil refinery at Come By Chance prompted two of his most ambitious ministers, John Crosbie and Clyde Wells, to leave Smallwood's cabinet in 1968.

Three years later his government was defeated, dramatically, by a revived Progressive Conservative party led by Frank Moores.

One example of 'forced growth' stands apart from all the rest: the spectacular hydro development at Churchill Falls, Labrador.[10] Smallwood had encouraged this mega-project from the early days of his premiership, leasing the falls in the early 1950s to the British Newfoundland Corporation, a largely British consortium put together by the Rothschilds. Since Quebec refused to allow transmission lines to run across its territory to customers in Ontario and the United States, and the federal government refused to intervene, BRINCO was forced to sign a 40-year sales contract with Hydro-Québec in 1968. The terms did not seem unreasonable at the time, but when

Premier J.R. Smallwood chats with Winston Churchill, Jr, at Labrador's Churchill Falls in 1966. Smallwood had promoted the hydro development as a project in the tradition of the British merchant adventurers, and the elder Churchill (who died in 1965) had provided practical support. But the hope that the Falls would turn Newfoundland and Labrador into a 'have' province has proved illusory. CNS, MUN.

Churchill Falls went on-stream in the mid-1970s and energy prices started climbing, Quebec began to reap mammoth windfall profits from the resale of electricity—profits that it continues to collect. For Newfoundlanders, the effective loss of one of the province's greatest assets prompted justifiable questions and unease about their place in Confederation.

Nevertheless, there were also success sto-ries. Like their counterparts 'from away', local entrepreneurs took advantage of government funding, and a few men—K.C. Irving, the McCain brothers, Frank Sobey, Harry Steele, and R.A. Jodrey in particular—launched suc-cessful corporations. The Stanfield govern-ment, through its state-sponsored Industrial Estates Limited, managed to persuade Euro-pean investors such as Volvo and Stora Forest

Industries to locate in Nova Scotia. With government help, Halifax, Port Hawkesbury, and Saint John emerged as superports. There was, however, a price to pay for jumping on the corporate bandwagon. To keep investors happy, Newfoundland and Nova Scotia passed restrictive labour legislation—the popular name of the Nova Scotia legislation, dubbed 'the Michelin bill', says it all—while K.C. Irving, whose oil, transportation, and media empire benefited greatly from government assistance, relocated in Bermuda to protect his personal wealth from Canadian taxation.

Politicians were fond of conjuring up visions of an 'Atlantic Community', but they often disagreed on programs designed to achieve regional development. Prince Edward Island felt cheated when the Atlantic Provinces Adjustment Grant was divided on a 30:30:30:10 ratio, and each province had its own ideas about which capital projects—Churchill Falls, Fundy tidal power, Chignecto Canal, Prince Edward Island causeway—should have priority if and when Ottawa could be convinced to fund them. In 1964 Robichaud added yet another controversial project to the mix: union of the Atlantic provinces. Such a move might well have raised eyebrows among his Acadian supporters, but it was popular in Ottawa where patience was growing thin with the rapidly proliferating demands from the region. At Robichaud's urging, the three Maritime premiers—Smallwood remained aloof—finally established a commission, chaired by John Deutsch, to study the issue in 1968. Not surprisingly, it recommended unification of the three Maritime provinces and, equally unsurprisingly, this advice was largely ignored. The Commission's

most important achievement was the Council of Maritime Premiers, established in 1971.

While politicians were commissioning studies and businessmen launching companies, ordinary Atlantic Canadians were living the post-war revolution. The impact of economic restructuring in this period is reflected in the statistical evidence. During the 1950s alone, the numbers of people in the region working in agriculture dropped by 49 per cent, in fishing and trapping by 37 per cent, in forestry by 24.5 per cent, and in mining by 22.2 per cent. Each sector had a cycle of its own, but all were reshaped to meet the demands of an increasingly bureaucratized, centralized, mechanized, and, ultimately, computerized world.

Long an endangered species, the family farm survived only by adopting corporate practices. Quotas, marketing boards, and national standards spelled the end of part-time farming. Whereas one in five people in the region had lived on farms in 1951, only one in fifty did so by 1981. Apple growers in the Annapolis Valley, faced with the permanent closure of the British market for their produce, were encouraged by generous government subsidies to uproot their trees and convert their acreage to mixed crops for a regional market. Most of them got out of farming altogether. On Prince Edward Island, the National Farmers Union and the Brothers and Sisters of Cornelius Howatt—a group named in honour of the island's most famous nineteenth-century anti-confederate—staged a protest in 1971 against the development policies that they believed had contributed to the decline of family farming. Although they succeeded in jamming the highway between Charlottetown and

Borden with their tractors at the height of the tourist season, this action had little impact on the general trends. Between 1951 and 1981, the proportion of people engaged in farming on the island dropped from nearly 50 per cent to less than 10, and the number of farms from 10,137 to 3,154.[11]

It was the same story in forestry, where mechanization had made it possible to fell and process more trees with fewer workers. Milling for the construction industry continued to thrive in New Brunswick, but even there, as elsewhere in the region, the major product was pulpwood. By the 1980s the 19 pulp and paper operations in Atlantic Canada depended on foreign markets and faced intense competition from other regions of Canada and the world. In the absence of tough environmental laws, companies were tempted to cut and run rather than invest in the more costly forestry practices that would ensure a sustainable industry. A side-effect of the over-exploitation of forest resources was a monoculture of softwood trees that invited periodic infestations of the dreaded spruce budworm.

In mining, restructuring produced mixed results. A growing demand for base metals such as lead, zinc, copper, and iron produced a mining boom in northern New Brunswick and Labrador. The most dramatic new frontier was off-shore oil and natural gas, which attracted investment from multinational oil companies that were in turn attracted by generous tax incentives. Newfoundland's government made a determined—but ultimately unsuccessful—attempt to claim ownership of the province's seabed resources, hoping to compensate for the disappointment of Churchill Falls and give a significant boost to

revenues. On the down side, the steady decline of the coal industry meant hard times for many communities. Mine disasters in Springhill in 1956 and 1958, which together took the lives of more than a hundred men, tragically documented the inadequacy of safety measures in the increasingly obsolete mines. The fluorspar industry on the Burin Peninsula appeared to be one of the region's success stories; but cancers caused by radon gas in the mines, together with the availability of cheaper ore from Mexico, closed it down in 1977. In the winter of 1982, the loss of 84 crew members when Mobil Oil's rig *Ocean Ranger* capsized in a fierce storm on the Hibernia oil field underscored the fact that new seagoing industries were no less life-threatening than the ones they had replaced.

The fisheries, for their part, experienced modernization, expansion, and collapse. In the early 1950s Europeans began sending freezer trawlers to the banks fishery, signalling a major transition in the region's oldest primary industry. Cod catches tripled, from an average of 500,000 tonnes a year in the first half of the century to 1,475,000 in 1968. With the emphasis on the offshore banks and fresh or frozen fish, on the plant rather than the fish stage, and overwhelmingly on the American market, saltfish production declined. Eager to tap a resource on its own doorstep, the Canadian government declared a nine-mile (15 km) limit in 1964, a 12-mile limit in 1970, then a 200-mile limit in 1977, and encouraged massive investment.

The number of Atlantic Canadians engaged in the fishery rose from roughly 31,000 in 1974 to nearly 55,000 in 1980, most of the increase taking place in Newfoundland. By the early

Trawlermen demonstrating in St. John's during the 1975 strike. Their key demand was that they should be recognized as employees of the companies on whose vessels they worked, rather than as 'co-adventurers'. The achievement of this concession was an important victory for the Newfoundland Fishermen, Food and Allied Workers Union led by Richard Cashin. CNS, MUN.

1980s Canada was the world's most important fish-exporting country, up from third in 1976, with the Atlantic provinces providing 65 per cent of the Canadian total. This proved to be a recipe for disaster. Overfishing, foreign and Canadian, depleted and in some cases destroyed fish stocks. In 1992 the Department of Fisheries, whose minister was Newfoundlander John Crosbie, placed a moratorium on cod fishing and stringent controls on the exploitation of other fish stocks. With 1,300 communities in the region almost entirely dependent on the fishery, its collapse precipitated a crisis of titanic proportions.

The expansion of employment in the fisheries notwithstanding, most of the jobs created in the new 'golden age' were in the burgeoning trade and service sectors, and were often tied to state spending. By the early 1960s government employment accounted for over 100,000 jobs in the Atlantic region—more than forestry and mining combined. The department of Defence, its budgets fattened by spending associated with the Korean and Cold wars, employed an additional 41,000 Atlantic Canadians. Many of the bases that had languished following the war received a new lease on life, and several new ones, such as Camp

Gagetown in New Brunswick, were established. While Nova Scotia led the region in dependence on defence jobs—over 11 per cent of its labour force were employed in defence in 1961—all four Atlantic provinces benefited economically from the federal government's decision to locate more than one-quarter of the nation's armed forces on the east coast.[12]

The transition from primary to tertiary industries was a difficult one for many Atlantic Canadians. Since unemployed farmers, fishermen, lumbermen, and miners often lacked the skills to fill the available jobs, they were obliged to seek work outside the region. Increasingly, skilled positions were taken up by immigrants. Jobs in areas traditionally dominated by women—clerical, teaching, nursing, social work—were also expanding rapidly. As more women entered the paid workforce, their subordinate positions and unfair wage scales became subjects of concern, as did changing gender relations within the family. At the same time the region's deeply rooted minorities—Aboriginal, Acadian, African—also called into question their unequal access to new economic opportunities.

The fortunes of the labour movement reflected structural changes in the workforce. From a high of 32 per cent in 1953, union membership dropped to a low of 21 per cent in the early 1960s. As white-collar workers—teachers, nurses, and government employees—began signing union cards, however, the percentage rose again. By the 1980s Newfoundland had the highest proportion of organized labour in the region—37 per cent—primarily because of a decision taken by the provincial legislature in 1971 to grant collective bargaining rights in the fishery.[13] The Newfoundland Fishermen, Food, and Allied Workers, under its feisty leader Richard Cashin, fought two successful actions: a strike at Burgeo in 1971 and a massive work stoppage by trawler crews in 1974–5. In 1982 the Maritime Fishermen's Union won collective bargaining rights in New Brunswick and, like its Newfoundland-based counterpart, was instrumental in making trawler-owners—increasingly, large multinational operations—responsible for the well-being of their employees, who until then had been treated as subordinate partners or independent operators. Even so, the union movement did not always present a united front. In Canso, a protracted strike led by the United Fishermen and Allied Workers' Union in 1970 won concessions in prices and berthing facilities for fishermen only to be challenged by the Canadian Food and Allied Workers Union, which wanted to represent workers in all facets of the fisheries.

Facing above. Alex Colville, 'Main Street', 1979, acrylic polymer emulsion on hardboard. At first glance, Colville's images may sometimes appear banal. As in this painting of Main Street in Wolfville, however, they invariably have a point to make. Here the women's preoccupation with shopping and the daily routines of life is set against a backdrop recalling the death and destruction of war that made the present peaceful scene possible. Copyright Alex Colville.

Facing below. David Blackwood, 'Abandoned Ancestors on Bragg's Island', 1970, etching, edition of 50. A native of Newfoundland's northeast coast, Blackwood has produced numerous images based on that region's harsh natural environment, its history, and the resilience of its people. Copyright David Blackwood.

Mary Pratt, 'Another Province of Canada', oil, 1978. A young Newfoundland fisherman delivers a monster codfish in the improbably pretty setting of the garden belonging to the artist—herself originally from New Brunswick. Copyright Mary Pratt.

Christopher Pratt, 'Benoit's Cove: Sheds in Winter', 1998, oil on board. A hard-edged evocation of the modern fishery on Newfoundland's west coast, with overtones of mechanization and modernization. Copyright Christopher Pratt.

Erica Rutherford, 'Earnscliffe' (1978). This colourful silkscreen print was clearly inspired by the landscape of Rutherford's Prince Edward Island home. Courtesy of the artist.

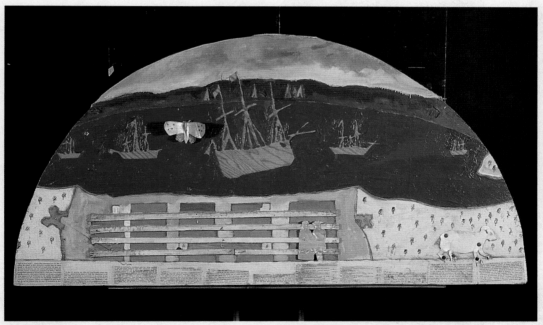

Janice Leonard, 'The Founding of Halifax', mixed media on wood, 1999. Two hundred and fifty years later, the British authorities' treatment of the Mi'kmaq is still a subject of controversy and bitter feelings. In this artistic rendering of the city's founding, Janice Leonard includes a Mi'kmaq encampment on the Dartmouth side of Halifax harbour. Purchased with funds provided by the Canada Council and the AGNS Gallery Shop, 1999. Collection of the Art Gallery of Nova Scotia, #1999.203.

Maud Lewis, 'Winter Sleigh Ride', oil on pulp board, n.d. Since the Second World War, Atlantic Canada has become home to a thriving folk art industry. One of the best-known of these folk artists is Maud Lewis, who despite extreme poverty and difficult living conditions produced countless colourful scenes such as this one. Gift of Louise Donahoe, Halifax, NS, 1996. Collection of the Art Gallery of Nova Scotia, #1996.50

Claude Roussel, 'La Famille', 1957, painted wood. The work of this sculptor, born in Edmunston in 1930, has been widely acclaimed and can be found in many public buildings in New Brunswick. The New Brunswick Museum, Saint John, NB, A69.1

The fishery was not the only industry troubled by inter-union conflicts. In the late 1940s members of the Canadian Seamen's Union fought pitched battles on the Halifax waterfront with goon squads from the Seamen's International Union, whose leader, Hal Banks, had been brought to Canada from the United States—with the blessing of both governments—to fight communist-dominated unions. Ironically, given the prevalence of multinational corporations in the region, nativist arguments were often used to blunt the recruiting efforts of international labour organizations. When the International Wood-workers of America tried to organize New-foundland forestry workers in the late 1950s, Smallwood intervened to put an end to the strike: 'How dare these outsiders come into this decent Christian province . . . amongst decent God-fearing people, and let loose [their] dirt and filth and poison. . . ?'[14]

The fact that the region's business and government leaders tended to treat ordinary people as just another natural resource to be exploited helped to build support for the New Democratic Party. Created in 1961 through a marriage of the old CCF Party—which had been all but wiped out in its Cape Breton stronghold by the Diefenbaker sweep of 1958—and organized labour, the NDP gradually gained strength in the region. Support came initially from Cape Breton but soon spread elsewhere as white-collar workers began reconsidering their traditional political allegiances.

By the early 1970s the voice of labour in Atlantic Canada had strengthened considerably, and governments took the side of capital at their peril. When Nigadoo Mines near Bathurst, New Brunswick, announced in January 1972 that it

was suspending operations and throwing 300 employees out of work, it precipitated an angry outburst from people in the area, who organized a 'Day of Concern'. As a result of this event, attended by Jean Marchand, the minister responsible for DREE, Premier Hatfield, and the leaders of both federal and provincial opposition parties, a $10-million temporary make-work program was created—testimony to the political climate of the day and the widespread belief that issues of poverty and unemployment must be addressed.[15]

The Day of Concern also reflected complex developments in New Brunswick's Acadian community. Among many working-class and younger Acadians, the gradualist approach taken by their leaders was increasingly coming under attack. In 1968, the refusal of Moncton's mayor, Leonard Jones, to consider making the municipality bilingual precipitated a confrontation between the city council and students from the Université de Moncton. Student unrest flared again early in January 1972 after a showing of the National Film Board's *L'Acadie, l'Acadie,* and together with the mine closures, precipitated the creation of the Parti Acadien, led by Euclide Chaisson. Although the new party's goal was more to politicize Acadians than to win seats, it fielded candidates in provincial elections between 1974 and 1984, and made headlines with its call for the creation of an Acadian province—Acadie—in northeastern New Brunswick. In the course of the 1970s Premier Hatfield's implementation of sections of the Official Languages Act helped to diffuse some of the anger and to confirm, once and for all, the bilingual character of the province.

Considerably fewer in numbers, Acadians

Student unrest hit the Atlantic region in February 1968, when students at the Université de Moncton boycotted classes for ten days to protest fee increases and then (with the silent blessing of university presidents) led a province-wide 'sit-in' at government offices in Fredericton. Centre d'études acadiennes, Université de Moncton.

in Prince Edward Island and Nova Scotia had more reason to be concerned about their cultural survival. While 90 per cent of New Brunswick Acadians claimed French as their mother tongue in 1960, only 45 per cent did so in Nova Scotia and Prince Edward Island. To focus their energies, Acadians in Nova Scotia formed the Fédération acadienne de la

Nouvelle-Écosse in 1967, while the Société Saint-Thomas-d'Aquin, established in Prince Edward Island in 1919, took on a more active political role. In 1968 the Prince Edward Island legislature became officially bilingual, and all provinces gradually made concessions in the area of French-language schooling. Francophone groups began to organize in Newfoundland and Labrador during the early 1970s, forming the Fédération francophone de le Terre-Neuve et du Labrador in 1973. With Moncton serving as the capital of the larger regional Acadie, French-language radio, television, arts, and cultural expression flourished.

As issues of human rights and social justice became part of the political agenda in the post-war period, the Black minority in the Maritimes began to protest its second-class status. The Nova Scotia Association for the Advancement of Coloured People was organized in 1945, and the following year it raised money to help Viola Desmond fight segregation in the province's movie theatres. Although her case was thrown out of court on a legal technicality, the incident created so much negative publicity that all such discriminatory laws were soon abandoned. In 1954 the Nova Scotia government, spurred by the civil rights movement in the United States, quietly dropped a clause in the province's education act sanctioning separate schools for its Black population. New Brunswick's smaller Black community formed their Association for the Advancement of Coloured People in 1959. In the 1960s all provinces in the region passed human rights legislation and established monitoring agencies.

Encouraged by the Black Power movement in the United States and galvanized by the deci-

sion of Halifax city council to demolish the Black community of Africville, African Nova Scotians stepped up their efforts to fight discrimination and crippling poverty. The Black United Front was founded in Halifax in 1969 after a visit to the city by Stokeley Carmichael and other leaders of the Black Panthers. Working with grants from both the federal and provincial governments, BUF leaders sponsored workshops and projects to help African Nova Scotians improve both their self-esteem and their material well-being. The Black Cultural Society, established in 1977, accomplished one of its major goals in 1983 with the opening of the Black Cultural Centre in Cherrybrook, on the outskirts of Dartmouth.[16]

The region's Aboriginal people also adopted a more activist approach in the 1970s. After three centuries of decline, their numbers had finally begun to increase in the twentieth century, reaching 18,000 by 1981. Following the Second World War, some of the more abhorrent features of the Indian Act had been dropped, and in 1960 status Indians were enfranchised. Ottawa's desire to abolish both the Indian Act and Indian status, articulated in an infamous 1969 White Paper, provoked a national effort to redress long-standing grievances and resist assimilation. In the Atlantic region, provincially based organizations sprang into existence—the Union of New Brunswick Indians, the Union of Nova Scotia Indians, the Native Council of Prince Edward Island, and the Association of Newfoundland and Labrador Indians—but often had difficulty defining common ground. A year after its founding in 1972, the Association of Newfoundland and Labrador Indians dissolved into the Labrador Inuit Association and

This cartoon by Josh Beutel, which appeared in the Saint John *Telegraph Journal*, 16 March 1985, captures some of the frustration that erupted over issues of official languages in the province of New Brunswick. PANB MC2806-1861.

the Federation of Newfoundland and Labrador Indians; the latter split into island and Labrador components, the Labrador group adopting the name Innu Nation in 1990. Native people living off reserves in the region organized separately. The Federation of Newfoundland Indians, for example, represents Mi'kmaq outside of Conne River, which became the

province's only reserve in 1987. Facing issues of status and employment unique to their gender, Aboriginal women both on and off reserves in Nova Scotia are represented by the Nova Scotia Native Women's Association, which held its first meeting in Sydney in 1972.

During the 1970s the National Indian Brotherhood—renamed the Assembly of First

Nations in 1982—and provincial associations pressured the government to give Native peoples responsibility for their own education and to recognize their land claims. Achievement of these goals was stalled by legal and bureaucratic processes, but the scales were tipped by shocking revelations about the treatment of Native children in residential schools, together with a series of court decisions recognizing Native title and the legality of eighteenth-century treaty agreements in the Maritimes. The complexity of Native issues was widened in the case of Sandra Lovelace, a Maliseet from the Tobique reserve in New Brunswick. Like all Native women subject to the Indian Act, she had lost her Indian status when she married a non-Native man. Denied housing when she returned to Tobique in 1977 after her divorce, she fought the case in the courts and was successful only after she appealed to the United Nations. The failure of white man's justice with respect to Native people became poignantly clear in the case of Donald Marshall, a young Mi'kmaq from Cape Breton who spent eleven years in jail, from 1971 to 1982, for a crime he did not commit.

Despite its poor economic prospects, the region continued to attract immigrants in the post-war period. War brides and their children, most of British background, were followed by refugees and displaced persons from Europe and domestics from the Caribbean. After Canada's immigration laws were reformed in the 1960s, Atlantic Canada became home to people from all over the world. Of those who stayed in the region, most settled in urban centres. A significant exception were the Dutch, who not only came in relatively large numbers—some 5,000 settled in the Maritimes between 1945 and 1960—but often

took up agricultural pursuits. During the Vietnam War (1965–75), the much discussed 'brain drain' of Canadians to the United States was reversed as 'draft dodgers' slipped across the border to avoid fighting in a war they did not support. The stranglehold of majority cultures on high political office was finally broken in 1986 when Joe Ghiz, whose family came from Lebanon, was sworn in as premier of Prince Edward Island.

In the Atlantic provinces as across North America, few developments in the post-war period were more dramatic than the changing status of women. Defying the unemployment cycle and all economic predictions, women flocked to jobs in the paid labour force, boosting the participation rate of the 25–54 age group in the region from less than 20 per cent in 1951 to nearly 70 per cent in 1986. Women also began entering the universities in unprecedented numbers, until by the 1980s they made up half of the region's enrolments. Meanwhile, the plummeting birth rate, escalating divorce rate, and increasing incidence of single motherhood prompted traditionalists to make dire predictions about the future of the family. Most women now had only one or two children, if they had any at all, and increasingly both parents worked outside the home. Following federal legislative reforms in 1969, gay and lesbian relationships began coming out of the closet, prompting more finger-wagging from traditionalists.

Even before the women's movement swept North America in the late 1960s, women in Atlantic Canada had begun the long process of recognizing their subordination and changing the structures that had sustained it. Aboriginal women gained the right to be elected to band councils in 1951. Provincial branches of the National Council of Women, Business and Professional Women's clubs, Women's Institutes, and Zonta pushed for reforms. By the late 1960s, married women were eligible for civil service jobs that had previously been denied them, and quotas restricting women's entry into law, medical, and engineering schools had disappeared. The achievement of Helena Squires, who had sat in the Newfoundland House of Assembly between 1930 and 1932, was finally matched in Nova Scotia when the former Kentville mayor Gladys Porter was elected to the province's legislature in 1960. In 1953 Muriel Fergusson, Fredericton's first female alderman, was named to the Senate, and in 1972 she became the first woman to be appointed Speaker. By that time the Royal Commission on the Status of Women, which reported in 1970, had made 167 recommendations for reform. Provincial governments eventually established commissions and advisory councils to address women's issues, passed legislation to ensure equal pay and a fairer division of marital property upon divorce, and provided funding for women's centres and shelters. No longer a laggard with respect to electing women to public office, the region produced one of the first female party leaders—Alexa McDonough, who was chosen to lead the Nova Scotia NDP in 1984—and the first elected female premier—Liberal Catherine Callbeck in Prince Edward Island in 1995. In Newfoundland, Lynn Verge was leader of the provincial Progressive Conservatives in 1995–6, having played a prominent role in the Peckford government.

Environmental issues also inspired dramatic new political approaches. In 1960 Halifax became one of the first cities in Canada to form a branch of the Voice of Women, an organization devoted to peace and disarmament. Its immediate goal was to stop nuclear testing in the atmosphere, which was causing radioactive contamination in Canada and around the world. Three years earlier, Pugwash, Nova Scotia, had become the site of a unique effort to stop the nuclear madness that defined the Cold War. Twenty-two scientists from around the world, including the United States and the Soviet Union, converged on the summer home of the Nova Scotia-born industrialist Cyrus Eaton to discuss nuclear disarmament. In 1995 the Pugwash Conference on Science and World Affairs, which had met regularly since 1957, would be awarded the Nobel Peace Prize for its efforts on behalf of world peace.

Nuclear fall-out was not the only environmental hazard that Atlantic Canadians had to face. In her highly publicized book *Silent Spring*, published in 1962, the American scientist Rachel Carson presented stunning revelations about the 'tide of chemicals born of the industrial age', singling out the 'rivers of death' created in New Brunswick by aerial pesticide spraying programs. In the 1970s Betty Kennedy mobilized opposition to budworm spraying in New Brunswick, which medical studies now showed was linked to the often fatal children's disease Reye's Syndrome. Elizabeth May led a similar campaign in Cape Breton.

Meanwhile, the International Fund for Animal Welfare under the leadership of New Brunswick's Brian Davis whipped up a storm over the seal hunt, arguing that the practice of clubbing white-coated seal pups was brutal and threatened the survival of an endangered species merely to satisfy the demand of the fashion industry. The issue was taken up by Greenpeace, which brought the French movie star Brigitte Bardot to the ice floes to make its point, provoking boycotts of seal products in Europe and the United States. People in Newfoundland and Labrador, outraged by the assault on a time-honoured practice, also used dramatic tactics, most notably satirical theatre productions by the St John's-based Mummers Troupe and Codco, but with less effect. With Cuddles the Cod eliciting far less sympathy than cute seal pups, the whitecoat hunt was banned and strict quotas were imposed on the killing of adult seals.

The fact that St John's supported two theatre groups in the late 1970s underlined the new vitality of cultural developments in Atlantic Canada. High and low, élite and popular, cultural production flourished in the region as never before, much of it drawing on local themes and talents. After a stint on the CBC-Halifax production *Singalong Jubilee*, Springhill native Anne Murray rose to fame with her rendition of 'Snowbird', composed by Prince Edward Island's Gene MacLellan. Beginning with Wilf Carter and Hank Snow, Nashville, Tennessee, welcomed a succession of country and western talent from the east coast. Others nurtured on the Nashville sound through radio and record, including Stompin' Tom Connors and Carol Baker, launched their careers in Ontario after 'going down the road' in the 1960s. Although Stan Rogers was born in Ontario, his Maritime roots were the inspiration for many of the songs, including 'Make and Break Harbour' and 'Barrett's Privateers', that made him a favourite on the North American folk circuit. Combining Acadian folk

In 1944 the Nova Scotia-born contralto Portia White (1910–68), who had already won national acclaim, made her New York debut. She later toured the United States, Europe, and the Caribbean. NAC, PA-192783.

traditions with rock 'n' roll, Caraquet's Edith Butler won acclaim in Canada and France. The region's Celtic traditions gave rise to a variety of popular entertainers, among them Rita MacNeil, John Allan Cameron, Rawlins Cross, Figgy Duff, and the Rankins. Following in the wake of Portia White, a gifted contralto whose international career included a performance at New York's prestigious Town Hall in 1944,

Every summer since 1972, the church of Sainte-Cécile, with its perfect acoustics and colourful interior, has hosted the International Festival of Baroque Music. That the festival draws baroque music-lovers from all over the world to Île Lamèque in northeastern New Brunswick is testimony to the growth of cultural tourism in the second half of the twentieth century. Shown here are Mathieu Duguay and François Codère, performing at the Festival in 1976. Centre d'études acadiennes, collection l'Evangeline, E8451.

African Nova Scotians, such as the a capella group For the Moment, found enthusiastic audiences at home and abroad.

Halifax's Neptune Theatre opened its doors in 1963, and in 1964 the highly successful Charlottetown Festival Theatre was launched in the Fathers of Confederation Building. Theatre New Brunswick followed in 1968. After struggling at a provincial level for a few years, symphony orchestras in Nova Scotia and New Brunswick pooled their resources in 1968 to create the Atlantic Symphony Orchestra. Post-war immigrants increased the region's cultural talent pool enormously. When, for example, Don Messer and his Islanders moved from radio to television in 1956, producer Bill Langstroth called on Gunta and Irma Buchta—dance teachers

Born in New Brunswick, in 1909, Don Messer was already a well-known radio performer when he moved to Charlottetown and formed 'The Islanders' for CFCY radio in 1939. 'Don Messer's Jubilee', which began airing on CBC television in 1959, became so popular that there were protests across the country when the show was cancelled in 1969. PEIPARO, 2320/40-4.

recently arrived in Halifax from Europe—to provide dancers for the show.

Literary output in the second half of the twentieth century also reflected a new cultural maturity. Poets and novelists such as Milton Acorn, Ernest Buckler, George Elliott Clark, Harold Horwood, Percy Janes, Wayne Johnston, Rita Joe, Alistair MacLeod, Antonine Maillet, Alden Nowlan, David Adams Richards, and Maxine Tynes have all drawn inspiration from the harsh realities of Atlantic life. Regional themes also inspired Don

Shebib's 1969 award-winning film *Goin' Down the Road*, which exposed the plight of working-class Maritimers in Ontario, and plays such as Gordon Pinsent's *John and the Missus* (1974), a gripping portrayal of outport resettlement in Newfoundland.

Artists such as Alex Colville and his students at Mount Allison University, including Christopher Pratt, Mary Pratt, and Tom Forrestall, developed representational painting in ways that have become internationally recognized as 'Atlantic realism'. Bruno Bobak,

Miller Gore Brittain, 'The Drinkers', 1947, oil on masonite.
Returning to his home town of Saint John from New York in
1931, Brittain became one of Canada's leading artists,
portraying ordinary people with warts and all. After the
Second World War, in which he served in the RCAF and
briefly as a war artist, his work took on surrealistic
overtones. Purchased with the assistance of the Viscount
Bennett Trust Fund and Paul Toomik. The New Brunswick
Museum, Saint John, NB, 994.5.

Molly Bobak, Miller Brittain, Jack Humphrey,
Goodrich Roberts, Fred Ross, and Ted
Campbell were only the leading names in the
vibrant artistic communities that had emerged
in Saint John and Fredericton by the middle of
the twentieth century. No longer focusing only
on the idyllic landscape, these New Brunswick
artists often revealed the harsher side of

Maritime life, as in Miller Brittain's 1947 painting 'The Drinkers'. The same was true of David
Blackwood, who gained widespread acclaim
for his images of the seal hunt and other
aspects of traditional life on Newfoundland's
northeast coast. In Prince Edward Island,
artists such as Erica Rutherford began to por-
tray the colourful island landscape in new and
exciting ways. Often excluded from formal
channels that promoted art education and
marketing in the region, Aboriginal artists
such as Ned Bear, Shirley Bear, Teresa
Marshall, Leonard Paul, Jonathan Sark, and
Alan Syliboy began to find receptive audiences, as did the Labrador Inuit artist Gilbert
Hay. The region's self-taught folk artists,
among them Maud Lewis, Joseph Norris, Arch
Williams, and Joseph Cullen, added yet
another dimension of artistic expression.

The lives of most Atlantic Canadians were
defined by ever-increasing years of formal education. In the 1950s school enrolments grew from
338,364 to 485,051. Stimulated by federal funding, vocational schools began proliferating
throughout the region in the early 1960s.
Universities were also transformed. At the end of
the Second World War, most of Atlantic Canada's
universities were small, private operations. Yet by
1970 Atlantic Canada boasted an impressive net-
work of state-funded universities and a total
enrolment of 15,820 students, up from 5,811
only a decade before. University restructuring
created the University of Prince Edward Island
out of Prince of Wales and St Dunstan's in 1970,
and moved St Thomas from Chatham to the
University of New Brunswick campus in
Fredericton. A branch of the University of New
Brunswick was opened in Saint John in 1964,
and the Sydney campus of St Francis Xavier

University gained autonomy as the University College of Cape Breton. One of Smallwood's first actions as premier was to grant degree-granting status to Memorial University College, founded to commemorate the Newfoundlanders who had died in the Great War. In the 1960s Memorial moved to a new campus on the outskirts of St John's, and in 1975 opened a branch campus in Corner Brook. In an effort to control the escalating costs and duplication of programs, Maritime governments established the Maritime Provinces Education Commission in the 1970s, but university enrolments and budgets continued to rise, helping to make higher education one of the most important industries in the Atlantic region.

In 1973 a global 'oil crisis', precipitated by the Organization of Petroleum Exporting Countries, signalled an end to the post-war 'golden age'. Together, rising government deficits and 'stagflation' prompted Ottawa to impose wage and price controls in 1975, and to cut back on its spending. Over the following decade, neo-liberal assertions that government assistance, whether to the poor or to outlying regions, was counterproductive gradually became conventional wisdom. Such views were reflected in the Royal Commission on Canada's Economic Union and Development Prospects, chaired by Donald Macdonald, a former Liberal finance minister. In its 1985 report, the commission suggested measures to mitigate the human misery caused by the dismantling of universal welfare state programs and the implementation of free trade with the United States, but they were conveniently forgotten. The principle of regional equity was also lost in the economic shuffle. It was each province for itself in the brave new 'information age'.

Nowhere was the new provincialism

more clearly manifested than in the ongoing constitutional talks intended primarily—but not exclusively—to accommodate Quebec's movement for independence. In the discussions leading up to the passage of the 1982 Constitution Act, which included a Charter of Rights and Freedoms and a new amending formula as part of the package designed to patriate Canada's Constitution, the three Maritime premiers met to discuss constitutional strategy. Newfoundland's Premier Brian Peckford, motivated by the expansion of the fisheries and investment in the Hibernia oil field, marched to his own drummer. Although the poorer provinces managed to entrench, in section 36 of the Constitution, the principle of equalization to 'ensure that provincial governments have sufficient revenue to provide reasonably comparable levels of taxation', and gained the right to pursue policies that would give existing residents preferential treatment in hiring, the notion that the federal government was responsible for ensuring regional equality fell victim to the new economic theories.

The Atlantic provinces made no co-ordinated effort to influence the deliberations of the MacDonald Commission. They also went their separate ways in the constitutional negotiations leading to the Meech Lake and Charlottetown accords. Newfoundland's Liberal Premier Clyde Wells used issues of regional disparity to justify his opposition to the Meech Lake Accord and the Canada-US Free Trade Agreement, but his position was not reflected in the Maritimes. Indeed, New Brunswick's Liberal Premier Frank McKenna defied his own party by supporting free trade. In the 1988 federal election, voters in Atlantic Canada gave only 41 per cent of the popular vote and 12 of their 32 seats to the Conservative government of Brian Mulroney, which had sponsored free trade. But the Conservatives won the election, and the Free Trade Agreement took effect on 1 January 1989.

By then the Atlantic provinces had settled into a comfortable, if unequal, relationship with the rest of Canada. Per capita income was no longer falling in relation to the national average but remained a surprisingly constant (two-thirds to three-quarters) distance behind.[17] As E.R. Forbes has noted, to have maintained this position on the economic escalator was clearly an achievement of sorts, given the impressive national growth in this period.[18] There is, of course, no way of knowing how the region would have fared in the absence of welfare and regional development programs, but the decision to abandon them at the end of the twentieth century may well reveal just how important they were to community well-being.

Nearly four hundred years after the first permanent European settlements were established in the region, Atlantic Canadians face the prospect of responding yet again to forces centred outside the region. While reform, retrenchment, and restructuring have been the mantra of the new world order, Atlantic Canada has embraced them more out of necessity than conviction. Few can dispute that the dismantling of the interventionist state has taken a heavy toll in a region where private institutions are ill-positioned to take up the slack. Toll highways, home-based health care, food banks, call centres, and corporate sponsorship of education and research may represent a brave new world to those converted to the religion of the marketplace, but many Atlantic Canadians regret the abandonment of the noble dream that made human welfare rather than corporate profits the measure of a civil society.

Another feature of the late twentieth century, linked to these changes, has been the emergence of Halifax as the capital not just of Nova Scotia but of the region as a whole. Prosperous, lively, expanding, Halifax has become a genuine metropolis, home of numerous corporate headquarters, regional federal offices, military installations, educational institutions, health care facilities, and film and television production. Its hinterland consists of all four provinces, and the other capitals are becoming its more or less resentful outports. What the implications of this trend may be for the region's future are unclear. There are some who fear Atlantic or Maritime union by stealth, particularly if Quebec secedes from the federation. Certainly the new economic and financial orthodoxies, combined with blows such as the fisheries crisis, the closure of the Cape Breton coal industry, and severe cuts in transfer payments, are forcing the provinces of Atlantic Canada to develop a more durable and effective regional consciousness. 'Where are we,' asked the Newfoundland writer Moses Harvey in 1885, 'and whither tending?'[19] The answer remains obscure, but the region is undeniably at another turning point in its long history.

NOTES

Introduction: A Region in the Making

1. Alan Wilson, 'Crosscurrents in Maritime Regionalism', in *Federalism in Canada and Australia: Historical Perspectives, 1920–1988*, ed. Bruce Hodgins et al. (Peterborough, ON: Frost Centre for Canadian Heritage and Development Studies, 1989), 366.

2. Phillip A. Buckner and John G. Reid, eds, *The Atlantic Region to Confederation: A History* (Toronto and Fredericton: University of Toronto Press and Acadiensis Press, 1994); E.R. Forbes and D.A. Muise, eds, *The Atlantic Provinces in Confederation* (Toronto and Fredericton: University of Toronto Press and Acadiensis Press, 1993).

3. J.Murray Beck, 'An Atlantic Region Political Culture: A Chimera', in *Eastern and Western Perspectives: Papers from the Joint Atlantic Canada/Western Canadian Studies Conference*, ed. David Jay Bercuson and Phillip A. Buckner (Toronto: University of Toronto Press, 1981), 147–68.

4. Janice Kulyk Keefer, *Under Eastern Eyes: A Critical Reading of Maritime Fiction* (Toronto: University of Toronto Press, 1987), 10.

5. Patrick O'Flaherty, *The Rock Observed: Studies in the Literature of Newfoundland* (Toronto: University of Toronto Press, 1979), 100.

6. Ian McKay, 'Of Karl Marx and the Bluenose: Colin Campbell McKay and the Legacy of Maritime Socialism', *Acadiensis* XXVII, 2 (Spring 1998), 3

7. David Weale, 'The Other Side', *Them Times* (Charlottetown: Institute of Island Studies, 1992), 5–7.

8. Francis Bolger and Elizabeth R. Epperly, eds, *My Dear Mr. M: Letters to G.B. MacMillan from L.M. Montgomery* (Toronto: McGraw-Hill Ryerson, 1980), 65.

9. Stephen H. Ullman, 'Nationalism and Regionalism in the Political Socialization of Cape Breton Whites and Indians', *The American Review of Canadian Studies* 5, 1 (Spring 1975), 66–97.

10. Marilyn Porter, *Place and Persistence in the Lives of Newfoundland Women* (Aldershot: Avebury, 1993).

11. Wallace Clement, 'A Political Economy of Regionalism in Canada', in *Modernization and the Canadian State*, ed. Daniel Glenday, Hubert Guindon, and Allan Turowetz (Toronto: Macmillan 1978), 89–110.

12. Thomas C. Haliburton, *The Clockmaker* (Toronto: McClelland and Stewart, 1958), 50.

13. Donald Savoie, *Regional Economic Development: Canada's Search for Solutions*, 2nd edn (Toronto: University of Toronto Press, 1992), 233–8.

14. David Alexander, 'New Notions of Happiness: Nationalism, Regionalism, and Atlantic Canada', *Journal of Canadian Studies* 15, 2 (Summer 1980), 29–42.

15. Ray Guy, 'A Christmas Story', in *That Far

Greater Bay, ed. Eric Norman (St John's: Breakwater Books, 1976), 101.

1: Beginnings

1. Ruth Holmes Whitehead, *Stories from the Six Worlds: Micmac Legends* (Halifax: Nimbus, 1988), 166–7.
2. *Rocks Adrift: The Geology of Gros Morne National Park* (Ottawa: Environment Canada, Parks Service, 1990).
3. Laing Ferguson, *The Fossil Cliffs of Joggins* (Halifax: Nova Scotia Museum, 1988); Harry Thurston, *Dawning of the Dinosaurs: The Story of Canada's Oldest Dinosaurs* (Halifax: Nimbus and Nova Scotia Museum, 1994).
4. A summary of recent scholarship on this period of the region's history can be found in Stephen A. Davis, 'Early Societies: Sequences of Change', in *The Atlantic Region to Confederation*, ed. Phillip A. Buckner and John G. Reid (Toronto and Fredericton: University of Toronto and Acadiensis Press, 1994), 3–21. See also Michael Deal and Susan Blair, eds, *Prehistoric Archaeology in the Maritime Provinces: Past and Present Research* (Fredericton: Council of Maritime Premiers, 1991); James A. Tuck, *Newfoundland and Labrador Prehistory* (Ottawa: National Museums of Canada, 1976) and Robert McGhee, *Ancient Peoples of the Arctic* (Vancouver: University of British Columbia, 1996).

2: Aboriginal Peoples

1. Cited in Ruth Holmes Whitehead, *The Old Man told Us: Excerpts from Micmac History, 1500–1950* (Halifax: Nimbus, 1991), 11–12.
2. Olive Patricia Dickason, *Canada's First Nations: A History of Founding Peoples from Earliest Times* (Toronto: McClelland and Stewart, 1992), 12.
3. Nicolas Denys, *The Description and Natural History of the Coasts of North America*, ed. William F. Ganong (Toronto: Champlain Society, 1908), 401.
4. A useful summary of Mi'kmaq culture at the time of European contact can be found in

Stephen A. Davis, *Micmac* (Tantallon, NS: Four East Publications, 1991), Chapter 3
5. Father Chrestien Le Clercq, *New Relation of Gaspesia With the Customs and Religion of the Gaspesian Indians,* ed. William F. Ganong (Toronto: Champlain Society, 1910), 239.
6. Ibid., 88–9.
7. Ruth Holmes Whitehead, *Stories from the Six Worlds: Micmac Legends* (Halifax: Nimbus, 1988), 8.
8. There were no moose in Newfoundland until they were introduced in the early twentieth century.
9. Cited in Eleanor Leacock, 'Montagnais Women and the Jesuit Program for Colonization', in *Rethinking Canada: The Promise of Women's History*, ed. Veronica Strong-Boag and Anita Clair Fellman (Toronto: Copp Clark Pitman, 1991), 16.
10. Nain station diary, 5 November 1772; quoted in J.K. Hiller, 'The Foundation and the Early Years of the Moravian Mission in Labrador, 1752–1805' (M.A. thesis, Memorial University, 1967), 163.
11. Cited in Ralph Pastore, 'The Sixteenth Century: Aboriginal Peoples and European Contact', in *The Atlantic Region to Confederation: A History*, ed. Phillip A. Buckner and John G. Reid (Toronto: University of Toronto Press, 1994), 24.

3: European Encounters: 1000–1598

1. Ruth Holmes Whitehead, *The Old Man Told Us: Excerpts from Micmac History, 1500–1950* (Halifax: Nimbus, 1991), 8.
2. Robert McGhee, 'Contact between Native North Americans and the Medieval Norse: A Review of the Evidence', *American Antiquity* 49, 1 (1984), 4–26; Thomas H. McGovern, 'The Archaeology of the Norse North Atlantic', *Annual Review of Anthropology* 19 (1990), 331–51.
3. Peter Pope, *The Many Landfalls of John Cabot* (Toronto: University of Toronto Press, 1997).
4. J.A. Williamson, *The Cabot Voyages and Bristol Discovery under Henry VII* (Cambridge: Hakluyt Society, 1962).

5. Felipe Fernández-Armesto, *Millennium* (New York: Scribner, 1995), 171, 257.

6. W.P. Cumming, R.A. Skelton, and D.B. Quinn, *The Discovery of North America* (New York: Elek Books, 1971), 74, 79.

7. James Axtell, 'At the Water's Edge: Trading in the 16th Century', in Axtell, *After Columbus: Essays in the Ethnohistory of Colonial North America* (New York: Oxford University Press, 1988), 145.

8. Darlene Abreu-Ferreira, 'Terra Nova Through the Iberian Looking Glass: The Portuguese-Newfoundland Cod Fishery in the Sixteenth Century', *Canadian Historical Review* 79, 1 (March 1998), 100–15.

9. Ralph Pastore, 'The Sixteenth Century: Aboriginal Peoples and European Contact', in *The Atlantic Region to Confederation: A History*, ed. Phillip A. Buckner and John G. Reid (Toronto: University of Toronto Press, 1994), 22.

10. Cited in Pastore, 'Sixteenth Century', 29.

11. As translated in Sally Ross and Alphonse Deveau, *The Acadians of Nova Scotia Past and Present* (Halifax: Nimbus, 1992), 3–4.

12. Axtell, 'At the Water's Edge', 177.

13. Pastore, 'Sixteenth Century', 39.

4: Colonial Experiments: 1598–1632

1. Peter Pope, 'Six Letters from the Early Colony of Avalon', *Avalon Chronicles* 1 (1996), 6.

2. Stephen Greenblatt, *Marvelous Possessions: The Wonder of the New World* (Chicago: University of Chicago Press, 1991), 9.

3. Alfred W. Crosby, 'Ecological Imperialism: The Overseas Migration of Western Europeans as a Biological Phenomenon', in *The Ends of the Earth: Perspectives on Modern Environmental History*, ed. Donald Worster (Cambridge: Cambridge University Press, 1985), 103–17.

4. Elizabeth Mancke and John Reid, 'Elites, States, and the Imperial Contest for Acadia', paper presented to the Atlantic Canada Studies Conference XIII, Halifax, 7 May 2000.

5. Patrick O'Flaherty, *The Rock Observed: Studies in the Literature of Newfoundland* (Toronto: University of Toronto Press, 1979), 10.

6. Naomi Griffiths holds that the name Acadia, or Acadie, derives from the Native word for the territory, but admits that this has been a matter of 'endless debate'. Given the Europeans' tendency to embellish their discoveries, it may also be derived from the word 'arcadia', which was first applied to the Atlantic seaboard by the Italian explorer Verrazano in 1524; Naomi Griffiths, *The Acadians: Creation of a People* (Toronto: McGraw Hill-Ryerson, 1973), 3, 88; Jean Daigle, 'Acadia from 1604 to 1763: An Historical Synthesis', in *Acadia of the Maritimes: Thematic Studies*, ed. Jean Daigle (Moncton: Centre d'études acadiennes, 1995), 2.

7. Elizabeth Jones, *Gentlemen and Jesuits: Quests for Glory and Adventure in the Early Days of New France* (Toronto: University of Toronto Press, 1986), 29.

8. Sally Ross and Alphonse Deveau, *The Acadians of Nova Scotia Past and Present* (Halifax: Nimbus, 1992), 11.

9. M.A. MacDonald, *Fortune and La Tour: The Civil War in Acadia,* 2nd edn (Halifax: Nimbus, 2000).

10. George Calvert to King Charles I, 19 Aug. 1629, in Gillian Cell, *Newfoundland Discovered: English Attempts at Colonization, 1610–1630* (London: Hakluyt Society, 1982), 295–6.

11. Denys Delâge, *Bitter Feast: Amerindians and Europeans in Northeastern North America, 1600–64* (Vancouver: University of British Columbia Press, 1993), 246.

12. Ramsay Cook, '1492 and All That: Making a Garden Out of a Wilderness', in *Consuming Canada: Readings in Environmental History*, ed. Chad Gaffield and Pam Gaffield (Toronto: Copp Clark, 1995), 62–80.

13. Cited in Ruth Holmes Whitehead, *The Old Man Told Us: Excerpts from Micmac History, 1500–1950* (Halifax: Nimbus, 1991), 39.

14. Alfred W. Crosby, *Ecological Imperialism: The Biological Expansion of Europe, 900–1900* (Cambridge: Cambridge University Press, 1986).

15. Cited in Peter Neary and Patrick O'Flaherty, *By*

Great Waters: A Newfoundland and Labrador Anthology (Toronto: University of Toronto Press, 1974), 10.

5: Imperial Designs: 1632–1713

1. Marcel Trudel, *The Beginnings of New France, 1524–1663* (Toronto: McClelland and Stewart, 1973), 192.
2. The most thorough discussion of this period of early French settlement can be found in John Reid, *Acadia, Maine, and New Scotland: Marginal Colonies in the Seventeenth Century* (Toronto: University of Toronto Press, 1981).
3. Andrew Hill Clark, *Acadia: The Geography of Early Nova Scotia to 1760* (Madison: University of Wisconsin Press, 1968), 90.
4. M.A. MacDonald, *Fortune and La Tour: The Civil War in Acadia,* 2nd edn (Halifax: Nimbus, 2000).
5. A synthesis of recent scholarship on pre-Deportation Acadia can be found in Jean Daigle, 'Acadia from 1604 to 1763: A Historical Synthesis', *Acadia of the Maritimes: Thematic Studies*, ed. Jean Daigle (Moncton: Chaire d'études acadiennes, Université de Moncton, 1995), 1–43.
6. Gisa Hynes, 'Some Aspects of the Demography of Port Royal, 1650–1755', *Acadiensis* 3, 1 (Autumn 1973), 3–17.
7. Luca Codignola, 'Competing Networks: The Roman Catholic Clergy in French North America, 1610–58', *Canadian Historical Review* 80, 4 (December 1999), 539–84.
8. Brenda Dunn, 'Aspects of the Lives of Women in Ancienne Acadie', in *Looking into Acadie: Three Illustrated Lectures*, ed. Margaret Conrad (Halifax: Nova Scotia Museum, 1999), 44.
9. N.E.S. Griffiths, 'The Acadians', *Dictionary of Canadian Biography* IV, xviii. For a more detailed discussion, see Naomi E.S. Griffiths, *The Contexts of Acadian History, 1686–1784* (Montreal and Kingston: McGill-Queen's University Press, 1992).
10. Jean Daigle, 'Nos Amis les ennemis: relations commerciales de l'Acadie avec Massachusetts, 1760–1711', (PhD thesis, University of Maine at Orono, 1975).
11. W. Gordon Handcock, *Soe longe as there comes noe women: Origins of English Settlement in Newfoundland* (St John's: Breakwater Press, 1989), 45.
12. Ibid., 37.
13. Bernard Pothier, 'Le Moyne d'Iberville', *Dictionary of Canadian Biography* II, 394.
14. John G. Reid, '1686–1720: Imperial Intrusions', in *The Atlantic Region to Confederation: A History*, ed. Phillip A. Buckner and John G. Reid (Toronto and Fredericton: University of Toronto Press and Acadiensis Press, 1994), 94.

6: Renegotiating the Atlantic Region: 1715–1763

1. Jerry Bannister, 'The Social Management of English Commerce: Benjamin Lester's Empire in Trinity and Poole, 1755–1775', paper presented to the conference of the Omohundro Institute of Early American History and Culture, 2000, 5.
2. N.E.S. Griffiths, 'The Golden Age: Acadian Life, 1713–1748', *Histoire Sociale* 17, 33 (May 1984), 21–34.
3. Cited in John G. Reid, 'Imperial Intrusions, 1686–1720', in *The Atlantic Region to Confederation: A History*, ed. Phillip A. Buckner and John G. Reid (Toronto and Fredericton: University of Toronto Press and Acadiensis Press, 1994), 100.
4. George Rawlyk, 'Cod, Louisbourg, and the Acadians', in *The Atlantic Region to Confederation*, ed. Buckner and Reid, 69.
5. James Pritchard, *The Anatomy of a Naval Disaster: The 1746 French Expedition to North America* (Montreal and Kingston: McGill-Queen's University Press, 1995).
6. Cited in G.F.G. Stanley, *New France: The Last Phase, 1744–1760* (Toronto: McClelland and Stewart, 1968), 65.
7. Earle Lockerby, 'The Deportation of the Acadians from Ile St.-Jean, 1758', *Acadiensis* XXVII, 2 (Spring 1998), 45–94.
8. Stephen E. Patterson, 'Colonial Wars and Aboriginal Peoples, 1744–1763', in *The Atlantic Region to Confederation*, ed. Buckner and Reid, 147.

9. Bannister, 'Social Management', 7–9.

10. Cited in M.A. MacDonald, *Rebels and Royalists: The Lives and Material Culture of New Brunswick's Early English-Speaking Settlers, 1758–1783* (Fredericton: New Ireland Press, 1990), 21.

11. G.P. Gould and A.J. Semple, eds, *Our Land: The Maritimes* (Fredericton: Sainte Annes Point Press, 1980), 177.

7: Community Formation: 1749–1815

1. D.W. Meinig, *The Shaping of America: Atlantic America, 1492–1800* (New Haven: Yale University Press, 1986).

2. J.M. Bumsted, *Land, Settlement, and Politics in Eighteenth-Century Prince Edward Island* (Montreal and Kingston: McGill-Queen's University Press, 1987).

3. Quoted in C. Grant Head, *Eighteenth Century Newfoundland: A Geographer's Perspective* (Toronto: McClelland and Stewart, 1976), 198.

4. Ernest Clark, *The Siege of Fort Cumberland, 1776: An Episode in the American Revolution* (Montreal and Kingston: McGill-Queen's University Press, 1995).

5. Ann Gorman Condon, '1783–1800: Loyalist Arrival, Acadian Return, Imperial Reform', in *The Atlantic Region to Confederation: A History*, ed. Phillip A. Buckner and John G. Reid (Toronto and Fredericton: University of Toronto and Acadiensis Press, 1994), 192.

6. D.G. Bell, *Early Loyalist Saint John: The Origins of New Brunswick Politics, 1783–1786* (Fredericton: New Ireland Press, 1983), 64.

7. James W. St G. Walker, *The Black Loyalists: The Search for a Promised Land in Nova Scotia and Sierra Leone*, 2nd edn (Toronto: University of Toronto Press, 1992).

8. Jennifer Reid, *Myth, Symbol, and Colonial Encounter: British and Mi'kmaq in Acadia, 1700–1867* (Ottawa: University of Ottawa Press, 1995), 34–5.

9. Graeme Wynn, *Timber Colony: A Historical Geography of Early Nineteenth Century New Brunswick* (Toronto: University of Toronto Press, 1981).

10. D.A. Sutherland, '1810–1820: War and Peace', in *The Atlantic Region to Confederation*, ed. Buckner and Reid, 237–8.

11. W.S. MacNutt, *The Atlantic Provinces: The Emergence of Colonial Society, 1712–1857* (Toronto: McClelland and Stewart, 1965), 122.

12. The southern Labrador boundary was moved from the River St. John to Blanc Sablon in 1825, and defined as a line extending north to connect with a line running due west along the 52nd parallel. Richard Budgel and Michael Staveley, *The Labrador Boundary* (Happy Valley-Goose Bay: Labrador Institute of Northern Studies, 1987).

8: Maturing Colonial Societies: 1815–1873

1. Joseph Howe, 'The Blue Nose', in *Joseph Howe: Poems and Essays*, ed. M.G. Parks (Toronto: University of Toronto Press, 1973), 145–6.

2. Phillip Buckner, 'Whatever Happened to the British Empire?' *Journal of the Canadian Historical Association* New Series, 4 (Ottawa, 1993), 3–32.

3. Douglas F. Campbell and David Niece, *Ties that Bind: Structure and Marriage in Nova Scotia* (Port Credit, ON: Scribblers' Press, 1979), 41.

4. Peter Toner, ed., *New Ireland Remembered: Historical Essays on the Irish in New Brunswick* (Fredericton: New Ireland Press, 1988); Thomas P. Power, ed., *The Irish in Atlantic Canada, 1780–1900* (Fredericton: New Ireland Press, 1991).

5. Cited in D.C. Harvey, ed., *Journeys to the Island of St. John* (Toronto: Macmillan, 1955), 105.

6. Cited in Jennifer Reid, *Myth, Symbol, and Colonial Encounter: British and Mi'kmaq in Acadia, 1700–1867* (Ottawa: University of Ottawa Press, 1995), 36.

7. Ralph Pastore, *Shanawdithit's People: The Archaeology of the Beothuks* (St John's: Atlantic Archaeology Ltd., 1992).

8. T.W. Acheson, 'The 1840s: Decade of Tribulation', in *The Atlantic Region to Confederation: A History*, ed. Phillip A. Buckner and John G. Reid (Toronto and Fredericton:

University of Toronto Press and Academic Press, 1994), 307–2.

9. A summary of the shipping industry in the region can be found in Eric W. Sager and Lewis R. Fischer, *Shipping and Shipbuilding in Atlantic Canada, 1820–1914* (Ottawa: Canadian Historical Association, 1986).

10. Shannon Ryan, *The Ice Hunters: A History of Newfoundland Sealing to 1914* (St John's: Breakwater Press, 1994).

11. T.W. Acheson, *Saint John: The Making of an Urban Colonial Society* (Toronto: University of Toronto Press, 1985), 24.

12. Douglas Baldwin, *Land of Red Soil: A Popular History of Prince Edward Island* (Charlottetown: Ragweed Press, 1998), 87.

13. R.J. Morgan, "Poverty, Wretchedness and Misery": The Great Famine in Cape Breton, 1845–1851', *Nova Scotia Historical Review* 6, 1 (1986), 93.

14. Judith Fingard, 'The 1820s: Peace, Privilege, and the Promise of Progress', in *The Atlantic Region to Confederation*, ed. Buckner and Reid, 270.

15. Judith Fingard, *Jack in Port: Sailortowns of Eastern Canada* (Toronto: University of Toronto Press, 1982).

16. A.J. Sandy Young, *Beyond Heroes: A Sport History of Nova Scotia*, Vol. 2 (Hantsport: Lancelot Press, 1991), 15.

17. Phillip A. Buckner, 'The 1860s: An End and a Beginning', in *The Atlantic Region to Confederation*, ed. Buckner and Reid, 377.

18. Ian Ross Robertson, *The Tenant League of Prince Edward Island: Leasehold Tenure in the New World* (Toronto: University of Toronto Press, 1996).

19. Cited in Phillip A. Buckner, 'The 1860s: An End and A Beginning', in *The Atlantic Region to Confederation* 360.

9: Industrial Challenges: 1873–1914

1. Eric W. Sager and Lewis R. Fischer, *Shipping and Shipbuilding in Atlantic Canada, 1820–1914* (Ottawa: Canadian Historical Association, 1986).

2. David G. Alexander, 'Economic Growth in the Atlantic Region, 1880–1940', in Alexander, *Atlantic Canada and Confederation: Essays in Canadian Political Economy*, comp. Eric W. Sager, Lewis R. Fischer, Stuart O. Pierson (Toronto: Memorial University and University of Toronto Press, 1983), 58–9; Alexander, 'Newfoundland's Traditional Economy and Development to 1934', in *Newfoundland in the Nineteenth and Twentieth Centuries: Essays in Interpretation*, ed. James Hiller and Peter Neary (Toronto: University of Toronto Press, 1980), 28.

3. Calculated from Alexander, 'Economic Growth'. See also Kris Inwood and John Chamard, 'Regional Industrial Growth During the 1890s: the Case of the Missing Artisans', *Acadiensis* XVI, 1 (1986), 101–17; and Kris E. Inwood, 'Maritime Industrialization from 1870 to 1910: A Review of the Evidence and Its Interpretation', *Acadiensis* XXI, 1 (1991), 132–55.

4. W.T. Acheson, 'The National Policy and the Industrialization of the Maritimes, 1880–1910,' *Acadiensis*, I, 2 (Spring 1972), 3–28.

5. Patricia A. Thornton, 'The Problem of Out-Migration from Atlantic Canada, 1871–1921: A New Look', *Acadiensis* XV, 1 (1985), 3–34.

6. Judith Fingard, 'The 1880s: Paradoxes of Progress', in *The Atlantic Provinces in Confederation*, ed. E.R. Forbes and D.A. Muise (Toronto: University of Toronto Press, 1993), 97.

7. Michael Staveley, 'Population Dynamics in Newfoundland: The Regional Patterns', in *The Peopling of Newfoundland: Essays in Historical Geography*, ed. John J. Mannion (St John's: Institute of Social and Economic Research, 1977), 59.

8. Larry N. Shyu, *Peoples of the Maritimes: The Chinese* (Halifax: Nimbus, 1997), 18.

9. Peter M. Toner, 'New Brunswick Schools and the Rise of Provincial Rights', in *Federalism in Canada and Australia: The Early Years*, ed. Bruce W. Hodgins, Don Wright, and W.H. Heick (Waterloo: Wilfrid Laurier University Press, 1978), 134.

10. N.E.S. Griffiths, 'Evangeline: A Tale of Acadie', in *The Canadian Encyclopedia*, 2nd edn (Edmonton: Hurtig, 1988), II, 729. See also Naomi Griffiths, 'Longfellow's *Evangeline*: The Birth and Acceptance of a Legend', *Acadiensis* XI, 2 (1982), 28–41.

11. Michael Hatfield, 'H.H. Pitts and Race and Religion in New Brunswick Politics', *Acadiensis* IV, 2 (1975), 46–65.

12. Quoted in Robert Craig Brown and Ramsay Cook, *Canada 1896–1921: A Nation Transformed* (Toronto: McClelland and Stewart, 1974), 25.

13. Margot I. Duley, *Where Once Our Mothers Stood We Stand: Women's Suffrage in Newfoundland 1890–1925* (Charlottetown: gynergy books, 1993), 24–34.

14. From a speech by Bishop M.F. Howley, quoted in Jiří Smrz, 'Cabot 400: The 1897 St. John's Celebrations', *Newfoundland Studies* 12, 1–2 (1996), 24.

15. Ian McKay, 'Strikes in the Maritimes, 1901–1914,' in David Frank and Gregory S. Kealey, eds, *Labour and Working-Class History in Atlantic Canada: A Reader* (St John's: Institute of Social and Economic Research, 1995), 190–232.

16. Ian McKay, 'The Five Ages of Nova Scotian Tourism', *New Maritimes* 5, 11–12 (1987), 8. See also Graeme Wynn, '"Images of the Acadian Valley": The Photographs of Amos Lawson Hardy', *Acadiensis* XV, 1 (1985), 65–9.

17. Ian McKay, *The Quest of the Folk: Antimodernism and Cultural Selection in Twentieth-Century Nova Scotia* (Montreal and Kingston: McGill-Queen's University Press, 1994), 225–6.

18. On Duncan, see Patrick O'Flaherty, *The Rock Observed: Studies in the Literature of Newfoundland* (Toronto: University of Toronto Press, 1979), 95–102.

19. Both quotations are from Gerald L. Pocius, 'Tourists, Health Seekers and Sportsmen: Luring Americans to Newfoundland in the Early Twentieth Century', in *Twentieth-Century Newfoundland: Explorations*, ed. James Hiller and Peter Neary (St John's: Breakwater Books, 1994), 47–78.

10: Crisis Years: 1914–1949

1. M. Stuart Hunt, *Nova Scotia's Part in the Great War* (Halifax: Nova Scotia Veterans Publishing Co., 1930), 302.

2. C.A. Sharpe, 'Enlistment in the Canadian Expeditionary Force 1914–1918: A Regional Analysis', *Journal of Canadian Studies* 18, 4 (1983–4), 15–29; 'The "Race of Honour": An Analysis of Enlistments and Casualties in the Armed Forces of Newfoundland: 1914–1918', *Newfoundland Studies* 4, 1 (1988), 27–55.

3. The difference in total casualty rates was similarly startling: 55.7 per cent for the Canadian Expeditionary Force, and 70.7 per cent for the Newfoundland Regiment.

4. Patricia R. O'Brien, 'Newfoundland Patriotic Association', *Encyclopedia of Newfoundland and Labrador* 4, 234.

5. Gale Denise Warren, 'The Patriotic Association of the Women of Newfoundland: 1914–1918', *Newfoundland Quarterly* XCII, 1 (1998), 23–32.

6. E.R. Forbes, 'Battles in Another War: Edith Archibald and the Halifax Feminist Movement', in *Challenging the Regional Stereotype: Essays on the 20th Century Maritimes*, ed. E.R. Forbes (Fredericton: Acadiensis Press, 1989), 67–89.

7. Janet F. Kitz, *Shattered City: The Halifax Explosion and the Road to Recovery* (Halifax: Nimbus, 1989), and Alan Ruffman and Colin Howell, eds, *Ground Zero: A Reassessment of the 1917 Explosion in Halifax Harbour* (Halifax: Nimbus and Gorsebrook Research Institute, 1994).

8. Women in Canada were granted the federal vote on the same conditions as men in 1918. The Maritime provinces followed suit: Nova Scotia in 1918, New Brunswick in 1919, and Prince Edward Island in 1922. Newfoundland adopted the British model of giving women over 25 the right to vote in 1925, but it was not until Confederation in 1949 that women and men were subject to the same voting regulations. New Brunswick also stands out from the other jurisdictions in its refusal to allow women to stand for public office until 1934; Sylvia

Bashevkin, *Toeing the Lines: Women and Party Politics in English Canada*, 2nd edn (Toronto: Oxford University Press, 1993), 5.

9. Ian McKay, 'The 1910s: The Stillborn Triumph of Progressive Reform', in *The Atlantic Provinces in Confederation*, ed. E.R. Forbes and D.A. Muise (Toronto: University of Toronto Press, and Fredericton: Acadiensis Press, 1993), 229.

10. Extract from *Periodical Accounts relating to the Missions of the Church of the United Brethren, 1919*, in Helge Kleivan, *The Eskimos of Northeast Labrador: A History of Eskimo-White Relations, 1771–1955* (Oslo: Norsk Polarinstitutt, 1966), 181.

11. Nolan Reilly, 'The General Strike in Amherst, Nova Scotia, 1919', *Acadiensis* IX, 2 (1980), 56–77.

12. Between 1920 and 1926, manufacturing employment in Amherst fell by 68 per cent, in New Glasgow by 77 per cent; E.R. Forbes, 'Misguided Symmetry: The Destruction of Regional Transportation Policy for the Maritimes', in *Challenging the Regional Stereotype*, 124.

13. This is Forbes's figure. Frank in Forbes and Muise, eds, says 122,000.

14. E.R. Forbes, 'Looking Backward: Reflections on the Maritime Experience in an Evolving Canadian Constitution', in *Les Provinces maritimes/The Maritime Provinces; Un regard vers l'avenir/Looking to the future*, ed. Donald A. Savoie and Ralph Winter (Moncton: Canadian Institute for Research on Regional Development, 1993), 13–37.

15. E.R. Forbes, 'The Origins of the Maritime Rights Movement', *Acadiensis* V, 1 (1975), 54–66; E.R. Forbes, *The Maritime Rights Movement, 1919–1927: A Study in Canadian Regionalism* (Montreal: McGill-Queen's University Press, 1979), 22–7. John G. Reid, *Six Crucial Decades: Times of Change in the History of the Maritimes* (Halifax: Nimbus, 1987), 164.

16. Forbes, *Maritime Rights*, 176.

17. David Alexander, 'Newfoundland's Traditional Economy and Development to 1934', in *Newfoundland in the Nineteenth and Twentieth Centuries: Essays in Interpretation*, ed. James Hiller and Peter Neary (Toronto: University of Toronto Press, 1980), 25.

18. E.R. Forbes, 'Prohibition and the Social Gospel in Nova Scotia' and 'Rum in the Maritimes' Economy During the Prohibition Era', in *Challenging the Regional Stereotype*, 13–40 and 41–7.

19. Ian McKay, 'Among the Fisherfolk: J.F.B. Livesay and the Invention of Peggy's Cove', *Journal of Canadian Studies* 23, 1–2 (1988), 23–45.

20. Gerald L. Pocius, 'Tourists, Health Seekers and Sportsmen: Luring Americans to Newfoundland in the Early Twentieth Century', in *Newfoundland in the Nineteenth and Twentieth Centuries*, ed. Hiller and Neary, 71.

21. E.R. Forbes, 'Cutting the Pie into Smaller Pieces: Matching Grants and Relief in the Maritime Provinces During the 1930s', in *Challenging the Regional Stereotype*, 151.

22. 'The Ignorant Masses', from the St John's *Liberal Press*, 1 Nov. 1928; quoted in James Overton, 'Self-Help, Charity, and Individual Responsibility: The Political Economy of Social Policy in Newfoundland in the 1920s', in *Twentieth Century Newfoundland: Explorations*, ed. James Hiller and Peter Neary (St John's: Breakwater, 1994), 79–122.

23. Gordon Handcock, 'The Commission of Government's Land Settlement Scheme in Newfoundland', in *Newfoundland in the Nineteenth and Twentieth Centuries*, ed. Hiller and Neary, 123–51.

24. James Overton, 'Brown Flour and Beri-beri: The Politics of Dietary and Health Reform in Newfoundland in the First Half of the Twentieth Century', *Newfoundland Studies* 14, 1 (1998), 15.

25. J.T. Jackson Lears, *No Place of Grace: Antimodernism and the Transformation of American Culture, 1880–1920* (New York: Pantheon Books, 1983).

26. E.R. Forbes, 'Consolidating Disparity: The Maritimes and the Industrialization of Canada during the Second World War', in *Challenging the Regional Stereotype*, 172–99.

27. James Lamb (RCN), quoted in Patricia O'Brien, 'World War II', *Encyclopedia of Newfoundland and Labrador* 5: 631.

28. Forbes, 'Consolidating Disparity'; Marc Milner, *North Atlantic Run: The Royal Canadian Navy and the Battle of the Convoys* (Toronto: University of Toronto Press, 1985).

29. On the Newfoundland experience, see Peter Neary, *Newfoundland in the North Atlantic World, 1929–1949* (Kingston and Montreal: McGill-Queen's University Press, 1988).

11: The Real Golden Age? 1949–1989

1. Eric Hobsbawm, *Age of Extremes: The Short Twentieth Century, 1914–1991* (London: Abacus, 1995), 6.

2. Margaret Conrad, 'The Atlantic Revolution of the 1950s', in *Beyond Anger and Longing: Community and Development in Atlantic Canada*, ed. Berkeley Fleming (Sackville and Fredericton: Centre for Canadian Studies, Mount Allison University and Acadiensis Press, 1988), 53–96; and 'The 1950s: The Decade of Development', in *The Atlantic Provinces in Confederation*, ed. E.R. Forbes and D.A. Muise (Toronto and Fredericton: University of Toronto and Acadiensis Press, 1993), 382–420.

3. Royal Commission on Canada's Economic Prospects, *Final Report* (Ottawa: Queen's Printer, 1957), 403.

4. W.S. MacNutt, 'The Fredericton Conference: A Look Backward and a Look Forward', *Atlantic Advocate* (September 1956), 11–13.

5. W.S. MacNutt, 'The Atlantic Revolution', *Atlantic Advocate* (June 1957), 11–13.

6. William E. Shrank, 'Benefiting Fishermen: Origins of Fishermen's Unemployment Insurance in Canada, 1935–1957', *Journal of Canadian Studies* 33, 1 (Spring 1998), 61–87.

7. Dalton Camp, *Gentlemen, Players and Politicians* (Toronto: McClelland and Stewart, 1970), 337; *Atlantic Advocate* (July 1957), 11.

8. Atlantic Provinces Economic Council, *Atlantic Canada Today* (Halifax: Formac, 1987), 125.

9. Della Stanley, 'The 1960s: The Illusions and Realities of Progress', in *The Atlantic Provinces in Confederation*, ed. Forbes and Muise, 421–59; D.M.M. Stanley, *Louis Robichaud: A Decade of Power* (Halifax: Formac, 1984).

10. Labradorians used the names 'Grand River' and 'the Grand Falls'. In the early nineteenth century the river became the 'Hamilton', after one of Newfoundland's governors. This name was eventually applied to the falls as well. In 1965 'the Churchill River and Falls' became the official designation.

11. *Atlantic Canada Today*, 31. See also Satadal Dasgupta, 'The Island in Transition: A Statistical Overview', in Verna Smitheram, David Milne, and Satadal Dasgupta, eds, *The Garden Transformed: Prince Edward Island, 1945–1980* (Charlottetown: Ragweed Press, 1982), 234–68.

12. APEC, *Defence Expenditures and the Economy of the Atlantic Provinces*, Pamphlet No. 9 (December 1965).

13. *Atlantic Canada Today*, 172–3.

14. Quoted in Harold Horwood, *Joey* (Toronto: Stoddard, 1989), 240.

15. John Reid, 'The 1970s: Sharpening the Sceptical Edge', in *The Atlantic Provinces in Confederation*, ed. Forbes and Muise, 479.

16. Bridglal Pachai, *Beneath the Clouds of the Promised Land: The Survival of Nova Scotia's Blacks*, Vol. II: 1800–1989 (Halifax: Black Educators Association, 1987/90), Chapter 4.

17. *Atlantic Canada Today*, 117.

18. E.R. Forbes, 'The Atlantic Provinces, Free Trade, and the Constitution', in *Challenging the Regional Stereotype: Essays on the 20th Century Maritimes* (Fredericton: Acadiensis Press, 1989), 213.

19. Moses Harvey, *Where Are We and Whither Tending? Three Lectures on the Reality and Worth of Human Progress* (Boston: Doyle and Whittle, 1886).

SELECTED BIBLIOGRAPHY

The historical literature on Atlantic Canada is so extensive that making a selection of sources is a difficult exercise. To conserve space, we have decided not to include the many fine biographies that have appeared in recent years; nor have we listed articles. Additional titles can be found in *Canadian History: A Readers' Guide*, 2 vols (Toronto: University of Toronto Press, 1994). Volume 1, *Beginnings to Confederation* (edited by M. Brook Taylor), is particularly useful for students of Atlantic Canada. Bibliographies are published regularly in the journals *Acadiensis* and *Newfoundland Studies*.

General Works

Buckner, Phillip A., and John G. Reid, eds. *The Atlantic Region to Confederation: A History*. Toronto: University of Toronto Press, 1994.

Forbes, E.R., and D.A. Muise, eds. *The Atlantic Provinces in Confederation*. Toronto: University of Toronto Press, 1993.

MacNutt, W.S. *The Atlantic Provinces: The Emergence of Colonial Society, 1712–1857*. Toronto: McClelland and Stewart, 1965.

Reid, John. *Six Crucial Decades: Times of Change in the History of the Maritimes*. Halifax: Nimbus, 1987.

General Essay Collections

Alexander, David. *Atlantic Canada and Confederation: Essays in Canadian Political Economy*, comp. Eric W. Sager, Lewis R. Fischer, and Stuart O. Pierson. Toronto: University of Toronto Press, 1983.

Bercuson, David Jay, and Phillip A. Buckner, eds. *Eastern and Western Perspectives, Papers from the Joint Atlantic Canada/Western Canadian Studies Conference*. Toronto: University of Toronto Press, 1981.

Bogaard, Paul A., ed. *Profiles of Science and Society in the Maritimes prior to 1914*. Fredericton: Acadiensis Press, 1990.

Brym, Robert J., and R. James Sacouman, eds. *Underdevelopment and Social Movements in Atlantic Canada*. Toronto: New Hogtown Press, 1979.

Buckner, P.A., and David Frank, eds. *Atlantic Canada Before Confederation: The Acadiensis Reader*, Vol. 1. 3rd edn. Fredericton: Acadiensis Press, 1999.

———, eds. *Atlantic Canada After Confederation: The Acadiensis Reader*, Vol. 2. 3rd edn. Fredericton: Acadiensis Press, 1999.

Candow, James E., and Carol Corbin, eds. *How Deep is the Ocean? Historical Essays on Canada's Atlantic Fishery*. Sydney: University College of Cape Breton Press, 1997.

Davies, Gwendolyn. *Studies in Maritime Literary History*. Fredericton: Acadiensis Press, 1991.

Fleming, Berkeley, ed. *Beyond Anger and Longing: Community and Development in Atlantic Canada*. Sackville and Fredericton: Centre for Canadian Studies, Mount Allison University and Acadiensis Press, 1988.

Forbes, E.R. *Challenging the Regional Stereotype: Essays on the 20th Century Maritimes*. Fredericton: Acadiensis Press, 1989.

Frank, David, and Gregory S. Kealey, eds. *Labour and Working-Class History in Atlantic Canada: A Reader*. St John's: Institute of Social and Economic Research, 1995.

Guildford, Janet, and Suzanne Morton, eds. *Separate Spheres. Women's Worlds in the 19th Century Maritimes*. Fredericton: Acadiensis Press, 1994.

Inwood, Kris, ed. *Farm, Factory and Fortune: New Studies in the Economic History of the Maritime Provinces*. Fredericton: Acadiensis Press, 1993.

McCann, Larry, ed. *People and Place: Studies of Small Town Life in the Maritimes*. Fredericton: Acadiensis Press, 1987.

———, and Carrie MacMillan, eds. *The Sea and Culture of Atlantic Canada: A Multidisciplinary Sampler*. Sackville: Centre for Canadian Studies, Mount Allison University, 1992.

Martin, Ged, ed. *The Causes of Confederation*. Fredericton: Acadiensis Press, 1990

Murphy, Terrence, and Cyril J. Byrne, eds. *Religion and Identity: The Experience of Irish and Scots Catholics in Atlantic Canada*. St John's: Jesperson Press, 1987.

Rawlyk, G.A., ed. *Historical Essays on the Atlantic Provinces*. Toronto: McClelland and Stewart, 1967.

Rawlyk, George, ed. *The Atlantic Provinces and the Problems of Confederation*. St John's: Breakwater, 1979.

Samson, Daniel, ed. *Contested Countryside: Rural Workers and Modern Society in Atlantic Canada, 1800–1950* (Fredericton: Acadiensis Press, 1994).

Toner, Peter, ed. *The Irish in Atlantic Canada, 1780–1900*. Fredericton: New Ireland Press, 1991.

Regional Monographs

Beattie, Betsy. *Obligation and Opportunity: Single Maritime Women in Boston, 1870–1930*. Montreal and Kingston: McGill-Queen's University Press, 2000.

Burrill, Gary. *Away: Maritimers in Massachusetts, Ontario, and Alberta*. Montreal: McGill-Queen's University Press, 1992.

Buckner, P.A. *The Transition to Responsible Government: British Policy in British North America, 1815–1850*. Westport CT: Greenwood, 1985.

Fingard, Judith. *Jack in Port: Sailortowns in Eastern Canada*. Toronto: University of Toronto Press, 1982.

Forbes, E.R. *The Maritime Rights Movement: 1919–1927: A Study in Canadian Regionalism*. Montreal: McGill-Queen's Press, 1979.

Howell, Colin D. *Northern Sandlots: A Social History of Maritime Baseball*. Toronto: University of Toronto Press, 1995.

Innis, Harold. *The Cod Fishery: The History of an International Economy*. 1940 rev. Toronto: University of Toronto Press, 1954.

Keefer, Janice Kulyk. *Under Eastern Eyes: A Critical Reading of Maritime Fiction*. Toronto: University of Toronto Press, 1987.

Ommer, Rosemary. *From Outpost to Outport: A Structural Analysis of the Jersey-Gaspé Cod Fishery, 1767–1914*. Montreal and Kingston: McGill-Queen's University Press, 1991.

Sager, Eric W., with Gerald E. Panting. *Maritime Capital: The Shipping Industry in Atlantic Canada, 1820–1914*. Montreal and Kingston: McGill-Queen's University Press, 1990.

Sager, Eric. *Seafaring Labour: The Merchant Marine in Atlantic Canada*. Montreal and Kingston: McGill-Queen's University Press, 1989.

Saunders, S.A. *The Economic History of the Maritime Provinces*. 1939 reprt. Fredericton: Acadiensis Press, 1984.

Taylor, M. Brook. *Promoters, Patriots and Partisans: Historiography in Nineteenth-Century English Canada*. Toronto: University of Toronto Press, 1989.

Thomas, Peter. *Strangers from a Secret Land: The Voyages of the Brig 'Albion' and the Founding of the First Welsh Settlements in Canada*. Toronto: University of Toronto Press, 1986.

Aboriginal Peoples

Bailey, A.G. *The Conflict of European and Eastern Algonkian Cultures, 1504–1700*. 2nd edn. Toronto: University of Toronto Press, 1969.

Coates, Ken. *The Marshall Decision and Native Rights*. Toronto: General Publishing, 2000.

Davis, Stephen A. *The Micmac*. Tantallon: Four East Publications, 1991.

Deal, Michael, and Susan Deal. *Prehistoric Archaeology in the Maritime Provinces, Past and Present*. Research Reports in Archaeology No. 8. Fredericton: Council of Maritime Premiers Maritime Committee on Archaeological Cooperation, 1991.

Gould, G.P., and A.J. Semple, eds. *Our Land: The Maritimes*. Fredericton: Sainte Annes Point Press, 1980.

Kleivan, Helge. *The Eskimos of Northeast Labrador: A History of Eskimo-White Relations, 1771–1955.* Olso: Norsk Polarinstitutt, 1966.

Mailhot, José. *The People of Sheshatshit: In the Land of the Innu.* St John's: Institute for Social and Economic Research, 1997.

Marshall, Ingeborg. *The History and Ethnography of the Beothuk.* Montreal and Kingston: McGill-Queen's University Press, 1996.

McGhee, Robert. *Ancient People of the Arctic.* Vancouver: University of British Columbia Press, 1996.

———. *The Native Peoples of Atlantic Canada: A History of Ethnic Interaction.* Toronto: McClelland and Stewart, 1974.

Paul, Daniel N. *We Were Not the Savages.* Rev. edn. Halifax: Fernwood, 2000.

Reid, Jennifer. *Myth, Symbol, and Colonial Encounter: British and Mi'kmaq in Acadia, 1700–1867.* Ottawa: University of Ottawa Press, 1995.

Tuck, James A. *Newfoundland and Labrador Prehistory.* Ottawa: National Museum of Man, National Museums of Canada, 1976.

———. *Maritime Provinces Prehistory.* Ottawa: National Museum of Man, National Museums of Canada, 1984.

Upton, L.F.S. *Micmacs and Colonists: A Study of Imperial Relations, 1713–1760.* Vancouver: University of British Columbia Press, 1979.

Whitehead, Ruth Holmes. *Micmac Quillwork.* Halifax: Nova Scotia Museum, 1982.

———. *The Old Man Told Us: Excerpts from Micmac History, 1500–1950.* Halifax: Nimbus 1991.

European Exploration and Early Settlement

Bumsted, J.M. *The People's Clearance: Highland Emigration to British North America, 1770–1815.* Winnipeg: University of Manitoba Press, 1982.

Cell, Gillian T. *English Enterprise in Newfoundland, 1577–1660.* Toronto: University of Toronto Press, 1969.

Conrad, Margaret, ed. *They Planted Well: New England Planters in Maritime Canada.* Fredericton: Acadiensis Press, 1988.

Cook, Ramsay. *1942 and All That: Making a Garden Out of A Wilderness.* Toronto: Robarts Centre for Canadian Studies, 1993.

Handcock, W. Gordon. *'Soe Longe as there comes noe women': Origins of English Settlement in Newfoundland.* St John's: Breakwater Press, 1989.

Head, C. Grant. *Eighteenth Century Newfoundland: A Geographer's Perspective.* Toronto: McClelland and Stewart, 1976.

McGhee, Robert. *Canada Rediscovered.* Hull: Canadian Museum of Civilization, 1991.

Pope, Peter. *The Many Landfalls of John Cabot.* Toronto: University of Toronto Press, 1997.

Reid, John. *Acadia, Maine, and New Scotland: Marginal Colonies in the Seventeenth Century.* Toronto: University of Toronto Press, 1981.

Acadia and the Acadians

Arsenault, Georges. *The Island Acadians, 1720–1980.* Charlottetown: Ragweed Press, 1989.

Basque, Maurice, et al. *Acadie au feminin: Un regard multidisciplinaire sur les Acadiennes et les Canadiens.* Moncton: Chaire d'études acadiennes, Université de Moncton, 2000.

Brebner, John Bartlet. *New England's Outpost: Acadia Before the Conquest of Canada.* New York: Columbia University Press, 1927.

Clark, Andrew Hill. *The Geography of Early Nova Scotia to 1760.* Madison: University of Wisconsin Press, 1986.

Conrad, Margaret, ed. *Looking into Acadie: Three Illustrated Lectures.* Halifax: Nova Scotia Museum, 1999.

Couturier, Jacques Paul, and Phyllis E. LeBlanc, dirs. *Économie et société en Acadie, 1850–1950.* Moncton: Éditions d'Acadie, 1996.

Daigle, Jean, ed. *Acadia of the Maritimes: Thematic Studies.* Moncton: Chaire d'études acadiennes, Université de Moncton, 1995.

Griffiths, N.E.S. *The Contexts of Acadian History, 1686–1784.* Montreal and Kingston: McGill-Queen's University Press, 1992.

———. *The Acadians: Creation of a People.* Toronto: McGraw Hill-Ryerson, 1973.

Harvey, Fernand, and Gérard Beaulieu, dirs., *Les Relations entre le Québec et l'Acadie de la tradition* à la modernité. Quebec: Éditions de l'IQRC/Éditions d'Acadie, 2000.

Johnson, A.J.B. *Life and Religion at Louisbourg, 1713-1758*. Montreal and Kingston: McGill-Queen's University Press, 1984.

Jones, Elizabeth. *Gentlemen and Jesuits: Quests for Glory and Adventure in the Early Days of New France*. Toronto: University of Toronto Press, 1986.

Landry, Nicolas. *Les pêches dans la péninsule acadienne, 1850–1900*. Moncton: Éditions d'Acadie, 1994.

MacDonald, M.A. *Fortune and La Tour: The Civil War in Acadia,* 2nd edn (Halifax: Nimbus, 2000).

McNeil, John Robert. *Atlantic Empires of France and Spain: Louisbourg and Havanna, 1700–1763*. Chapel Hill: University of North Carolina, 1985.

Moore, Christopher. *Louisbourg Portraits: Life in an Eighteenth-Century Garrison Town*. Toronto: Macmillan, 1982.

Ross, Sally, and Alphonse Deveau. *The Acadians of Nova Scotia Past and Present*. Halifax: Nimbus, 1992.

New Brunswick

Acheson, T.W. *Saint John: The Making of an Urban Colonial Society*. Toronto: University of Toronto Press, 1985.

Bell, David G. *Early Loyalist Saint John: The Origins of New Brunswick Politics, 1783–1786*. Fredericton: New Ireland Press, 1983.

Condon, Ann Gorman. *The Envy of the American States: The Loyalist Dream for New Brunswick*. Fredericton: New Ireland Press, 1984.

MacDonald, M.A. *Rebels and Royalists: The Lives and Material Culture of New Brunswick's Early English Settlers, 1758–1783*. Fredericton: New Ireland Press, 1990.

MacNutt, W.S. *New Brunswick: A History*. Toronto: Macmillan, 1984.

See, Scott W. *Riots in New Brunswick: Orange Nativism and Social Violence in the 1840s*. Toronto: University of Toronto Press, 1993.

Spray, William, *The Blacks in New Brunswick*. Fredericton: Brunswick Press, 1972.

Toner, Peter, ed. *New Ireland Remembered: Historical Essays on the Irish in New Brunswick*. Fredericton: New Ireland Press, 1988.

Wright, Esther Clark. *The Loyalists of New Brunswick*. Wolfville: Wright, 1955.

Wynn, Graeme. *Timber Colony: A Historical Geography of Early Nineteenth Century New Brunswick*. Toronto: University of Toronto Press, 1981.

Newfoundland and Labrador

Blake, Raymond B. *Canadians at Last: Canada Integrates Newfoundland as a Province*. Toronto: University of Toronto Press, 1994.

Cadigan, Sean T. *Hope and Deception in Conception Bay: Merchant-Settler Relations in Newfoundland, 1785–1855*. Toronto: University of Toronto Press, 1995.

Duley, Margaret I. *Where Once Our Mothers Stood We Stand: Women's Suffrage in Newfoundland, 1890–1925*. Charlottetown: gynergy books, 1993.

Fitzhugh, Lynne D. *The Labradorians: Voices from the Land of Cain*. St John's: Breakwater, 1999.

Greene, John P. *Between Damnation and Starvation: Priests and Merchants in Newfoundland Politics, 1745–1855*. Montreal and Kingston: McGill-Queens University Press, 1999.

Hiller, James, and Peter Neary, eds. *Newfoundland in the Nineteenth and Twentieth Centuries: Essays in Interpretation*. Toronto: University of Toronto Press, 1980.

———, eds. *Twentieth-Century Newfoundland: Explorations*. St John's: Breakwater Books, 1994.

Kealey, Linda, ed. *Pursuing Equality: Historical Perspectives on Women in Newfoundland and Labrador*. St John's: Institute for Social and Economic Research, 1993.

McDonald, Ian D.H. *'To Each His Own': William Coaker and the Fishermen's Protective Union, 1908–1925*. St John's: ISER, 1987.

Macpherson, Alan G., and Joyce Brown Macpherson. *The Natural Environment of Newfoundland, Past and Present*. St John's: Department of Geography, Memorial University of Newfoundland, 1981.

Mannion, John J., ed. *The Peopling of Newfoundland: Essays in Historical Geography*. St John's: Institute of Social and Economic Research, 1977.

Neary, Peter. *Newfoundland and the North Atlantic World, 1929–1949*. Montreal and Kingston: McGill-Queen's University Press, 1988.

Neary, Peter, and Patrick O'Flaherty. *By Great Waters: A Newfoundland and Labrador Anthology*. Toronto: University of Toronto Press, 1974.

Noel, S.J.R. *Politcs in Newfoundland*. Toronto: University of Toronto Press, 1971.

O'Flaherty, Patrick. *The Rock Observed: Studies in the Literature of Newfoundland*. Toronto: University of Toronto Press, 1979.

———. *Old Newfoundland: A History to 1843*. St John's: Long Beach Press, 1999.

Overton, James. *Making A World of Difference: Essays on Tourism, Culture and Development in Newfoundland*. St John's: Institute of Social and Economic Research, 1996.

Porter, Marilyn. *Place and Persistence in the Lives of Newfoundland Women*. Aldershot: Avebury, 1993.

Rowe, Frederick W. *History of Newfoundland and Labrador*. Toronto: McGraw Hill-Ryerson, 1980.

Ryan, Shannon. *Fish Out of Water: The Newfoundland Saltfish Trade, 1814–1914*. St John's: Breakwater, 1986.

———. *The Ice Hunters: A History of Newfoundland Sealing to 1914*. St John's: Breakwater Press, 1994.

Nova Scotia

Beck, J. Murray. *The Politics of Nova Scotia*, 2 vols. Tantallon NS: Four East Publications, 1985/88.

Brebner, John Bartlett. *The Neutral Yankees of Nova Scotia*. Toronto: McClelland and Stuart, 1969.

Bruce, Harry. *An Illustrated History of Nova Scotia*. Halifax: Nimbus, 1997.

Campbell, D., and R.A. MacLean. *Beyond the Atlantic Roar: A Study of Nova Scotia Scots*. Toronto: McClelland and Stewart, 1974.

Conrad, Margaret, Toni Laidlaw, and Donna Smyth. *No Place Like Home: The Diaries and Letters of Nova Scotia Women, 1771–1938*. Halifax: Formac, 1988.

Cuthbertson, Brian. *Johnny Bluenose at the Poles: Epic Nova Scotian Election Battles, 1758–1848*. Halifax: Formac, 1994.

Donovan, Kenneth, ed. *Cape Breton at 200: Historical Essays in Honour of the Island's Bicentennial, 1785–1985*. Sydney: University College of Cape Breton Press, 1985.

———, ed. *The Island: New Perspectives on Cape Breton's History, 1713–1975*. Fredericton: Acadiensis Press, 1990.

Fingard, Judith. *The Dark Side of Life in Victorian Halifax*. Porters Lake, NS: Pottersfield Press, 1989.

Fingard, Judith, Janet Guildford, and David Sutherland. *Halifax: The First 250 Years*. Halifax: Formac, 1999.

Gwyn, Julian. *Excessive Expectations: Maritime Commerce and the Development of Nova Scotia, 1740–1870*. Montreal and Kingston: McGill-Queen's University Press, 1998.

Hornsby, Stephen. *Nineteenth-Century Cape Breton: A Historical Geography*. Montreal and Kingston: McGill-Queen's University Press, 1992.

Macgillivray, Donald, and Brian Tennyson, eds. *Cape Breton Historical Essays*. Sydney: University College of Cape Breton Press, 1980.

McKay, Ian. *The Quest of the Folk: Antimodernism and Cultural Selection in Twentieth-Century Nova Scotia*. Montreal: McGill-Queen's University Press, 1994.

MacKinnon, Neil. *This Unfriendly Soil: The Loyalist Experience in Nova Scotia, 1783–1791*. Montreal and Kingston: McGill-Queen's University Press, 1989.

Morton, Suzanne. *Ideal Surroundings: Domestic Life in a Working-Class Suburb in the 1920s*. Toronto: University of Toronto Press, 1995.

Neal, Rusty. *Brotherhood Economics: Women and Cooperatives in Nova Scotia*. Sydney, NS: University of Cape Breton Press, 1999.

Pachai, Bridglal. *Beneath the Clouds of the Promised Land: The Survival of Nova Scotia's Blacks*, 2 vols. Halifax: Black Educators Association, 1987/90.

Pryke, K.G. *Nova Scotia and Confederation, 1864–74*. Toronto: University of Toronto Press, 1979.

Rawlyk, G.A. *Nova Scotia's Massachusetts: A Study of Massachusetts-Nova Scotia Relations, 1630 to 1784*. Montreal and Kingston: McGill-Queen's University Press, 1973.

Walker, James W. St G. *The Black Loyalists: The Search for a Promised Land in Nova Scotia and Sierra Leone*. 2nd ed. Toronto: University of Toronto Press, 1992.

Prince Edward Island

Baldwin, Douglas, and Thomas Spira, *Gaslights, Epidemics and Vagabond Cows: Charlottetown in the Victorian Era*. Charlottetown: Ragweed Press, 1988.

Bolger, Francis. *Canada's Smallest Province: A History of PEI*. Charlottetown: Prince Edward Island Centennial Commission, 1973.

Bumsted, J.M. *Land, Settlement, and Politics in Eighteenth-Century Prince Edward Island*. Montreal and Kingston: McGill-Queen's University Press, 1987.

Clark, Andrew Hill. *Three Centuries and the Island: A Historical Geography of Settlement and Agriculture in Prince Edward Island*. Toronto: University of Toronto Press, 1959.

Hornby, Jim. *Black Islanders*. Island Studies Series No. 3. Charlottetown: Institute of Island Studies, 1991.

MacDonald, Edward. *If You're Stronghearted: Prince Edward Island in the Twentieth Century*. Charlottetown: Museum and Heritage Foundation, 2000.

Robertson, Ian Ross. *The Tenant League of Prince Edward Island: Leasehold Tenure in the New World*. Toronto: University of Toronto Press, 1996.

Smitheram, Verner, David Milne, and Satadal Dasgupta, eds. *The Garden Transformed: Prince Edward Island, 1945–1980*. Charlottetown: Ragweed Press, 1982.

INDEX

PLEASE NOTE: Page numbers in italic type refer to illustration captions.